ICE

Akureyr

Reykjavík

MILES

R.L.W.

Kuopio

L. SAIMA

Jyväskylä

Viipuri

Leningrad

HELSINKI

Porkkala

Tampere

Turku

Hangö

Riga

FINLAND

GULF

ÅLAND

Gävle

UPPLAND

Uppsala

L. MÄLAR

STOCKHOLM

BALTIC

SEA

Visby

GOTLAND

ÖLAND

Kalmar

Danzig

Falun

Grängesberg

Karlstad

S

W

Göta Canal

L. Vättern

Jönköping

SMÅLAND

Vänern

Trollhättan

Gothenburg

SKÅNE

Lund

Malmö

ZEALAND

FALSTER

Elverum

Hamar

OSLO

Moss

ØRESUND

Elsinore

COPENHAGEN

Roskilde

Great Belt

LALAND

Kristiansand

Bergen

Rjukan

N

Haugesund

Stavanger

Ålborg

Århus

JUTLAND

Esbjerg

Odense

FYN

DENMARK

The American Foreign Policy Library

Edwin O. Reischauer, Editor

Scandinavia

Franklin D. Scott

Harvard University Press

Cambridge, Massachusetts
and London, England
1975

*To the memory of
my father*

Foreword

The five Scandinavian countries—Denmark, Finland, Iceland, Norway, and Sweden—contain only a very small part of the world's population, but their experience, especially in recent decades, constitutes a very significant aspect of the human effort to solve the problems men face. Placed between the rival power blocs of East Europe and the Atlantic, the Scandinavian nations have found a variety of accommodations to the resulting dual pressures. Denmark, Norway, and Iceland have developed close associations with the Western European community and NATO; Sweden has maintained its strict neutrality; and Finland has managed to combine independence with circumspection in its dealings with its great Soviet neighbor. More important, all of the Scandinavian lands have proved to be imaginative leaders in seeking to find a just balance in their own societies between economic equality and individual freedom. Relatively small and extremely homogeneous as they are, they have served in a sense as test tubes for social and economic innovations that may prove highly relevant for other more numerous peoples in their groping efforts to find a safe way into the future.

When the Foreign Policy Library of the Harvard University Press was first organized, in the early years after the Second World War, in order to produce broad, interpretive volumes on the nations and regions that loomed largest in American foreign policy, it was natural that Scandinavia should have been among the first regions selected for treatment. Professor Franklin D.

Scott's *The United States and Scandinavia* appeared in 1950 to meet this need. For a quarter of a century it has been a classic in its field. The intervening years, however, have added an abundance of new material and have altered perspectives. The experiences of World War II and the cold war have receded into the background. On the other hand, the problems of the balance between individual equality and freedom within nations have become considerably more acute, making the Scandinavian experience in this field all the more significant.

Professor Scott has wisely chosen not just to update his earlier book but to rewrite it. The result is a new look at Scandinavia, embracing much of the material from his original volume but adding to this the extensive record of the past quarter century and evaluations of the whole experience from the contemporary point of view. Because the changes have been so extensive, it has seemed appropriate to give the work a new title—*Scandinavia*.

Edwin O. Reischauer

Preface

Exciting and controversial developments have focused much attention on Scandinavia. One observer warns in ominous tones that the whole Western world is headed for the rigid authoritarianism of the Swedish socialist elite. Next door to the USSR, Finland maintains a kind of stubborn independence on a leash. Denmark builds garden suburbs and tries to create *gemytlighet* along with urbanization. Norway's bonanza of North Sea oil bids fair to give her the capital for more rapid strides into industrial prosperity and twentieth-century problems. Iceland, after centuries of withdrawal, diversifies and internationalizes her economy. All the Nordic countries intensely pursue the quest for justice and individual equality and have initiated some institutions such as the ombudsman that have found imitators around the globe. Medical services are among the best in the world, and the longevity of the descendants of the Vikings tends to verify the fact. Innovative ideas find expression in social organization, in arts and crafts, in technology and industry. Do these small countries of the North, no longer wasting their resources in the struggle for power, constitute the frontiers of a new society?

My own concern with Scandinavia began with a study of Bernadotte and Napoleon, under the inspiration of Professor Charles Kingsley Webster. Gradually my interest broadened from diplomatic history to the entire spectrum of Nordic life—its culture and economy, its political and social systems, and the interrelations of its peoples with one another and with the United States.

Through forty-odd years of observation it has been fascinating to watch the transformation of tradition-oriented communities into modern change-oriented societies keenly aware of their position in the world.

To provide a basis for understanding these unusual developments is the purpose of this volume, as it was the purpose of its predecessor twenty-five years ago. But the rapidity and extent of change have made this a new and different book.

Acknowledgments of assistance in the learning process of nearly five decades could themselves fill a volume. Here I can mention only a few of the special obligations. For the original publication I owe much to Sumner Welles and Donald C. McKay, to Adèle Heilborn, Folke Lindberg, and Howard Wilson; more recently to Lars Kritz, Sture Lindmark, Steven Koblik, and Jerry Voorhis for critical reading of the new manuscript and helpful suggestions. The endpaper maps were done by R. L. Williams and the map in the text by Mrs. Marjorie Sommers. Gratitude is happily acknowledged to various foundations that have aided in one or more of some fifteen trips to northern Europe: the American Scandinavian Foundation, the Viking Fund, the American Philosophical Society, the Ford Foundation, and the Social Science Research Council. The work could not have been carried on without the long-continued support of Northwestern University, nor without the continuing help of the staffs and resources of the Northwestern University Library, the Honnold Library in Claremont, the Library of International Relations in Chicago, and, of course, the many archives, libraries, and government departments of Scandinavia, most particularly the University Library in Oslo, the Uppsala University Library, and the Royal Libraries of both Copenhagen and Stockholm. Thanks are due also to the many students who through the years have tried to keep me on the right track and to my wife for her labors on the index—and for much more.

F. D. S.

Claremont, California
January 1975

Contents

1 *Northern Lands and Peoples*

It is "the rooftop of the world." Once the home of ruthless Vikings, now it is a haven of peace; once isolated off the routes of travel by land and sea, now on main air traffic lanes; once poor, now productive and prosperous beyond the average; barbarous late into European history, now an admired pattern of enlightened society. This is Scandinavia, Norden, the North.

In its widest and truest compass Scandinavia includes the central core of Denmark, Norway, and Sweden, the eastern flank in Finland, the western outposts in the Atlantic Ocean: the Faroes, Iceland, and the Danish colony of Greenland. The area reaches from the Russian border to the shores of North America. It is flanked on one side by polar seas, and on the other by the Atlantic and the states of continental Europe. The twenty-two million people who inhabit it have a common cultural tradition, have been in and out of various political combinations with one another, and think of themselves as a group. They have their differences, each of the five nations is an entity, yet each is far more different from other nations outside the group than it is from any of the brother nations within the group. Its unity is based on geographical position and community of culture.

When Scandinavia was on the frontier of civilization and conflict the people could choose whether they wished to play the game of international war and politics, or stand aloof. When they did choose to play they could usually do so on other people's grounds. Swedes like to claim, for instance, that their country has never been invaded, and even though the claim is not literally accurate, it is almost so. Does this aloofness of the past have significance in the mid-twentieth century? Is the idea of the marginal position of northern Europe merely an illusion to which wishful thinking clings? What are the geographical realities of today, the pressures, the protective barriers which affect this section of the earth?

The countries of the North have been praised to the skies as lands of the middle way and damned to the depths as selfish and blind in a confused and embittered world. Neither view is correct. But what is correct? How have the peoples of the North created their high standard of living out of the meager resources available to them?

The answers cannot be given in easy simplicities. To understand these peoples one must assume certain fundamentals: common sense, education, honesty, cooperativeness, hard work, a dash of good luck, far-sighted planning, careful spending, a creative talent, independent spirit, and democratic processes. Progress has been hampered sometimes by distance from supplies and markets, sometimes by pride and stubbornness, sometimes by an overdose of the independent spirit. Difficulties from the outside (plagues, wars, blockades) repeatedly have harassed the Scandinavians. But progress has been real throughout the area. Perhaps the elements of that progress have meaning for the rest of the world.

What Scandinavia Is

A Mercator projection map pulls Scandinavia apart and distorts the northern shapes. Only a globe can picture something of the basic geologic and geographic unity of the area.

Far back in geologic times the "North" lay buried under the great ice sheet. Slowly the frozen mass receded under the warmth of the sun. The dynamic of geology asserted itself and the land rose, released of its crushing burden. The Baltic Sea took shape as an inland lake in the heart of Fenno-Scandia, the entire land mass comprising what is now Finland, Denmark, and the Scandinavian Peninsula. The Baltic then rose higher and at last broke through a channel to reach the North Sea. Thus was formed Öresund (the narrow sound between Denmark and Sweden), the Danish lands were separated from the Scandinavian Peninsula, and the waters of the Baltic made contact with the Atlantic.[1] Boats could then traverse the Baltic and sail out to the British Isles, to Iceland and Greenland and Vinland. The Baltic itself was a northern Mediterranean, providing pathways for travel and commerce and nurturing a common culture.

The barriers were not the sea but the vast forests and swamps which lay between Finland and the inhabited parts of Russia. High mountains, marshes, and broad barrens were what man could not cross. Fenno-Scandia was thus insulated from the East and interconnected within itself and with the West. The region was and remains a natural area of community of culture, its entire history intricately intertwined. The islands in the Atlantic were separated by greater distances, yet lay within easy reach of Viking seamen, and have borne the stamp of Scandinavian culture for over a thousand years.

As one looks at this area on a globe he is impressed by how far north it lies, and he wonders how an active modern society with large towns can prosper in latitudes more northerly than Labrador, some of the land above the Arctic Circle. The Atlantic Ocean is the answer. Aided by winds from the west, it keeps the Scandinavian peninsula warmed and watered. The Gulf Stream gives an added touch. But it is the whole breadth of salt water that modifies the winds, creates the temperate marine climate, and makes the lands to the east livable. To the west of the Atlantic, Labrador suffers under cold winds blowing off the northern plains.

Tromsö in northern Norway (above latitude 69° N.) has a winter temperature averaging about 37° and a summer average

---

1. A note on pronunciation:

å is pronounced like o in cold. Basically Swedish, used in Norwegian, and, since the spelling reform of 1948, in Danish.

ä is like the ai in fair.

ö (Swedish)⎫
ø (Danish) ⎬ are like the ö or oe of German; there is no real English equivalent.

just above 50°. Spring flowers bloom there in February. The mountain backbone of the Scandinavian Peninsula blocks off some of this ocean warmth, but never all of it. Even the west coast of Finland feels something of the moderating influences from the west, though by the time the winter breezes reach Finland's eastern border they have lost their delicacy, and a northern "continental" climate prevails. Generally the Fenno-Scandian area has a climate stern but not capricious. Hurricanes and sizzling heat and earthquakes are unknown, floods and drought are rare. Moderation is there a habit of nature, though weather has always exceptions.

Summer in these northern lands brings days which linger through long twilight far into the night. In the northernmost parts, for weeks before and after the summer solstice one may see the sun which never sets but merely glides low to the horizon and rises again. This is the compensation for the long nights of darkness in the winter, and helps to explain the sun worship in ancient ritual and on modern beaches.

The warmth, the sun, the moisture dropped in frequent rains from the western winds, make crops grow quickly where the soil is good. Yet the glacial terrain of Finland and the Scandinavian Peninsula often leaves only small patches of arable land, sometimes in inner valleys like Gudbrandsdal in Norway or in strips between water and rock in the western fjords, sometimes along quiet river mouths in northern Sweden, or in clearings in Finland's forests. The ice sheets scraped off the earlier topsoil, and the present thin covering is geologically recent—on top of rocks 300,000,000 years old (the Alps, for comparison, are but 50,000,000 years old).

Iceland has vast stretches of barren land, and Greenland is only a name given by that early genius of real estate promotion, Eric the Red. Greenland's real claim to fame is her "icy mountains," one of the determining forces in the climate of the world. The major food-producing area of Scandinavia is in southern Sweden (Skåne) and in the fertile fields of Denmark on the sedimentary rock plains. Contrasts are great between the grandeur of the western Norwegian fjords with their perpendicular walls and the green shores of the Danish islands creeping out of the sea.

In Scandinavia sea and land exist together, complement each

other. Man lives on the land but draws sustenance from the sea and makes it serve his needs. The sea is not only his highway of commerce, his connective link within Scandinavia and with the lands which lie beyond; it is also his most dependable source of nourishment. "Norway has plenty of food—but it's all fish" is exaggeration based on fact. The fishers of the Lofoten Islands and of the whole long coast, like the fishermen of Iceland who provide that country's most important export, attest the importance of the sea.

It is through the Baltic Sea that ships carry pulp, paper, and prefabricated houses to the markets of the world. It is because the Baltic flowed to the west and opened a sea route through the Danish Sound (Öresund) that Finland maintains an active trade with the United States, 4,000 miles away, and it is the North Sea which makes Britain the best customer for Danish butter and eggs.

The coast lines of the Scandinavian countries are long and they are usable. Harbors are as full of boats as the streets of Copenhagen are full of bicycles. When the Vikings began to build streamlined seagoing ships in the ninth and tenth centuries they were simply learning how to use the natural advantages of their harbors; the fjords led to the ocean, and the ocean continued to the lands beyond. It is no accident that these northern countries are leaders in seamanship and that Norway has one of the largest merchant fleets of the world.

It is because of the sea that the Scandinavian lands have built a basic cultural unity and maintained it through the centuries; it is because of the sea that they are "oriented" to the south and the west. Their Christianity came to them from the South, from Rome. Finland quite naturally received both her first baptism and her Protestantism across the Gulf of Bothnia from Sweden, while Russia was Christianized from Constantinople. The line of religious division ran down the eastern border of Finland and the Baltic states, a line that was also normally a demarcation of linguistic, economic, and political division; while the Gulf of Bothnia, the Baltic, and the North Sea tied these shores to one another, just as the Atlantic tied western Europe and eastern America.

Scandinavia stands, therefore, united geographically as well as historically. The peoples of the North have intermixed, have carried on their interchange of commerce and ideas among themselves, and have fought their family quarrels. In the greater and more diverse world clan of nations Scandinavia is like a family among and yet apart from the rest.

What, then, are the characteristics of these peoples of the North? The Danes, the Swedes, the Norwegians, the Icelanders—these are the Scandinavian peoples proper, these are the folk whom the racial anthropologists call Nordic. The men tall and blond, the women fair. The racists went too far in apotheosizing this northern type and disregarded too much the varieties within the type. Nevertheless, by whatever standards one wishes to apply—health, strength, endurance, size, intelligence, even subjective beauty, the Scandinavians must rank high, and here the Finns must be included.

Originally these Scandinavians (except for the Finns and the Lapps) must have been one people. Perhaps their ancestors came northward from Asia Minor or the Balkans and founded the great Teutonic family. As the last ice sheet receded, small groups crept northward to hunt and fish and to settle. Tribal differentiations developed, and by the Age of the Migrations (beginning in the second century B.C.) we know of the Cimbri and soon of the Goths; a few centuries later of Angles and Saxons and Jutes, of Svear and Götar and of the Norse Vikings. As late as A.D. 700 the runic inscriptions found in the three central countries indicate that the people used exactly the same language, but in the Viking period (c. A.D. 800–1100) there grew a consciousness of the oneness of Norway and of distinction between Danes and Swedes.

Gradually environment played its subtle part in selection and modification; immigrating groups (Scots, Walloons, Germans, and others) affected communities differently; variation in personalities and in experience changed habits and traditions. Hence people and speech are not now the same in urban Copenhagen, in the mining town of Kiruna in northern Sweden, and in the rural valley of Setesdal in Norway.

Books of one country can be more easily read in the other countries when they are translated, but translation is a matter of convenience rather than necessity. Any Dane, Swede, or Norwegian can travel in the neighbor countries, use his own speech, and be understood without too great difficulty. In fact, these peoples do not try to learn each other's language, but at their various common gatherings each speaks his own, with an occasional bow to some special idiosyncrasy of his neighbor. Skåne has been a Swedish province for about 300 years and it speaks and writes Swedish; but it was long Danish territory and still has close cultural and economic ties with Denmark—enough so that a scholar at the Swedish university of Lund can claim he has less language difficulty in Copenhagen than he has in Stockholm.

With Iceland the story is different, for the Icelanders, basically of Norwegian stock since the Viking Age (although many probably stemmed more distantly from the ancient Herules, and some from the Irish), have really retained their ancient speech. At least their language is most closely akin to that of the ancient skalds (poets) and the saga-writers. Danish, Norwegian, and Swedish have succumbed to modernization within themselves and to acceptance of a number of words from German, French, and English. The Icelanders are proud to say that they, like the Greeks, always have a word for it. Even for such an invention as the radio the Icelanders utilized one of their own root-words and called it *utvarp* (out-casting) and for television used the ancient *sjón* (sight, vision).

Language illustrates one of the many ways in which continuity and originality blend, and similarities and differences exist side by side.

The Finns, related culturally and geographically to their western neighbors, are of different origin. Their ancestors moved, in prehistoric times, westward across the Russian plains, then north into Estonia and Finland. Perhaps their homeland was around the Caspian Sea or in the Ural Mountains. Related tribes are still scattered along the Volga, and the Hungarians probably originated from the same stock. The languages of these groups are at least distantly related, and belong to a distinct development, as do the peoples themselves, not Slavic, not Teutonic. They are all part of the separate Finno-Ugrian group. They are tall, blond, and virile, with broad cheekbones. When they moved across the Gulf of Finland they probably found settlements of Germanic peoples already in their destined country. The Finns absorbed some of these peoples, but the Swedish communities on the west and south coasts have remained distinct in blood and speech. The Finns themselves have retained definite tribal characteristics in several of the provinces (*landskap*). Others have moved on and have spread into northern Sweden and Norway and mixed to some extent with the Lapps. Still other related peoples, the Karelians, have occupied sparsely the cold forest area east of Finland, but their contact with the Finns is slight.

Within Finland a self-conscious minority retains Swedish speech and customs, and the Finnish and Swedish languages are equal before the law. These Swedes have been for centuries officials and farmers and fishers and have clung to their two coastal areas in west and south. Finland was converted to Christianity from Sweden, and for 600 years was an integral part of the Swedish state. The national culture is therefore strongly impregnated with Swedish elements, now so thoroughly absorbed that they seem indigenous. The "pure Finns" developed a strong nationalistic consciousness in the nineteenth century and, although the nationalist antagonism was and is directed primarily against Russia, the Swedish minority has also suffered from it occasionally. The Finnish element is in an overwhelming majority and many Swedo-Finns seek identification with the predominant group by adopting Finnish names; in intermarriage the tendency is toward Finnicization. Whereas early in the twentieth century something like 12 percent of the population was Swedish-speaking, the proportion has declined by the 1970s to about 7 percent. The most solid remaining area of Swedish predominance within Finnish boundaries is the Åland Islands. In most things there is no conflict between the two different peoples, and together they make one of the proudest and most self-assertive nationalities in Europe.

Life is difficult in the northern forests. Returns may seem meager to some; to the Finns they are enough. With patient will and a strength which transcends the physical these people have through centuries of hardship and of war with their eastern neighbors hardened their courage, their *sisu*. They dislike to admit impossibility, their backs are broad and unbending. They love their land with the passion of generations who have suffered to conquer the woods and the swampland, and who can suffer for centuries still. Sibelius' *Finlandia* is a mirror of the popular spirit— somber, strong, intense.

Even these lands of the northern border have their minorities problems. The outstanding example is the Swedish minority in Finland, but Finnish migration to Sweden both old and new involves large numbers, and the recent immigration from southern Europe to the factories and shops of the North is a social and economic factor of major importance.

Most colorful and ancient of the minorities are the Lapps, less than 40,000 all told (c. 22,000 in Norway, 10,000 in Sweden, 2,500–3,000 in Finland, and 1,500–2,000 in Russia). In northwestern Russia, all across northern Scandinavia and reaching southward along the mountainous dividing area between Norway and Sweden, the Lapps have roamed for centuries with their reindeer. Perhaps they were the original inhabitants of Scandinavia. These small dark people have a unique culture and speak a language of their own, partly borrowed from ancient Finnish, and also one or more of the modern Nordic tongues. The more "advanced" peoples who claim sovereignty over the land (Finns, Swedes, and Norwegians) feel a sense of responsibility toward these "little brown brothers," and allow them special legal privileges such as direct access to the king.

But a Lapp boy of the late twentieth century is not likely to grow up to herd reindeer on the tundra as did his grandfather and perhaps his father. He will no longer wander freely in the twenty-four-hour daylight of the northern summer across the Arctic borders that mean no more to him than to his animal herds. He and his sister will go to schools dedicated to the majority culture and will probably learn more about the Chinese and the Africans than about their own ancestral culture. They will probably settle in some remote village and become foresters or farmers, and in old age will go to a home for the elderly instead of being left sitting on a rock while family and herds move on. Their rights to water and grazing lands will have gone when they no longer raise reindeer, and the lands will have been taken over by others for mining and timber and power stations along the rivers. A nomadic culture based on reindeer is obsolete in the technological age. The attitude of the dominant society toward these simple but proud people is indifference or condescension, and only in recent years have some of the younger Lapps begun to resent and protest. Their people have enjoyed a legal position better than that of the American Indian, but in many ways their situation is as cruel.

As to the major peoples of the North, despite certain superficial differences they remain much alike—more than most of them wish to admit. In social customs and outlook on life they are closer to each other than New Englanders to Southerners—even in speech perhaps not much farther apart! In religion all the Scandinavians once worshiped Odin and Thor together; they passed together from paganism to Christianity. Now they are Lutherans—better than 90 percent throughout the area, although the ties are weakening. The legal systems come from common origins and are dominated by a common philosophy; many modern social laws are formulated in common.

The basic common ideal of individualism is modified in practice by the varying degrees of socialism in each of the five states. Literacy is, for all practical purposes, 100 percent throughout, and nowhere in the world can one find a higher per capita production and consumption of books. Freedom of expression is an ideal and a practice. Poverty, one might say, is one of the few things "verboten," and great wealth is taxed with severity.

Perhaps the most obvious inherent characteristic of the Scandinavians is their pervasive practicality. They can dream, yes, but they are likely to dream of worldly things. They are scientists and technologists; they are architects and designers, shipbuilders and sailors, skillful, resourceful; they are administrators, long successful in the art of governing themselves.

Exceptions there are, of course: Emanuel Swedenborg was one of them, and Hans Christian Andersen, and Edvard Grieg. Henrik Ibsen recognized and portrayed the inner conflict of man's spirit; in *Peer Gynt* fancy dominates reality, and often a Northerner likes to think he has a good bit of Peer Gynt in himself, though 99 percent of them suppress the little imp most effectively. Abstract thinking is rare, and a materialistic attitude toward life is deep rooted. A profound love of nature and of the physical is visible, expressing itself in literature and art, in competitive sports and hiking, bicycling, boating, and skiing in the high fjelds.

Essentially united as one family, but with strong intrafamily differences too. Unity is prized, but each member-nationality in the family group has an individuality to maintain even while cooperating with the group.

The Five Countries

The diversity which exists within the overall unity can be understood by a brief introduction to each of the individual countries.

Denmark is the geographic link between the European continent and the North. Denmark has been in closest contact with Germany and western Europe. This is evident in a speech which has been affected by Low German elements, in manners cosmopolitanized by trading and cultural contacts with France, and in architecture influenced noticeably by the Netherlands.

The Danish land seems as openhearted and as smiling as the people who enjoy themselves in Copenhagen's open-air playhouse, Tivoli, or who jostle one another as they stroll along commercial *Strøget* or seaside *Lange Linie*. Springtime views reveal the character of the countryside: green fields dotted with white cottages, thatched or red-tiled, with red window frames; families working together in the fields; cows and their calves, horses and their colts; square-towered white rural churches, solid-built, well-proportioned; wide reaches of sandy beaches; close-packed fishers' villages; an occasional stork's nest pitched high on the roof; dunes and stretches of heath being slowly reclaimed for cultivation; sometimes a small forest of beech or low wooded hills; a folk high school here and there; factories, breweries, shipyards; roadways built in three sections instead of two, one for pedestrians, one for automobiles and wagons, and one for the thousands of bicycles on which Danes go to work or to church or to play.

It is a gently rolling landscape, somewhat like northern Illinois, with only enough woods or undulating country to shelter the cottages from the west wind. Occasional sections are as rugged as southern Iowa, but the highest point in the country is only 568 feet above sea level. This modesty of the landscape seems comfortably appropriate. As Bishop Grundtvig put it: "No towering peaks thundered over our birth: it suits us best to remain on earth."

In the west of Denmark is low-lying Jutland, turning her back to the North Sea (the only important port there is Esbjerg, a mod-

ern "made" town though another and larger port may soon be
built). In southern Jutland Germans and Danes have pushed and
shoved at each other for generations. Eastward lie the islands
great and small which make up the bulk of the country: Fyn, with
busy Odense and, across the Great Belt, Zealand, on the east shore
of which is Copenhagen. To the south are Laaland and Falster
and a number of smaller islands; far to the east in the Baltic Sea is
ancient Bornholm. On Zealand was the castle of Hròthgar and the
scene of the Beowulf epic; to the north, at Elsinore, the ramparts
paced by Hamlet.

Across the Sound boats ply busily, as they have for centuries, to
the nearby Swedish shores, and through Öresund goes the shipping from the lands of the Baltic out to the world's markets. Copenhagen is a natural crossroads, like Constantinople and Singa-
pore. The sea is in and around Denmark, inviting commerce and
travel and fishing.

The Faroe Islands are the last remnant left in Scandinavian
control of the once extensive Norwegian holdings in the British
Isles. Here some 40,000 sheepraisers, farmers, and fishermen of
Norwegian ancestry live under Danish suzerainty, but with a high
degree of local autonomy. They have their own flag and they
enjoy membership in the Nordic Council, but they also send two
delegates to the Danish Folketing. Their green hills, mist-
enshrouded, have not attracted foreign invasion, except during
World War II when Great Britain took them under temporary
protection. Far to the west is Denmark's great island, Greenland,
but of that more later.

The total population of Denmark is about 5,000,000, of whom
1,350,000 live in metropolitan Copenhagen. There is no second
city in Denmark, but rather a group in third place, each rapidly
growing in the late twentieth century: busy and cultured Århus
(245,000); Odense (168,000); cement- and akvavit-manufacturing
Ålborg (155,000); Esbjerg built for fishing and commerce
(78,000); and a number of small towns.

Denmark is a land not of luxurious abundance but of a carefully nourished sufficiency. Her people live within their means. In
times of stringency they export their butter and eat margarine,
they boil barley to stretch out the coffee, and they forgo fancy new
cars and their grilles with the "dollar grin." Perhaps centuries of

experience have taught them to accept limitations. The Danes keep happy doing the necessary.

Sweden. Across the narrow Sound from Denmark lies the southern tip of the northward-reaching Scandinavian Peninsula. This southern province of Skåne, separated yet intimately linked with Denmark both culturally and geologically, has deep rich soil not scoured off by the ice sheets. Here is the breadbasket of Sweden, where the wheat is raised, the oats for the morning oatmeal, the sugar beets, and the vegetables. It is the region of beech trees and of the chateaux of the old landed aristocracy. The rolling landscape and the trim white cottages make one wonder if he is not still in Denmark.

Immediately to the north of Skåne begins a new landscape: the beech ceases to flourish, coniferous trees begin to dominate, and the surface of the earth is strewn with rock. Underneath is a different geologic substructure; it is the land of granite and other crystalline rocks, still asserting themselves after thousands of years of erosion. Sediments have filled in enough to support farming areas, but sometimes only enough to allow the roots of trees to gain foothold in pancake formation, and often naked rock permits no growth. The south central Swedish province of Småland was less abundant in its production of crops than of people, and from this rock and forest area came a large portion of Sweden's immigration to the United States.

Northward, in a broad belt running from the west coast in a northeasterly direction toward Stockholm and the ancient plains of Uppland, is again a fertile agricultural area. The mouths of the northern rivers provide strips of rich delta land, slowly increasing as they rise out of the sea.

For the most part the northern half of the country is timbered, and the slow-growing pines provide Sweden's greatest natural wealth. Lying within the rock in both central and northern Sweden are rich deposits of iron, copper—now almost gone—gold, silver, and a variety of other minerals. It is in the north, too, that the great series of parallel rivers flowing to the Gulf of Bothnia provide resources of waterpower to give light and energy to the south and to drive the trains of the country.

Variations are numerous, for the total length of Sweden from south to north is almost 1,000 miles, comparable to the distance from the southern tip of Italy's toe to the German Baltic coast. East to west the breadth at most is 300 miles, and the total area is 173,300 square miles—almost the size of prewar Germany, 10 percent larger than California, and ten times the size of Denmark. So in May, while the farmers till their fields in Skåne, city workers can vacation on skis in the mountains of the north and enjoy the midnight sun.

Sweden's physical and political boundaries are significant. In the south the sea connects her with Denmark and with Germany; in the west it opens a wide window to Britain and across the Atlantic. Toward Norway in the west rises the Keel, a long high range of mountains, unfortified and peaceful since 1814. In the east the border with Finland is defined but not defended by the fjelds (the upland moors) and the waters of the Torne river and by the wider waters of the Gulf of Bothnia. Sweden's east and south coast on the Baltic is blessed with skerries and harbors. For many centuries it has been the starting point for adventurers and traders to sail across to the neighbor lands; it has held for Sweden the islands of Öland and Gotland; and it has led fishermen out for many a catch. The same coast has attracted invasion, too, but it was the ancient habit of the Swedes to get there first.

One of the magnificently situated cities of the world is Stockholm, built on islands and cliffs of rock where sprawling Lake Mälar enters the narrow end of the widening Stockholm archipelago. The early medieval trading center was at Birka, an island in Lake Mälar, but Birger Jarl (thirteenth century) sensed the strategic importance of the Stockholm site and built a new city. In the last generation it has grown with especial rapidity, and now Greater Stockholm numbers 1,350,000 (1973). The second city in Sweden, westward-looking Gothenburg, is a kind of Scandinavian San Francisco, cosmopolitan, commerce-minded, with busy shipyards. The population is 688,000. Malmö, with a population of 450,000, is third, building ships, too, and carrying on the active import and export trade of Skåne.

Norway's heritage is much of nature's magnificence and little of resources (until oil). The country stretches 1,100 miles in direct line from south to north, 2,100 miles along the coast; the whole coastline, if one measures the fjords and bays, is about 12,000 miles, protected on the west by a long chain of outlying islands. The land is shaped like a squash with an abnormally long and bumpy neck. The end of that neck, up beyond Kirkenes, curls farther to the east than the easternmost limits of Poland or Rumania.

In width the land varies from 4 miles to 267, and the total area of Norway proper is 124,556 square miles, about three-quarters the size of Sweden, or a little smaller than Montana. The only long land frontier is the mountainous eastern border with Sweden, well marked but unfortified (1,028 miles). Farther north Norway marches for 460 miles with Finland across a rugged country of reindeer, Lapps, and occasional settlers. In the far northeast there is a frontier of 110 miles with Russia, since Finland ceded Petsamo in 1944. But it is the long western frontier of the coast, with its wealth of protected harbors and its deep-cut fjords which opens Norway to the Atlantic Ocean, Britain, the world of the West.

There is no complete road to the far north. Ferries are frequent, and the burden of north-south transportation is borne by coastal boats. The sea so dominates communications and life that an English visitor once insisted that Norway was really an island like Britain. It is the sea which holds the Norwegian land together; it is the sea which has made Norway a nation; and it is sea and rock together which give Norway its grandeur. Norwegians send out their fishing boats to the Arctic and the Antarctic and catch and process everything from sardines to whales (now only in the North Atlantic). They have created one of the world's largest merchant fleets.

The earliest settlements in Norway, and probably in all Scandinavia, were made in the far north, where wanderers from Asia came in along the ice-free coast. Here there were birds and fish, perhaps wild animals, and it may be that man lived in this coastal fringe even while the great ice sheet covered the mountains behind him and the whole land south into Denmark. When the later Teutonic and Mediterranean peoples moved up from the south, they too came along the warm coastal belt and moved inward through the rock-walled fjords, finding their small patches of fertile loam and living by fishing, hunting, and a little agriculture. As the population increased, men had to seek the inner valleys, where narrow strips of soil along lakes and streams were separated from each other by vast areas of barren, windswept fjeld. Intercommunication was difficult, and each cloistered valley tended to inbreed its people and its speech.

The larger unity of Norway was accepted the more easily because nature guaranteed each valley a high degree of autonomy. Whether up in his inland valley, or in a cove of a deep fjord, or in a fishing village on an island in Lofoten, the Norwegian has had the opportunity, and the need, to be independent. He has built his self-sufficient farm on a narrow mountainside, often on the only soil in sight. Like the American pioneer, the Norwegian has had to struggle alone to carve his destiny. For in Norway only 3 percent of the land is tillable, 1 percent is good for pasture, 25 percent is covered with productive forest, and 71 percent is for hunting, skiing, and photography.

From the Keel, the ridge which divides the Scandinavian Peninsula both politically and geographically, Norway slopes to the west, and the Norwegian slope is as precipitous as the eastern Swedish slope is gradual. At Narvik, for example, the railroad climbs steeply about four miles up from the fjord to the mountain divide, then takes hours to come down to sea level on the Swedish side.

Norway is first to feel the warming winds and the rains off the Atlantic; the clouds in the blue sky may shower rain at any moment. In the southern bulge of Norway the valleys are broader and closer together but still embraced by mountains. Water cascades from the fjelds in magnificent abundance. Far out in the North Sea, across a great deep, lie the new oil fields. Mineral resources are scarce compared with the deposits in Sweden, but through Narvik much of Swedish iron ore is shipped to foreign markets.

The cities of Norway are built, therefore, not on industry as much as on commerce, and they are neither so numerous nor so large as the cities of the neighboring lands. Population increase in recent years has likewise been less rapid in the cities than in the rural districts, but there has been a considerable increase in both. Oslo has a population of about 470,000, Bergen 214,000, Trondheim 133,000, and Stavanger 84,000. Norway as a whole numbers just under 4,000,000.

By an international agreement of 1920 Norway was granted

sovereignty over Svalbard, a group of islands 250 miles to the north, of which West Spitsbergen is the most important. Norwegians and others had fished and hunted whale in the surrounding waters for years before coal was discovered. An American company operated mines there in 1906–07, but sold out to Norwegians in 1916. The Dutch and the Swedes tried it, too, but since World War II the active exploiters have been Russians and Norwegians. 1972 estimates indicated coal reserves of 50–100,000,000 tons.

In the nineteenth and twentieth centuries the exploring zeal and the whaling skill of the Norwegians drew them to still more distant lands of ice. Nansen and Sverdrup and Amundsen found new seas and ocean currents. Large reaches of Antarctica were staked out by the venturesome Norsemen, and the surrounding seas were once the scene of great whaling expeditions. East Greenland was wanted, too, but in 1933 the World Court at The Hague decided that Denmark held sovereignty over the entire island, whether settled or not.

Bordering Norway and Sweden on the east is Finland. "Oh, why did our forefathers fall in love with these lakes and woods and settle here? Why didn't they keep on moving west? Then someone else could be Russia's neighbor."

Many Finns may agree with this plaint of one of them, but the forefathers did stay and took possession of the stern land. It is the northernmost country in the world, and one of the most sparsely settled: 4,600,000 (1971) people in a land that stretches 720 miles from north to south and 400 miles from east to west. In Europe only Norway spreads out its people more generously; in comparison with an American state the density is about the same as in Minnesota. The northern sections are more thinly populated than the southern, partly for climatic reasons, partly because settlement moved in from the southwest and south. Here in the middle of the western coast and along the southern shores still live the 7 percent of the population who retain their Swedish language and character.

The people have grown from 500,000 in 1740 to 1,000,000 in 1811, 2,000,000 in 1880, 3,000,000 in 1910, 4,000,000 in 1950, and to the 4,600,000 of 1971. The impressiveness of that growth is emphasized when it is recalled that since 1893 about 350,000 have emigrated to the United States and Canada and many to Sweden. The greatest rate of increase came in the stimulating and hopeful first years of independence, 1920–1940, and the population peaked in the early 1970s; projections indicate decline from 1975 to 1990.

The land is low lying and nearly 10 percent is covered with lakes. These factors added to the influence of the Atlantic winds give Finland a climate more moderate than is usual in such northern latitudes. In climate and flora as in several other respects Finland is a transition zone, intermediate between Scandinavia and the east European plains region. Her wealth is in her forests, on which are based her natural industries and her export trade; minerals, fisheries, and agriculture play a comparatively minor role.

Finland has three long land frontiers: 333 miles with Sweden along the Torne and Muonio rivers, 460 miles with Norway along the Tana River and the watershed between the Atlantic and the Gulf of Bothnia, and 775 miles in the east with the Soviet Union. This new-drawn frontier with the USSR mainly follows the watershed between the White Sea and the Baltic, but at several points it cuts in two economic and old cultural communities.

Finland's industrial centers are many but her cities are few. Helsinki (Helsingfors) is capital and metropolis with a population of 830,000; Tampere (Tammerfors) with a population of 228,000 is a lumber and textile town; while Turku (Åbo), about 225,000, is the chief western port, and a center of the old Swedish culture.

Iceland, in mid-Atlantic, lies only 180 miles from the coast of Greenland; the northernmost point reaches to the Arctic Circle. The island is a rough oval, deeply cut by fjords and bays, almost 300 miles in length and 194 miles in width and growing wider by about one inch each year. The total area of 40,000 square miles is less than that of Cuba and about the same as Virginia, but the people live in the lowlands, comprising only 7 percent of the land. The interior is starkly magnificent, with a hundred mountains up to 6,400 feet in height and geysers, sulphur springs, waterfalls, volcanoes. Not only Surtsey but the 1973 eruption on Haemey in the Westmann Islands attest the continuing violence of vast undersea forces. The weather is even more uncertain than in most parts of the world but not at all as cold as the country's name implies. The climate is strongly influenced by the Gulf Stream and by a northern current which brings drift ice and mist. Rainfall in the south averages almost fifty inches a year, but the north is dry though often foggy like the east.

The geographical-technological revolution has affected this northern island directly. Just as it was on the route of the Vikings westward, much more now Iceland lies athwart vital strategic routes. In World War II it was a gathering place or way station for convoys sailing from the west to Murmansk; it was a stopping place and an emergency base for planes between North America and the British Isles or Germany. In the crucial northern hemisphere, in a period of waterborne and airborne commerce and warcraft, Iceland occupies a key position; isolation is no longer conceivable.

Holding this crossroads position is a population of 213,000 (1973)—homogeneous, literate, highly intelligent, well-governed folk, alert to the changing world in which they live. More new books are published in Iceland, per capita, than in any other country. The "per capita" may not be much, but the significant things are that publication is a habit and that since the saga age the children of Iceland, girls and boys, have been taught to read and write. The chief city is Reykjavik (the Smoky Bay), the capital, grown rapidly from a population of 6,600 in 1900 to 84,000 in 1973, with handsome new buildings for the university, and extensive modern concrete housing. The city and its suburbs together contain well over half the country's people. In the north is Akureyri, a fishing port of 10,000 population, and several towns slightly smaller.

The contacts of the Icelanders have been largely with Danes and Norwegians, but British traders and pirates disregarded prohibitory regulations and visited the island, and Americans edged into a small trade there beginning in 1809 and gained a special license in 1815. But in general the Danes held close control over trade and government.

In the nineteenth century a nationalist movement, inspired by Jón Sigurdsson, forced gradual concessions from Denmark. In the 1830s a consultative assembly was established, and in 1874, when Iceland celebrated the 1000th anniversary of settlement, King Christian IX gave this assembly, the Althing, additional legislative powers. In 1903 the Althing won the right to control the ministry, and in 1918 Iceland became a kingdom, united with Denmark through a common sovereign and using the Danish foreign service to represent its interests abroad. It was then conceded that Iceland might become completely independent by mutual agreement after twenty-five years. World War II hastened the realization of that ambition; Iceland steered her own course after April 9, 1940, and became a sovereign republic on June 17, 1944.

Greenland is the western outpost of the Scandinavian area, only a short jump across the Davis Strait from the North American mainland. (Because the island must be neglected in later sections of this volume it will be considered generously at this point.)

The world's largest island has an area of 840,000 square miles; it is larger than the combined area of Spain, France, Germany, and Italy. From Cape Farewell in the south to Cape Morris Jesup in the north is 1,650 miles, and the greatest width is 690 miles. From the northernmost point it is but 439 miles to the North Pole. Of its vast surface 86 percent is covered by the inland ice cap, which reaches heights up to 10,000 feet. The ice averages about 5,000 feet in thickness; at the edges it is usually some 100 feet above sea level, and throws off icebergs from its glaciers directly into the sea or into the in-reaching bays and fjords which indent the coast. Some of these more southerly glaciers move at speeds of 65 to 125 feet per day.

Atop the ice sheet the temperatures are always low, but in the coastal regions there is great variation: within the month of February Upernivik has had temperatures as high as 60.8°F. and as low as −44.°F. Precipitation varies from as little as six inches per year (Danmarkshavn) to as much as forty-six inches (Ivigtut), and it is almost all snow.

Current life on the island has come from the West, both the sparse flora and the animal life of land and sea: reindeer, fox, caribou, polar bear, whales, seal, ptarmigan, even the native Greenlanders, whose Eskimo ancestors came across from northern Canada.

In two areas an ice-free coastal strip is wide enough and conditions are favorable enough so that settlements of people can exist: (1) West Greenland, really the southern stretch of the west coast, where the ice retreats as much as 95 miles from the shore, and where in some places islands dot the coast; (2) East Greenland, about one-third of the total ice-free land, where in one place (Scoresby Sound) it is 186 miles from sea to ice. In East Greenland the land is even more rugged than in the west, with many peaks of over 6000 feet.

Along these two coastal strips a population of some 48,000 scatters itself in small communities; a few Eskimo, a few Danes, mostly a mixture of the two called Greenlanders.

Eric the Red made his permanent establishments (985) in the southwest, first in the "Eastern Settlement," now the Julianehaab District, and soon additional immigrants built up the "Western Settlement," now the Godthaab District. In these two settlements around the year 1000 may have lived 2000 people, Icelanders and Norwegians all. It was Eric's son Leif who led the first expedition to explore Vinland; and it was from these Greenland settlements that successive attempts were made by others in the next few years to colonize in North America. But that was too far, demands for more land were not pressing enough; the Vikings had reached their western limits.

The colony seemed to prosper moderately until the thirteenth century, and we read in European literature of the importance of Greenland falcons. But Greenland became increasingly dependent on Norway and in the mid-thirteenth century was forced to accept Norwegian overlordship (about the same time as Iceland), though the local Althing was kept. The Norwegians promised to send at least one ship a year, but frequently the ship was lost. When the Black Death scourged Norway in the mid-fourteenth century no ship went out for several years, "the long forgetfulness." An expedition to the Western Settlement in 1350 found only wild cattle and sheep, no human beings.

At last, in 1355, Paul Knutson was sent from Norway to try to check the decline of Christianity, for King Magnus said, "We will not let it perish from the earth." He did not find much, although the Eastern Settlement still existed. Knutson evidently wrote no report on his expedition, and mystery surrounds both of its exploits in North America and the last phases of life in Icelandic-Norwegian colonization in Greenland. Possibly the people, few in numbers and weakened by malnutrition, were overcome by the Eskimo. Possibly they migrated to the American mainland and were lost. The colony ceased to exist.

Greenland's "rediscovery" dates from an expedition sent out by Christian I of Denmark in 1472 or 1473, which was attacked by Eskimo in East Greenland, near Angmagssalik (East Greenland being completely different from the old "Eastern Settlement"). The king's purpose was to find a northwest passage to China, which was also the primary aim of later explorers such as Frobisher, Davis, and Baffin. Commercial interest grew as English, Dutch, and Danes learned from the Basques the art of harpooning whales. The Danish-Norwegian king became annoyed with Dutch claims in Greenland. So in 1666 the Greenland symbol, the polar bear, was added to the Danish royal coat of arms as a reminder to others to keep out. The first new settlement was established in 1721 by the Norwegian Hans Povelsen Egede, named Royal Missionary, and backed by a Bergen trading company.

Trade rivalries and conflicts over fishing led to the declaration of a royal monopoly on trade in 1776. The purpose of the monopoly was to assure the interests of the Greenlanders in culture and trade, and many commissions and self-sacrificing administrators have done their best. Greenlanders have themselves participated in local and district advisory councils. Schools and churches and hospitals have been established. But the people remained poor. Monopoly and the rigidity of controls were criticized both in Greenland and in Denmark as stifling to development.

In the mid-twentieth century the whole monopolistic system was being abandoned, trade put on a basis of free competition, and private Danish capital invited to enter the field. In 1953 Greenland ceased to be a colony and became an integral part of the Danish kingdom. The economic and political reorientation was stimulated to some extent, probably, by the impact of United States soldiers and others in Greenland. Internal reasons had to do with a moderation of the climate; the diminution of seals, which had made possible a self-contained economy; the increase of cod fishing, which required sale on a world market; and sheep raising. The changed basis of the economy has been accompanied by a doubling of the population in less than twenty-five years.

Disputes and complications concerning sovereignty over Greenland have continued. The Norwegian claim was rejected in 1933. The United States, when it purchased the Danish West Indies in 1917, renounced claims to the territory discovered in the north by Admiral Peary. Then came World War II and the German occupation of Denmark. One year after that occupation, April 9, 1941, the Danish Minister in Washington, Henrik Kauffmann, signed an agreement with the United States Secretary of State which established a wartime protectorate over Greenland by the United States and permitted the United States to establish military and meteorological bases. But the United States reasserted that Denmark remained sovereign over all Greenland.

The importance of this vast ice-covered island is largely strategic. Most of the native products are of no outside significance, not even the furs are important in world trade, though the natives dress in fox or bearskin trousers, eat the meat, use skins for boats, and in general live from animals. Coal is mined, but only for local consumption. In 1948 the discovery of uranium in East Greenland was reported. For some years the only important export was cryolite from the mine at Ivigtut, but that has ceased.

Strategically, the island has a double importance. In the first place, the enormous field of ice is a powerful influence on the winds and weather of the North Atlantic, and therefore on northern and western Europe. A number of scientific expeditions, primarily Danish and American, have sought there to fathom the mysteries of weather. During World War II the Germans did their best to establish a meteorological post. In the second place Greenland, like Iceland, is on the Great Circle air route between America and Europe and lies along the pathway of a potential Arctic submarine route. Greenland is in the strategic center of conceivable Arctic warfare.

The Unity of the North

The great expanse of land and sea from Greenland in the west to Finland in the east is unified historically and geographically. The Viking longboats, raiding and crusading, made it one. Language affinities and political institutions attest the interrelationships. Shippers and fishers of all the North mingle in each other's ports. But the pilots and planes of the air have created the real modern counterpart of the sea routes of old. Through changing times and varying techniques the Scandinavians have retained intimate relations within their area and have preserved their institutions. The borders have from time to time been threatened and are threatened in the twentieth century, but so far they have held with tenacity. In a five-way political division the essentials of cultural unity have been deeply engraved. Outside rule has been repelled; immigrants have been absorbed.

These lands and peoples of the North are closely related to each other; they are also closely related to the other countries of western Europe, particularly those bordering on the Baltic and the North Sea. Age-old bonds of culture and commerce connect them with Germany and Britain, and they feel keenly any break in those established and natural ties.

The "island" character of each of the Scandinavian lands influences its entire life. Iceland is the only one which is technically an island. Denmark, however, is made up of many islands and a peninsula connected with the continent by only a narrow neck. The Scandinavian Peninsula and Finland are land-connected only through wide swaths of forest and swamp (except in the isthmus between Lake Ladoga and the Gulf of Finland, where Finland and Russia meet). The insular nature of the area, therefore, emphasizes the importance of the sea as a link with other lands and peoples, and has made of the Scandinavians seafaring peoples, using the sea for commerce and fishing and war.

Other pervasive characteristics are sparsity of settlement and vastness of distance; only Denmark is tightly settled, and the distance from Copenhagen to Norway's North Cape, in a straight line, is longer than that from Berlin to Constantinople. Winters lack crippling cold, but in the northern portions they are long and dreary and dark.

The air age and polar flying have come to minimize distance and to add air to sea as a new medium of communication. Airplanes not only knit more closely the territory of the North, they also transform Scandinavia's strategic position. The region was on the edge of land or sea conflicts of the past between the great powers; it now lies under the Great Circle air routes between East and West.

Political shifts outside Scandinavia reinforce the changes wrought by air transportation and a new technology. When four to six powers on the continent vied with one another in the balance of power and bid for the aid or neutrality of the northern states, they had a chance to protect themselves. They were then, as individual nations, relatively strong enough to deserve respect. But now there are not four to six powers juggling the diplomacy of Europe. The power centers lie outside Europe proper and the theater is not Europe but the world. Scandinavia's strategic position has deteriorated politically as well as geographically.

Consciousness of this change has accentuated among the small states of the North a sense of their need for each other and has emphasized their common heritage and outlook. They know they do not now lie on the border as much as they once did. Each has different neighbors with whom to deal, and each has its own individual interests. But each has also a feeling of kinship in the group and of common concern. In the present generation the idea of unity has reached far enough to be institutionalized in the Nordic Council (but just so far and no farther).

2 *The Heritage*

The essence of Scandinavia's historical background may be seen in terms of four fundamental shaping forces: *war* which has created states, and fixed boundaries; *religion* which has held people together and encouraged ideals beyond the present and the material; *law* which has defined the relationships of individuals to one another and established order and justice; the *economy* by which men live and through which they have organized for material well-being. These four, expressed in institutions, in literature, in arts, in tradition, afford an insight into a total culture.

War

In the dawn of civilization in Scandinavia it was war which decided the preeminence of the Nordic invaders over the "little brown folk" who inhabited the inner lands of Sweden or the coasts of Norway. Perhaps tribes like the Herules had fled from the Danube because they had been defeated and decimated in war; new struggle faced them in the North. A reverse movement occurred when the Cimbri moved south out of Jutland and ravaged large areas of the Roman Empire before they were subdued and absorbed. The Svear and Götar and the Danes extended their sway by war and even by the enslavement of conquered peoples.

The Beowulf Saga pictured a warlike society, and the Vikings became the terror of their age.

The Viking raids were the second outward thrust of the Scandinavian peoples. The earlier migrations of the Cimbri and the Goths were surges of mass humanity from a backward area into the more highly civilized Roman Empire. The forays of the Vikings were mixtures of trading and raiding carried out not by tribal groups but by small bands of men, sailing in the finest ships of the day, seeking profit and booty and adventure. In the central thrust they raided the coasts of Britain and France, took over the Faroes, Orkneys, Shetlands, Hebrides, and the Isle of Man, and established a kingdom in Ireland; they fought on the shores of Portugal, and Normans won control of Sicily. The fleeting raids with which they began in France became large-scale operations and ended at last in the establishment of the duchy of Normandy in 911 under Rollo. From there a century and a half later the mixed descendants of that enterprise went on to conquer England.

In the eastward thrust there was more of trading and less of raiding, when the Swedish Vikings or Varangians traversed Russia via the Dvina and the Dnieper and sailed on through the Black Sea to Miklagard (Constantinople). Here they traded their honey and furs and pitch for the gold and the luxurious products of Byzantine and Oriental civilization. Here in Miklagard some of them stayed for a time and served in the Varangian Guard, elite soldiery of the Byzantine emperors and empresses. These "axe-bearing barbarians" fought throughout the Mediterranean, and one of them even carved runic inscriptions on the huge body of a lion statue in the Piraeus. To the northward their fellows left runic monuments on the Volga. Others under Rurik and his partners first built an orderly state among the Russian Slavs. Their very name, for the Varangians were called Rus by the Slavic tribes, became at length the name of those tribes themselves and of the modern Russians.

Far westward across the North Atlantic went another major thrust of the Vikings. Here their shapely longboats carried warriors and pioneers to Iceland and on to Greenland, and farther yet to Vinland. In their previous expeditions to the south and east, however numerous the Vikings may have been, they lost their northern identity; but in Iceland they created a society which retained their customs and their language longer than did the home lands.

The whole "movement" of these three thrusts was a prodigal dispersion of power, never centrally directed, never quite focused, but with far-reaching results impossible to calculate. In east and west the constructive aspects are clear; in the central push the coasts of western Europe were laid waste, the Carolingian Empire was shattered, and one knows not how much the northern strength and northern ideas of law may have contributed to the process of reconstruction. Nor can we measure the effects of this violent outburst on the lands back in the north. Something was learned of Christianity, and the booty brought back in only one or two raids was often greater than the taxes collected through years from peasants and fishermen.

Medieval Scandinavians had their wars and their empire-building nearer home, too. In warfare within the North, Denmark first occupied the central position, and the weight of power swung back and forth like a pendulum. Denmark was the bridge between south and north; also she lay athwart the routes of war and commerce between east and west. Germans pushed north through Jutland, where the still-used central roadway shows evidences of invasion and strife through centuries of both prehistoric and modern times. Across the base of the Jutland peninsula lay the ancient land route for trade between France, the North German cities, and the Baltic area, and that region was fought over repeatedly by princes and city states. The Kiel Canal is but a modern device to utilize more fully this age-old route.

Denmark too stood guard over the narrow water passage from North Sea to Baltic and so through many centuries played a pivot position in the naval wars of commerce which involved England, Spain, France, and Holland on the west, Sweden, Russia, and the German cities on east and south in all conceivable changing combinations. Denmark's existence hung upon her own agility and the fate of foreign rivalries. The near-by Germans in their periods of both weakness and strength were the main external influence in Danish affairs. Slesvig (Schleswig in the German spelling) and Holstein, symbol and center of this continual conflict, passed back and forth. War gave and war took away. When, through her own strength and that of her allies, Denmark won, she evidenced her prosperity in extensive building and in an increasing population; when she lost, her people suffered privation and waited for another chance.

Denmark did not, however, stand as a passive participant, but was often the aggressor—not only in the raids of the Vikings but in the migratory movement of the Angles and Saxons and Jutes, in the later establishment of the Danelaw in north England and in the creation of the North Sea Empire of King Canute in the eleventh century. For a fleeting moment Canute conquered and ruled over Denmark, Norway, and the British Isles. But these lands were too diverse and Denmark was too weak to hold them together. When shorn of this empire ambitious Danish kings strove to extend their power throughout the north and east. Norway and her colonies were united with Denmark in 1389 not by war but by marriage and the diplomacy of Queen Margaret. With control emanating from Copenhagen the Danes held the southern parts of the Scandinavian peninsula, directed Norwegian forces from the west, and won dominion over Gotland and in the lands on the eastern shores of the Baltic.

Thus for a brief period following 1389 the Danes realized the recurrent dream of a Scandinavian empire and exercised hegemony in the famous Union of Kalmar. For 400 years they played an active game of diplomacy and war. Sweden Finland was boxed in between the encircling Danes and Norwegians and their frequent allies, the Russians. But Sweden gained the occasional support of Denmark's western neighbors, the Dutch, and she showed a rapidly developing internal strength. By the seventeenth century, Denmark was pushed back from her eastern position; she was left only Norway and the western possessions in the Atlantic. The Swedes had taken the initiative from their cousins in the south.

The early wars between tribes and traders in central Sweden are beclouded in legend and uncertainty. We know only that out of strife the Swedes and Goths made themselves masters over the other tribes in the east-central area of the Scandinavian peninsula. In the twelfth century the prolific and vigorous Swedes pushed on in a movement of conquest and colonization to control and Christianize the Finns and to establish in their forest frontier permanent institutions of western culture.

With colonies also on the islands and on the coasts of the Baltic countries to the south of Finland, it was natural that the Swedish expansionists should seek power there and inevitable that they should come into conflict with both the eastward-reaching Danes and the westward-pushing Russians.

In 1523 Gustav Vasa, contemporary of Henry VIII of England, of the Emperor Charles V, and of Martin Luther, by war established Sweden's independence from Denmark, built a national state and a national church, and laid the foundation for further growth. Generations of warfare around the Baltic and the creation of a wide-spreading Baltic Empire led at length to continental conflict. Gustav II Adolf (Gustavus Adolphus), "lion of Protestantism," feared that Hapsburg-Catholic success in Germany would threaten the political-religious independence of the North.

In a remarkable speech to the Swedish Riksdag in 1630 as he was about to lead his forces south, Gustav Adolf explained that though the Holy Roman Empire had no fleet at that moment and could not cross the Baltic it would quickly build such a fleet once it reached the northern shores of Germany. Sweden's best protection, said the King, was to fight the enemy on German soil, before she had become too strong and while the north German states could still be of help as allies. It was the 1940–41 argument of "defend America by aiding the Allies" in a seventeenth-century setting. Gustav Adolf lost his life, but his policy triumphed, and Sweden won territory in Bremen and Pomerania. The Swedish king also contributed improved techniques and a new mobility to the art of warfare.

Gustav Adolf's successors used the increased power and prestige of the kingdom for further victories: most important was the winning of the southern provinces of Skåne, Halland, and Blekinge from Denmark. It was in this war that King Charles X, after a frustrating campaign in Poland, led his army across Germany, north into Jutland, then on ice across the Little Belt and the Great Belt in a spectacular island-hopping operation, over passages which froze hard enough for such a transit once in a hundred years. In that crucial year, 1658, nature obliged the Swedes, and the stunned Danes could not defend Copenhagen. Sweden thus won the agricultural land of the south and the commercial coast of the west and widened what had been but a narrow wedge of coast between Denmark and Norway.

But the victories of Gustav Adolf concentrated jealousy against a nation with small resources. A half century later Charles XII found himself confronted with a formidable coalition of enemies, and his dashing brilliance in battle was not enough to save Sweden from disaster. Charles conquered for himself only an undying admiration from the romantic heart of the "little man," who still thinks of the impulsive boy wonder as Sweden's greatest king. But Sweden alone was not strong enough to carry through a policy of force. The states of the continent had more men and more guns. Charles lost his soldiers and his empire deep in the plains of the Ukraine. Years later he made a spectacular dash back to the north but was killed on the Norwegian frontier, and Sweden's age of imperial greatness was over.

Expansion of the power of any state tends to increase the number of its enemies and to consolidate them in opposition. A small state cannot long survive against pressure from all sides. Both Denmark and Sweden had their brief days of brilliance and power, but they were weakened by internal rivalries and divisions and they lacked the essential bases of manpower and industrial resources for lasting imperial dominion. In the years to come they were even played as pawns in the rivalries of the great powers with one another.

After Charles XII was killed and the Swedish Baltic empire came to its inglorious end in 1721 two small kingdoms were left in the north: Sweden with Finland, and the combined kingdoms of Denmark-Norway. The Norwegian border had been pushed back to the mountain ridge which still marks a natural division between Sweden and Norway; Jämtland and Härjedalen had become parts of Sweden. In the south, too, the Swedish state had expanded, at the expense of Denmark, and occupied the whole of the lower end of the peninsula; Skåne, Halland, and Blekinge were incorporated into the Swedish state. Denmark-Norway held dominion over Greenland and Iceland and the Faroes—but the Danish king had been forced to mortgage the Norwegian-settled Orkneys and Shetlands for dowry when his daughter married King James III of Scotland (1468). They were never recovered.

In the long struggle for supremacy in the Baltic Sweden had forged ahead, held Pomerania on the North German coast, and won back from Denmark the island of Gotland, "Pearl of the Baltic." She lost to Denmark her brief grip on the southern island of Bornholm and finally lost to Russia the littoral of Estonia and Latvia where German barons and the merchants and warriors of both Denmark and Sweden had long fought for mastery. To Denmark one imperial right remained: the Danish king continued, as he had since 1429, to collect "Sound Dues" from every ship passing Elsinore between the North Sea and the Baltic.

The external boundaries of Scandinavia in the 1970s are surprisingly similar to those of 1721, though intermediate and internal changes have taken place. Slesvig-Holstein was then connected with Denmark and now only the northern section is so connected. Finland's eastern and northern borders were then approximately as today, with Viborg belonging to Russia and with the Russian frontier in the north marching for a brief distance with Norway and cutting off Finland from the ocean.

During the centuries of Danish and Swedish imperialistic rivalry Finland and Norway played subordinate roles. The Finns, directed by the Swedes, made no effective protest against their leadership and participated as Swedish soldiers in the wars against Russia and in Gustav Adolf's campaigns in Germany.

The warfare of the Norwegians was mostly an internal affair, chieftain against chieftain striving for authority over the whole of Norway. Unity came with Christianity out of the wars of the tenth to twelfth centuries: Harold Fairhair united the kingdom about 900, but the divisive elements were still strong; Olav Tryggvason and Saint Olav used Christianity as a means of winning a common loyalty; King Sverre at last broke the power of both aristocracy and bishops and established the prestige of kingship. The fighting was bloody and significant, both in the building of Norway itself and in the expansion of Norway overseas. Many independent nobles, defeated or outmaneuvered by the centralizing kingship, then sailed off to build new careers in the islands of the Atlantic, all the way from the Faroes through Iceland to Greenland. In the fourteenth century the male line of Norse kings died out and Norway was united with Denmark. Theoretically Norway remained independent, but the common king resided in Copenhagen and Danish officials directed the fate of the northern partner.

Norway was used repeatedly to threaten Sweden's rear when Denmark allied with Russia to try to drive the Swedes out of the Baltic. The uncertain borderland, for a time taking Norway to within thirty miles of the Gulf of Bothnia, was a place of pillage and burning and terror until a shift in power in the seventeenth century drove the frontier westward to the mountains. The common border between Norway and Sweden has been unchanged since 1660, and a certain détente between these two states was reached by 1721.

The eighteenth century was dominated by the imperialistic wars of the great powers, and the Scandinavian states played cagily for self-preservation. They accepted subsidies from Britain or France, joined one alliance or another, battled with or against each other, cautiously sought a chance to win territory or to expand trade. It was a transition stage in which they reluctantly abandoned the policy of power and turned to the less venturesome, much safer, system of neutrality.

During the general turmoil of the Revolutionary and Napoleonic period, war again brought significant changes in Scandinavian boundaries. First, as a result of agreement between Napoleon and Alexander I of Russia, the Bear walked into Finland. Battle and treachery combined to yield a swift decision, and Finland was taken from Sweden; the Russians drew the Finnish border to include the Swedish-populated Åland Islands in the Baltic, and in the north swung the frontier far around Sweden toward the Atlantic. This blow to Swedish pride and power, depriving her of the province which she had regarded as part of herself for over 600 years, led to revolution and reorientation. Gustav IV Adolf was removed in a coup d'état by a group of nobles and officials (1809).

A peculiar sequence of events led within a year to the choice of the French marshal, Bernadotte, as Crown Prince and real ruler. But Bernadotte, now Prince Carl Johan, was unhampered either by Swedish tradition or by love of Napoleon. He saw that Sweden had little hope of regaining Finland from mighty Russia. He also entertained the geographic concepts of the French Revolution which meant to him that Norway and Sweden, joined in the same land mass, formed a "natural" geographic entity. Therefore Finland must be forgotten, and Norway must be united with Sweden. The fact that Norway was then united with Denmark could hardly mean much to a soldier who had participated in the wars of the Revolution and of Napoleon and in the recent reorganization of Germany. War must establish what nature intended.

King Frederick of Denmark followed an understandable but foolish policy. When Denmark was attacked in 1807 by Great Britain he saw Britain as the continuing enemy and clung stubbornly to an alliance with Napoleon, the real threat to all small states. This made it possible for Carl Johan, convinced that Napoleon was soon to collapse, to win agreement from Russia and Prussia and Great Britain that Norway should be separated from Denmark and added to Sweden. This was the price which the Swedish Prince and military genius demanded and received for his alliance in the last coalition against the Emperor of the French.

The Frenchman turned Swede revolutionized the policy of his adopted country. At Åbo, Finland, in August 1812 an unprecedented spectacle took place: the Crown Prince of Sweden and the Czar of Russia embraced each other in the friendship of common interest. Alexander turned to watch Napoleon's army destroy itself in the desolating Moscow campaign, and Carl Johan faced about to plan for the final drive on the continent and the conquest of Norway.

After the success of the allies on the continent and the Napoleonic downfall at Leipzig, Bernadotte took his mixed army of Swedes, Russians, and a few others to Denmark and in January 1814 forced King Frederick to renounce Norway. The Norwegians tried to reestablish their long-lost independence, drew up the constitution of Eidsvold, and elected their Danish statholder as king. It took a short summer campaign and appeals to the pledges of his allies for Carl Johan to assure the union of Norway with Sweden. His conciliatory policy left the Norwegians with the feeling that the essentials of national freedom had been won. He left the constitution unchanged, and the day of its original proclamation, May 17, is still the national holiday of Norway. Norway remained united with Sweden under a common king until 1905; the Norwegians then insisted on being independent. The Swedish attitude was summed up: "Let the erring sister depart in peace." Divorce came with bitterness and regret, but without war.

Denmark had, in 1814, by clever diplomacy kept for herself the Atlantic possessions of Norway, but her power and her ambitions had been given an irretrievable blow. In 1848 and in 1864 she was forced to fight against desperate odds to retain the provinces of Slesvig and Holstein. Pan-Scandinavian sentiment was strongly with her, but sentiment did not check the Prussian soldiers. Except for a small occupying force in 1848 the government of Sweden-Norway kept hands off, to the chagrin of the king and of many a citizen; and in 1864 Denmark lost again. Ibsen composed some anguished charges, but Slesvig-Holstein was gone, and even the Prussian promise of a plebiscite went unfulfilled until 1920. Except for these two local, defensive wars in Denmark, the Scandinavians kept out of war from 1814 to 1914, and, except for Finland, on to 1940.

War forged the boundaries of the North; war determined who should control the trade routes and the fisheries; war repeatedly tested the strength of kings and aristocracy. In war were released the pressures of personal ambition and adventure which were later contained temporarily in treaties of peace. Protestantism and the desire for religious independence influenced both the Danish and Swedish phases of the Thirty Years' War. Both personal and national aggrandizement played their parts in the wars of Charles XII and Gustav Adolf and Waldemar Atterdag, the fourteenth-century Danish conqueror. As in warfare everywhere, one finds in that of Scandinavia a blend of economic forces and limitations, population pressures, religious and nationalistic ideologies. The peasants asserted their rights in local and national risings and thus tried to maintain or improve their status. Denmark and Norway were parted by war; Norway and Sweden were for ninety years united by means of war. Finland was torn from Sweden by war and by war gained at last a new independence. Iceland was settled by refugees from internal strife in Norway. Warfare did much to shape the North.

But gradually conflicting forces became balanced within Scandinavia. Boundaries and relative power were established. It became fruitless for the Scandinavian peoples to war among them-

selves, and dangerous for them to fight such neighbors as
Germany and Russia. Out of the fires of experience they learned
the destructiveness and the futility of war; they had sufficient intelligence and sufficient inner political stability to reject it "as an
instrument of national policy." But they could not escape it when
it came from outside.

Religion

"We obey the Law and bow before Christ." These words are
from an old motto, displayed at Eidsvold in Norway with the picture of a kneeling soldier.

Less tangible than war, but no less an influence in Scandinavian
life is religion—both as an impelling force and as a basis of the
social structure. The Swedish conquest of Finland was a Crusade,
and missionaries marched with soldiers; Christianity formed one
of the bonds thereafter tying the two peoples together. In the
Thirty Years' War it is impossible to disentangle the intertwined
elements of religion, politics, and strategy. In Norway from the
time when Olav Tryggvason gave the chieftains a choice of sword
or cross on to the resistance movement of World War II nearly a
thousand years later Christianity and the Christian church have
been inextricably linked with the state and the vital interests of the
people.

The religion of the ancient gods was bound in closely with the
lives of the people of the North. Odin the All-Father was the
fountainhead of wisdom; Thor with his miracle-hammer, the god
of thunder and of war, was dear to the Viking heart, and so was
Loki, the trickster, and Freya, the life-force mother, and the Val-
kyrie, who made pleasant the deaths of warriors in Valhalla. All
Northerners believed in these same gods, the Aesir, a democratic
family community of super-beings, whose lives and loves and
hates helped to epitomize and explain the mysteries of the unex-
plainable on earth.

Beliefs were strongly individualistic, each person having the
right to choose his own god-protector. Chieftains, military
leaders, chief peasants, acted in the religious rites, and there arose
no separate powerful priesthood. Along with this general religious structure persisted beliefs in the *norns* or the spirits that
inhabited the forests and the swamps.

The Vikings learned to associate Christianity with the prosperity and the higher culture of the lands they plundered, and foreign traders brought in new religious ideas. Ansgar came north from a Saxon abbey in the ninth century to Christianize Denmark and Sweden, but the converts he won tended to backslide when the missionary had moved on; the ideas he brought were foreign ideas. Then Vikings converted in England or France began to exert their influence at home.

Thus Olav Tryggvason came with power and prestige to Norway, and slaughtered those who would not be baptized; it was through him that Leif Ericson became a Christian and was sent to Greenland, where he had more success with the other colonists than with his stubborn father. Many of Olav's conversions were obtained very suddenly, with no real conquest of heart; conversions of the battlefield did not strike deep.

Not surprisingly many of the chieftains combined against the next unifying and Christianizing king, Olav Haraldson, reasserting paganism and their own rights. This new Olav was cut down at the battle of Stiklestad in 1030, but the sequel showed what a ferment had begun to work. Miracles were reported from Olav's body, and at the same time people began to feel the pinch of foreign authority. Half-convinced already, the chieftains and the people began to rethink their deeds and decided that Olav must have been right. They repented their victory, regretted the death of the national leader and the Christian, made him "Saint Olav," and erected Trondheim (Nidaros) Cathedral over his grave. In his memory they joined in a move to reunite Norway.

"The blood of the martyrs is the seed of the church." But as people came haltingly to a recognition of the new faith, so they came with painful gradualness to an acceptance of the teaching of Jesus.

Christ himself was preached at first as a lord of strength, able to humble and to shatter the power of mighty Odin. The apostles were represented as the bodyguard of Jesus, Armageddon as Ragnarök, and Paradise as the old Valhalla. The story of the death of Balder the Good and the Beautiful may well have been an early attempt to reconcile something of the heathen beliefs with the story of Jesus. The annual festivals celebrating the coming of spring and praying to the god of the harvest were so natural to folk dependent on rain and sunshine that they have been merely transformed and kept in a Christian environment; fires still burn on Swedish hillsides on Valborgsmässoafton, and Midsummer Eve has elements of pagan mysticism even if followed by a church service on Midsummer Day. The worship of the sun left traces far into the Christian epoch, when the radiant sun symbol was blazoned on altar cloths in medieval churches. Intricately beautiful wood carving on church doors and pagan dragons flaunted atop roofs attest the continuing power of the old traditions as well as the old art forms.

Gradually Christianity, allied with the centralizing policy of the kings, struck firm roots. About 1100 Lund was made the seat of an archbishopric for all the North, and the foreignness of Christianity began to lose significance. Bishops and kings often worked together, even as in those more "civilized" lands to the south. Perhaps most notable is the case of Absalon, bishop of Roskilde in Denmark, foster brother of King Waldemar, who is credited with discovering the site of the merchant city of Copenhagen. The later establishment of separate archbishoprics for Denmark, Sweden, and Norway was both a recognition and a stimulus to the development of national unity. The conquest of Finland in the twelfth century combined the pious efforts of an English missionary, Henry, and the expansionist energies of Swedish armies.

The adoption and extension of Christianity encouraged an increased cultural borrowing and absorption from the continent and facilitated the growth of peaceful trade. Through Christianity and the Christian Church Scandinavia became culturally integrated with Europe. Yet at the same time Christianity became something different in Scandinavia, for there, as in all the other lands of earth into which it expanded, it adapted itself somewhat to native beliefs and to pagan customs.

Individualism was one of the aspects of the old beliefs of the Scandinavians which was retained and emphasized in Christianity as they interpreted it. Luther's "priesthood of all believers" was among them an established concept, therefore some of the theological disputes of the Protestant Revolution were less disturbing in the North than elsewhere. Protestantism came easily. Also it came hand in hand with a reinvigorated nationalism. The Danish attempt to maintain the Union of Kalmar reached an intolerable climax for Sweden in the massacre of 1520 (Stockholm's Blood Bath), when the leaders of the defeated Swedish party were slaughtered after an amnesty, and Gustav Vasa found Protestantism a useful means of augmenting the popular strength of the national rising. The confiscated property of the church was a royal blessing first in Sweden and then in Denmark. For after a decade of defeat and turmoil Denmark too became Lutheran, and then forced Norway to accept the reform.

This element of outside pressure was the most difficult part of the Reformation for Norway; here national sentiment rose in opposition to the change, a futile opposition in the long run. The carrying out of Denmark's policy demoralized faith and national feelings, but it did reinvigorate the Danish language in the northern kingdom. Danish became entrenched as the official and the written language, and Norwegian was forced to be but a "tongue-language," without a written usage.

In theology and intellectual life in general the Reformation was an invitation to new influence for Scandinavians. In Denmark Niels Hemmingsen interpreted the Scriptures to students from all over Europe and was visited by King James VI of Scotland. Olaus Petri had been a student at Wittenberg and he became Sweden's reforming theologian and a writer of renown in both philosophy and style. A rational and practical attitude gained new strength.

Then gradually coldness and indifference grew within the churches as a result of their secure position, and the clergy sometimes lost contact with the real soul of the people. Inevitably came reaction from folk who yearned for a more emotional religious experience. In Norway this expressed itself in the popular pietistic movement led by Hans Nielsen Hauge in the early nineteenth century. The "Haugeans" held cottage meetings with prayer and singing, but they did not renounce allegiance to the national church. Nevertheless the established clergy were annoyed, and conservative elements were fearful. Hauge spent ten years in prison for preaching without a license, but his influence expanded.

Discrimination and contempt widened the cleft between religious groups, and dissenting sects like the Quakers found converts. Such groups took a major part in the emigration which began with the sailing of the *Restauration* to America in 1825. In

Sweden (and Finland also) similar movements roused the peas-
antry and the Eric Jansonists were forced to seek a new home, set-
tling at Bishop Hill in Illinois. The ferment in Scandinavia
brought first repression, then reform; in Norway lay preaching
was permitted in 1842 and religious toleration was granted in
1845; in Sweden the Methodists won a number of followers in the
1840s. Events took a different turn in Denmark, perhaps because
of the dynamic personality of Bishop Grundtvig, who reinvigorated spiritual life and gave impetus to the broad program of
the folk high schools. Religion and education went hand in hand,
both geared in closely with the state churches.

In the course of centuries the church established itself in each
of the Scandinavian countries as the most inclusive organization
outside the state itself. In many ways it is coextensive with the state
and functions as a part of the state. The church is still "established" in each of these countries, and a person is born into the
church as he is into the political society. A citizen can declare himself a member of another religious organization, but even then,
for example in Sweden, the records of his birth, his marriage, and
his movements are kept by the parish priest. Only in the 1970s is
the church gradually being separated from the state.

In Norway as well as in Sweden one government department
for generations administered the affairs of both church and education. Religious instruction is given in the schools, but it is increasingly general and nonindoctrinating. Nevertheless the common tradition strengthens the sense of national uniformity and
homogeneity. Well over 90 percent of the people in each of the
northern countries is at least nominally Lutheran, though it is
becoming comparatively easy to opt out of membership. The very
comprehensivenss of church membership permits a wide range of
thought and of individual liberty. It also puts certain religious
matters under the control of political bodies, introduces some
compulsion on the individual, and produces a certain passivity.
People support the church through taxes rather than through
voluntary contributions, and hence may not feel the highest degree of responsibility for the maintenance of either the establishment or the faith.

The official position of the church and the passivity and reserve
of the membership have made some observers think that the

Northerners are non-Christian, even outright pagan. Many of the socialist leaders are anticlerical, occasionally atheist. One critic has pointed an accusing finger at the sheer physical display of Vigeland's nude humanity in Frogner Park in Oslo. Scandinavians are likely to say that they simply treat the body in a natural, not a pagan, way; instead, they express horror at the worship of the machine and the dollar in New York.

The fact is that the free churches, though small, are vital, and that many religious influences express themselves without separating their followers from the state organization. The Salvation Army, for example, has astonishing strength, particularly in Sweden. Various lay groups have active mission stations both at home and in the far corners of the world.

Most dramatic illustration of the power of the church and of the basic Christian spirit was the fight of the church in Norway during World War II. It was a fight not just for self-preservation but, as Bishop Eivind Berggrav wrote, "a spiritual struggle against violence and lawlessness." Against a government which defied God the Norwegian Christian was called upon to "obey God rather than man." Both teachers and ministers renounced their state appointments and salaries but agreed to fulfill their educational and religious functions anyway. The church issued a bold statement of position, "The Church's Foundation," which condemned nazism and was read in churches throughout the land. Of the 858 clergymen of the state church 797 resigned their places; the people of the parishes took over their support, and the government dared not carry out its threats. Some 28 percent of the pastors were punished in various ways, and two died as a result of treatment in concentration camps. Seven or eight hundred Jews were taken to Germany; only a handful survived to return to Norway. The church spoke boldly against such brutalities and helped many others to escape capture. Operating "underground" and in persecution the old church rekindled faith and inspired resistance and hope; it could not be intimidated or subdued.

But the war was an experience of the now older generation, and in Sweden war did not hit as poignantly as in the other countries. In Sweden especially, secularism plus a combination of antagonism and indifference are eroding the position of the church. Yet there is also a tenacity of loyalty and concern. In 1973, in connection with constitutional revision, a government commission recommended separation of church and state. Some church leaders thought a divorce, which would put emphasis on voluntary church adherence, might make religion more meaningful. But the proposal aroused such an overwhelming popular opposition that it had to be shelved. People do not attend church and they often reject the claims of religion, but they nevertheless regard Christianity and its institutions as an irrenounceable part of their heritage and the church-state relationship as unseverable. Church structures are community monuments. Nevertheless, pressures for severance are sure to continue.

Law

> With law shall the land be built,
> not by lawlessness laid waste.
> —Frostathing Law

Law regulates the relationships of individuals within a community; it is given its character by the moral standards and ideals of society and is thus closely associated with religion.

In Scandinavia the development of law preceded the establishment of the state. Farther back in time than we can know the chieftains and freemen met in periodic "Law Things" to decide cases and to formulate rules of conduct. The Things were district meetings of the farmer-freemen which brought the force of public opinion to bear upon criminals, and which slowly built up bodies of law which were carefully phrased and just as carefully preserved. In ordinary civil disputes the Thing often acted as a court of conciliation or arbitration, getting the opposing parties to agree on a reasonable settlement.

When a murderer was brought before the Thing both his partisans and his enemies had a chance to present their case; by a clanging of shields the assemblage gave judgment. If the man was judged guilty he was outlawed; there were no police to enforce a verdict, but private individuals might do so if they wished—and if they could. It was a system of controlled personal vengeance, with community sanction through the Law Thing a matter of vital importance. Gradually there developed rules of conduct that were clear and just, and later real government to enforce the rules.

When the Norwegians settled in Iceland and were faced with new problems of adjustment it was natural that they should go a step farther than they had yet gone and make of the court meeting a full-fledged legislative body, a parliament, the Althing. This oldest legislature in the world, founded in 930, celebrated its thousandth anniversary in 1930. When other Norsemen went to France and won control of the duchy that was to be called Normandy, it was not surprising that they should there pool their own experience and methods with those of the natives and that the jury system should develop therefrom—a system of inquest and judgment by one's peers developed in Normandy, taken from Normandy to England, from there overseas to America, and thence back to Norway in the nineteenth century and to Denmark in the twentieth century.

As the chieftains gained power some of them became petty kings, then slowly gave way before the centralizing tendencies of the strongest. The kings in Sweden and Denmark gradually took over the administration of justice, but in Norway the Things persisted. There the kings came to propose laws which the freemen in the Things discussed and often adopted. Sometimes the freemen enforced their collective will against the king, as when Torgny the Law-man was their spokesman at a Thing after an argument over fighting in the east or in the west:

We freemen wish that you, King Olof, make peace with Olaf Digre, Norway's king, and give him your daughter Ingegärd to marry. But if you want to reconquer the kingdom in the east that your forefathers have owned, then we will all follow you. If you do not wish to do as we say, so will we go against you and kill you, for we will not tolerate lawlessness or disorder of you. So have our ancestors before us done. They threw five kings in a well at Mora Thing, when they were full of presumptuousness as you now are toward us. Say quickly, which you will choose.

A great clatter of arms affirmed the agreement of the assemblage, and the king bowed.[1]

Out of the traditions of the old law and the revised formulations there grew in Norway four basic law codes, unified into one

---

1. E. Ingers, *Bonden i svensk historia,* I (Stockholm: Lantbrukets Tidskriftsaktiebolag, 1949), 31–32. This and all succeeding translations are mine unless otherwise noted.

code for the entire country in the 1270s. Some of the clauses of one of these four, the Frostathing Law, reflect not only the law itself but also the kind of society which then existed and the philosophy on which it was based:

IV. 5.   All free men shall enjoy security in their homes.
VI. 1.   The first provision in our law of personal rights is, that every one of our countrymen shall be inviolate in his rights and in his person, both in the kingdom and outside the kingdom.
IV. 58. In three places, in the Church, at the Thing, and at a merrymaking, all men are equally sacred.
II. 4.   Every man in the king's dominions must be a Christian.
VII. 1. It is the king's right to command and to forbid, but he must rule according to law.

Landholding was most carefully regulated, each man holding land as the representative of a family; in case of sale the land had to be offered first to relatives, and if sold outside the family it could under certain conditions be redeemed. Slaves were recognized, but had few rights. A freeman had three fundamental duties: to serve in the *leidang* or army, to help in road mending, and to aid when necessary in church construction; he could not refuse an appointment to meet at a Law Thing, and he could not bring ale to a Thing.

These laws of the Norse Things were primarily rural in nature, while rules concerning commerce were most highly developed in the later law of Birka, named after the merchant island in Lake Mälar in Sweden. Maritime law owed much to the later development of the Sea Code of Visby, the Hanseatic center on Gotland.

In such a society of equals, making laws for all in great open gatherings, there was no place for absolute monarchy. The idea of divine right was occasionally claimed, but it did not become fixed. In Denmark at last in 1660 the king became really an autocrat, absolute ruler in law and in fact, but this extremity of power was all but unique in the North and was abolished in the revolution of 1848. The basic concept was that the king should be chosen by the people, and strict rules of inheritance were not adhered to: the Swedes chose Gustav Vasa in the sixteenth century and a French soldier in 1810; the Norwegians elected a Danish prince in 1905. Only in Denmark does the royal line date from the Middle Ages.

The Scandinavians never wholly forgot the precept that the king must rule according to the law, and they considered themselves to be exercising a natural right when, for example, they dethroned Gustav IV Adolf in 1809 in Sweden.

Most significant of all was the attitude of common responsibility and participation in the making and enforcement of the law. As Nils Herlitz writes:

> Sweden was a school of self-government, where the people were educated to look upon the state and the municipalities neither as foreign, hostile powers nor as instruments for promoting their own interests, but as a common concern, for which they had to share the responsibility.[2]

Throughout Scandinavian legal systems runs a general affinity due to common origins and a somewhat parallel experience and need; on this has been built in the twentieth century a more conscious unity through commissions working to make similar or coordinated laws for each of these countries in social affairs. The total result has been the creation of socially responsible states, but with a citizenry closely critical of the acts of government. There is meaning in the fact that the most common book next to the Bible in a Scandinavian home is a book of law.

Out of these ideas and experiences have grown the governments of present-day Scandinavia, two republics and three monarchies, yet all democratic in nature.

Sweden had the earliest of the written constitutions in the North, one drawn up at the time of the overthrow of the Vasas in 1809. Here were embodied the principles of individual liberty, freedom of speech and the press, and the limitations on the king which made possible the further development of constitutional monarchy. The Riksdag, dating probably from 1435, was left with its division into four estates: the nobility, the clergy, the burghers, and the farmers. In 1866 this obsolete structure was changed to a two-house system, with a First Chamber indirectly elected, and a Second Chamber elected by direct vote, each house equal in authority. In 1971 it was "modernized" into a single chamber. In legislation the constitution provided for agreement between king and Riksdag, each having an absolute veto. Both executive and

2. *Sweden: A Modern Democracy on Ancient Foundations* (Minneapolis: University of Minnesota Press, 1939), p. 90.

judicial authority were vested in the king. Within this framework
the pressures of democracy in the nineteenth and twentieth centuries transferred the real power from the hands of the king to
the parliament, the cabinet (or ministry), and the supreme court,
and a virtually new constitution came into effect in January 1975.
Universal male suffrage was won in 1909 and also proportional
representation. Woman suffrage together with woman's right to
sit in the Riksdag came in 1921.

In Denmark the absolutism established in 1660, though complete in theory, was for the most part patriarchal and benevolent
in practice, and administration was in the hands of a bourgeois
bureaucracy. Denmark's misfortunes in foreign politics both discredited the system and for a time fixed it the more firmly on a de-
spondent people. Reform and reaction alternated, influenced
heavily by German thought and German officials.

After 1814 a sweeping school reform in Denmark democratized
education, and gradually the opposition to absolutism gained
overwhelming power. A great jurist, Anders Orsted, demanded
that the courts consider the meaning of the law, not only its letter
or spirit. Grundtvig called for freedom of conscience and political
liberty—"Let freedom be the watchword in the North, freedom
for Loki as well as for Thor." The July Revolutions of 1830 encouraged demands for a free constitution in Slesvig-Holstein, and
in 1831 consultative provincial chambers were established in the
duchies. The rigidity of the absolutist system was thus broken,
and in 1841 parish and county councils were granted. The European revolutions of 1848 gave the necessary impetus to the next
step.

A constituent assembly met, and on June 5, 1849, a new constitution was enacted, abolishing absolutism and setting up a constitutional monarchy. A two-house legislature (Rigsdag) was established with an upper house, the Landsting, elected indirectly
and a lower house, the Folketing, elected directly; the basis of voting was equal suffrage of all males over thirty years of age. The individual won the rights of freedom of speech and of worship and
of habeas corpus; the privileges of nobility were abolished; and
the executive, legislative, and judicial powers were separated and
defined. Such a constitution went far toward real democracy: it

was too much for the middle class of the towns, not enough for the small farmers. In 1866 a reactionary constitutional act introduced property qualifications in voting for the upper house, and made the Landsting a bastion of Conservative power.

Against this reversion toward aristocratic authority the industrial workers and the small farmers gradually consolidated their strength and built powerful political parties. By 1884 the Liberal Left (Venstre) had sixty-nine seats in the Folketing, the Right only nineteen, and the Social Democrats won two seats. The Left, in its struggle for recognition, sabotaged everything except social reform and at long last, in 1901, the Conservative ministry resigned. The Conservative party had only eight seats by that time, the Social Democrats fourteen, and the Left seventy-six. A new ministry was appointed in line with the legislative majority. Like the sudden changes of 1660, 1849, and 1866, this one too came without bloodshed, but it was nevertheless a revolution: parliamentary government, with full ministerial responsibility, became an established fact.

For Norway governmental power before 1814 had rested in Copenhagen. Norway had kept her legal system, and was theoretically a kingdom, but in reality was governed as a Danish province. Liberal ideas did not perish, and nationalism gained force before 1814, wringing from the king, for example, a Norwegian university in 1811. The consitution of Eidsvold, May 17, 1814, was a thoroughly Norwegian document, combining centuries-old traditions and ideals with the latest thought and practice in Europe and America.

The leaders from different branches of Norwegian life gathered at a country estate north of Oslo that reminds one of Mount Vernon or Monticello. These bureaucrats and farmer-statesmen had read Montesquieu and Rousseau and Locke, as had the framers of the American constitution. The men of Eidsvold knew also the great work of Philadelphia, the Federalist papers, and the various constitutions of the French Revolution. Their document breathed the northern ideal of law-bound liberty and provided for a government of careful checks and balances. Carl Johan accepted this constitution with only slight changes necessary to the acceptance of the King of Sweden as King of Norway. The electorate was at first only 7 percent of the population but by 1898 male suffrage was universal, and by 1913 women as well as men over the age of twenty-three could vote without restrictions.

Norway, like Denmark and Sweden, experienced steady advance in democratic processes through the nineteenth century. The greatest single step was the winning of parliamentary government in 1884, under the decisive leadership of Johan Sverdrup, a veritable Gladstone of the North. Like her sister states, and even earlier than Sweden, Norway built strong political parties, and like the others she built a multiparty system with the Social Democrats gaining steadily increasing power. The safeguarding of freedom is so important that in Norway as in the United States the Supreme Court has won for itself, without explicit constitutional sanction, the right to question the constitutionality of laws.

Finland, for hundreds of years an integral part of the Swedish kingdom, shared in the constitutional history of Sweden. Finns had the same rights as Swedes, and were represented in the Riksdag of the Four Estates. When Russia conquered Finland in 1809 the liberal Czar Alexander I guaranteed the preservation of Finnish liberties and the country became an autonomous archduchy, continuing independently the laws and political institutions formerly shared with Sweden. Until the Russification policy of the very end of the nineteenth century these pledges were fulfilled; there has been no break, therefore, in the continuity of the Scandinavian legal tradition in Finland. Even local government has borne much the same character of independence and responsibility as in the countries to the west. It was not until 1906, however, that Finland was able to discard the antiquated system of the Four Estates. At the same time she established, as the first country in Europe, complete suffrage for men and women. She then set up the one-chamber parliament which she retained when she won independence.

Iceland's pioneering experience as an independent law-built society was interrupted in the thirteenth century, when Norway made Iceland a dependency, yet internal institutions were not changed. Then control passed to Denmark and the most significant effect was a relaxation of local political activity, finally overcome in the nineteenth century under the leadership of Jón Sigurdsson. Population and prosperity increased and democratic forces were given new inspiration and new vitality. Subservience to Denmark was abandoned in 1918, when the kingship was left as the only legal bond. Independence was declared in 1944.

The Scandinavian peoples have lived for centuries with similar traditions of freedom and justice, and their political institutions have differed more in detail than in principle. The pace of political development has often speeded reforms in one country and retarded them in another, but each has so closely watched its neighbors that progress in one has had an invigorating effect on each of the others. They have experimented with forms but they have clung tenaciously to fundamental principles. On this foundation they have created the modern socially responsible state.

Economy

Hunting, fishing, grazing, and agriculture were the early bases of economic life in the North as everywhere. Ancient Denmark's garbage heaps, euphemistically called kitchen middens, give evidences of the life men lived: the bones of fish, oyster shells in vast quantity, well-shaped tools and weapons of bone and stone, and later of iron, and musical instruments such as the *lurs*. Along the shores of Norway and Sweden are found remains from later periods, among them rock carvings of animals of the forest and of men in boats.

Primitive methods of earning a livelihood survived longer in the Scandinavian peninsula than in many parts of the world, for it was exceptionally difficult there to bend nature to man's will. Man had to use what he found. Slowly he did win patches of soil from the forest and supplemented fishing with a few small crops. As the numbers of men increased and pushed farther inland and northward, the bear and the deer retreated or were wiped out, and their economic importance almost disappeared—except for the reindeer which are still wealth to the Lapps, and a welcome meat to all.

Fish remained throughout the centuries the dependable standby in the waters all about the Scandinavian countries. In the Middle Ages the great market fish was the herring, taken during their run through the Sound along the southern coast of Sweden (then Denmark). These fish when salted were shipped throughout Catholic Europe and helped to build the fortune of many a

Hanseatic merchant. Control of the fishing grounds became a matter of political importance and a cause of wars. Then suddenly in 1477 the herring for some unknown reason abandoned their Baltic spawning fields and dispersed into the vastness of the North Sea and the Atlantic. Their move upset the economic balance in northern Europe. But fish remained vital in home consumption and domestic economy, and gradually a new world trade was built.

In the early spring of the year the fishing banks of Lofoten off the coast of northern Norway have produced their wealth for centuries, and more and more have gained a place on the world market. In the south of Norway the tiny *brisling* (sardines) have been netted by the million, and canned and sent round the world (labeled still with the picture of King Haakon). In the belts and sounds of Denmark and on the rough sea men have continued to fish, and fishwives have sold the eels and the green-boned horn-fish and herring and dozens of other varieties in the odorous fish-markets of Copenhagen and lesser towns. To the north men fished for trout and salmon in the inland rivers and lakes and for *strömming* (a small herring) in the waters of the Baltic. The Icelanders have built their export trade from the great fishing banks near by.

Farther afield the Norwegians hunted for whale and made themselves the world's great whalers. It was a Norwegian Vestfold fisherman who constructed the first harpoon gun for whales in 1868. In 1904 whaling west of Norway was forbidden by law, for the fishermen feared that if the whales were all killed off there would be nothing to drive the small fish in toward land. Then the whalers sought new fields, the richest of them in distant Antarctica, until those too were exhausted by international competition and overkill. The great whaling ships now rot at the quays of Kristiansand.

Forestry must be as old as fishing, providing at first only the humble necessities of logs for cabins and fuel for the fires in the dirt-floored dwellings. It was wood which made the Viking longboats and the oars. Logs were sectioned and fashioned into chairs; dishes were made of wood, and plows; benches were built for eating and sleeping, playthings were carved in the shapes of horses and chickens. Farmsteads had only a few acres under tillage, many acres in slow growing, precious forest. The great tracts of woods distant from settlement were claimed by the kings or the states.

Not all the North had forests. Denmark soon exhausted her beech forests, and Iceland's woods disappeared. Norway had to supply both Iceland and Greenland with wood for boats and building, and she traded wood to Denmark for grain.

From the forests of Norway and Sweden and Finland came the pitch, turpentine, resin, tar which were large items in the trade of the Varangians with the East and in the later trade of Scandinavia with England. Timber was sent to the continent and to England for buildings and for boats. The British navy and merchant marine found the straight Swedish and Norwegian spruce trees strong and good for masts, and Englishmen bought shipload upon shipload of timber for pitprops in their mines. By the seventeenth century the rivers were being used to float logs down to crude sawmills at their mouths, and here the export trade developed.

Mining is likewise an art inherited from ancient times. At first men merely picked up flints off the surface of the earth in Jutland and fashioned them into hammers and axes. When they found iron over on Fyn the center of population and power shifted to the island where the raw material was available for new tools and weapons. In Sweden bog-iron was found in the marshes and lakes of the south; smelting with charcoal from the forests and adding fine craftsmanship, the Vikings of the iron age made armor and swords of wide renown.

Sweden's great copper mines at Falun provided the basis of royal wealth and power in early modern times, and were the chief support for the armies of Gustav Adolf in the Thirty Years' War. The mines were chartered in 1347 to the Stora Kopparbergs Bergslag, which claims to be the oldest corporation in existence today. For although the copper is almost exhausted, there is still mining for by-products such as the red clay from which paint is made, which is the reason the Swedish countryside is dotted with deep-red cottages and barns. The copper supplied the shining pots and pans which have hung on kitchen walls for generations.

Other metals and minerals such as gold and silver and nickel are of recent development in Scandinavia, but on the basis of copper, and more especially of iron, manufacturing industries came early to occupy an important place. The Norwegians had a large iron stove industry in the eighteenth and nineteenth centuries. The Swedish Riksdag started a cutlery industry in 1751 (under the old mercantilistic principles). In 1771 the privileges of Eskilstuna, favored center of this industry, were widened, and it became the Sheffield of Sweden, manufacturing fine cutlery for a world market. During the eighteenth century the state granted subsidies to shipbuilding and to many industries and towns, fostering industrialization and urbanization. Textile industries and others which lacked a natural resource base had difficulties, but industries based on wood and iron saw greater and greater opportunities opening before them in the nineteenth and twentieth centuries.

Agriculture grew from its original position as a supplement to hunting and fishing to become the backbone of economic life. Even fishermen found that it was useful to have some ground to till. The man who built his life upon the land could also hunt and fish, could raise a few pigs and cattle in grassy clearings, and cut timber for his own use or for sale. There was a mutual interdependence in these simple activities, and with them all in proper balance a village of a few families could be almost self-sufficient. Such was a necessity in the isolated fjords and upland valleys of Norway and only a little less so elsewhere.

Oats and barley were the staple crops of early tribesmen, and they have been cultivated in the fields of Jutland, Skåne, and Upland in central Sweden since soon after man entered those fertile regions. After the discovery of America the potato was brought north and in due course was raised to equal dignity with fish; today not even the Irish eat such quantities of potatoes as are raised and consumed in Norway, Denmark, and Sweden. Wheat came, too, and rye, but wheat has thrived less well than the old staples. Berries have grown in abundance, especially in the Scandinavian peninsula and in Finland. In Greenland and Iceland agriculture has remained secondary to fishing, but vital nevertheless. Even a meager crop may stave off famine when export products fail.

Land was of such importance that much of the early law is the law of landownership and inheritance. In Norway individual landownership was the rule, for who but an owner and lover of the mountainside patch could make it yield at all? The odal law assured to a family continuance of ownership and safeguarded against partitioning of patches already too small. In Denmark, favored with wide flat fields in the islands and east of the morainic ridge in Jutland, there was more temptation for squires to acquire large areas and to have them worked by peasants. Landowners grew rich on the toil of tenants and beautified the fertile countryside with their castles. Not until the nineteenth and twentieth centuries were those great estates broken up into small holdings, worked by the little men on their own land. Sweden occupied a middle position, with conditions in Skåne comparable to those in Denmark and with conditions in the northern districts similar to those in Norway. In Finland the forest is still being invaded by the plow and settlement is extended by farmer-foresters.

But nowhere is there land enough. Scarcity of land and food is the foundation for the epic of emigration and perhaps also the basic reason for the careful methods of exploitation of all resources.

Despite their marginal position and their small resources the Scandinavians for centuries have been active traders. They traded for art objects to faraway Cathay and their merchants operated on the lower Volga in the Middle Ages. They took honey, furs, and pitch to Miklagard and received coins and luxury articles from the East and from Rome. They were the middlemen who brought to the courts of medieval Europe the fish and falcons of Iceland and Greenland, and the Hanseatic League did a large business in its "kontor" (branch office and stores) in Bergen and through its merchants in Gotland and Stockholm. Visby, the capital of Gotland, was one of the chief cities of the Hansa, the league of continental merchant cities, and middleman for the entire Baltic. Ger-

man merchants were so numerous in Stockholm that they had
their own German church in the heart of the old "city between the
bridges," and held half the seats in the city council.

Foreign trade, however, was based upon the raw products of
the North—fish from the sea and the simple products of the
forest. Very slowly did the Sandinavians learn to make for export
the products of their hands, and much of their early imports were
but loot from the raids of Viking warriors.

After the Viking period the German merchant cities long held
Scandinavia in economic subjection, and it took war as well as economic development to break their hold. The Danes fought to gain
trade, while Swedes and Finns long accepted a passive role. Norway
suffered most from a persistent rurality, sinking from medieval
prosperity to poverty and stagnation, milked both by the German
merchants and by Danish officials. Economic and intellectual ste-
rility followed the greatness of the saga age. Many explanations
have been offered, such as change of climate and the theory of
outworn institutions and inability to establish the democracy
which the times demanded. The Black Death (1346–1350) also
played its tragic part, destroying a third of the population. Most
plausible of all theories is that of Wilhelm Keilhau who held that
Norway simply was too completely rural, suffering from structural weakness. The people were farmers and fishermen, lived in
isolated small communities, and seemed unconcerned about the
conflicts or the culture of the world outside. Because of this rurality the kings had been forced to grant foreign traders special privileges which became in the end burdensome to the Norwegian
people.

The Hanseatic merchants were interested in immediate profits,
and they did not feel the community of interest in the development of the country as a whole which was essential to prosperity.
The attitude of the Germans and the feeling of the Norwegian
ruler, concerned about the utility of trade for his realm, are illustrated by the speech of King Sverre at Bergen in 1186 after some
riots in the town: "We thank Englishmen who have brought
wheat, flour, honey and cloth, and those who brought flax linen
wax or kettles, and any who have brought useful goods, as well as
our friends from Orkneys, Shetlands and Iceland. But the Germans take out cod and butter and thus create want, and bring

wine, which produces evil and no good. Some of our people have lost lives or been dishonored or beaten. If these Germans wish to keep their lives or their goods they will have to depart immediately, as their visit has been of little benefit to us and to our realm." [3]

The Hansa bled not only Norway but the entire area, and this mercantile league became involved in repeated wars with the Scandinavian states and succumbed at last only because of its political weakness. Then Scandinavia took a new lease on life. Ironworks were built in the sixteenth century, new inventions were made— such as the long line with 2000 hooks for fishing—and the Norwegians gained from Denmark control of their own export of fish and sawn timber. Sweden regained independence in the sixteenth century and launched into expansion both political and economic. The peoples of the North vigorously increased their exports and took their place as competitors in world trade. Monarchs and businessmen made common cause under the money banners of mercantilism. Progress was slow but it was steady through the eighteenth and nineteenth centuries.

The most noteworthy accomplishments of the northerners were on the sea, in this later period as in their earlier lustful forays into the world outside. Settlement had come by way of the sea, the routes of the Vikings were by river or sea, the life-giving fish came from the sea, and even the amber of the medieval traders. For many the sea was home.

Shipbuilding was a fine art among the Scandinavians when the peoples of the South were making slow and top-heavy vessels. The Viking longboats were superb in strength and streamlined beauty, swift and seaworthy. One of them, the resurrected Gokstad ship now in the Viking ship museum at Bygdø, near Oslo, served as model for a new-built vessel which sailed the North Atlantic in 1893 to the Chicago Exposition. The Vikings of the tenth century sailed such ships at will through the Baltic, the North Sea, the Atlantic, and into the Mediterranean and the Black Sea.

The Scandinavians continued to build ships, after a lapse in the

3. Quoted in Wilhelm Keilhau, *Norway in World History* (London: Macdonald, 1944), p. 88.

later Middle Ages, changing their patterns to meet the changing techniques of sail and steam and the changing demands of commerce. They made sturdy fishing boats and special whalers and freighters. Their ports were crowded with boats from their own lands and far-off countries.

Norway lost some 1100 ships in the Napoleonic wars; she had enough shipbuilding capacity so that in 1815 she still had 1673 vessels. Through building and buying she had some 8100 ships by 1880 and ranked third in the world; in 1914 she had 3050, two-thirds in steamships, and she ranked fourth in world tonnage. Sweden and Denmark were close behind Norway, all active world traders who participated in the East India business as well as in European and American commerce.

Certain persistent characteristics of this whole economic development can be brought into focus.

The pre-twentieth-century economy of the northern communities was founded directly upon natural resources and involved little processing, except for the small domestic market. Foodstuffs were raised at home, and imported "colonial goods" such as coffee and sugar and tobacco were for a long time rare luxuries. Agricultural life flourished abundantly in Denmark, but on the wind-blown, rocky farms of the more northerly lands farming was a perpetual pioneering. The activities of mines and factories were small scale. The richest profits were often reaped by the foreign buyers and processers of iron, lumber, and fish. For the natives a precarious self-sufficiency was possible on the basis of a meager life.

In resources, psychology, and organization the Scandinavians had the fundamentals for the flowering that was to come. They had soil and sea, timber and ore, and abundant water power. They had learned as people with little that they must stick together and work together. The more isolated they were the more they realized the value of cooperation—as small groups building a house or a boat; as crews on a fishing boat, sharing the catch. They blended individualism with cooperation.

The part played by the state was an interesting prelude to later developments. The state owned much of the forests and took an active interest in support of commerce. The Greenland trade was

a state monopoly both in the Middle Ages and again in the nineteenth and twentieth centuries, until 1948. The state had guided
the foundation of many industrial establishments, and the primary natural resources were regarded as state or community
property. The state guided landholding policy and finally provided legislation to keep the land from passing out of the hands of
the peasants who worked it, or, as in Denmark, to enable the peasants to gain land. The modern socialistic state is in many ways the
natural heir of the paternalistic state of the Middle Ages and of
the mercantilistic epoch.

Yet there was freedom for initiative. "Who is chief among you?"
a Viking was asked. He replied, "None, we are all chiefs here." Individual freedom was preserved within a voluntary, deeply trea-
sured, social and economic organization. It is the experience with
this kind of system and the belief in its possibilities, or even in its
necessity, that prepared the Scandinavian people for the "middle
way."

Still other facets of Scandinavian culture confirm and widen the
impressions of such an analysis. Art gives expression to the individual's love of beauty; and art is not a monopoly of "artists" but a
possession of the people. The Swedish program of *vackrare varor
för varje dag* (more beautiful things for every day) encouraged appreciation of useful beauty; the flowers which brighten Danish
and Norwegian cottages and apartments evidence a love of beauty
for its own sake, and a pride in appearance. Literature is a heritage of deep interest and power; it helps to maintain ideals and
traditions of ancient and self-conscious peoples and is a vehicle
for constant self-criticism and improvement. Migration has
spread people and ideas from the North to all corners of the earth
and has enriched Scandinavia with the ideas of the wide world.

So we turn to an investigation in more detail of these forces of
cultural interchange and of the twentieth-century society the
Scandinavians have built on the foundations of this heritage.

3 *Functioning Social Democracy*

Cultural stability in the North is deeply rooted in time. Survival demands change, yet people cling to the past even as they reach out for the future. It is almost as the college student wrote of Dante—"He stood with one foot in the Middle Ages while with the other he saluted the rising star of the Renaissance." In ways just as bizarre the processes of democratic change transform society while peoples hold fast to the forms of monarchy; and atheism is professed while the church is supported. Even toward the end of the twentieth century Scandinavia retains institutions hallowed by time yet in other ways leads the van along the speedway to change. On their age-old foundation stones they have built new structures to meet the demands of the individual and of society—just as in purely architectural terms men built the royal castle of Stockholm and Elsinore in Denmark on stones laid down centuries ago. And everything is still in flux as they search and experiment.

Fundamental for the Scandinavians in their planning of change is the individual and his needs. This fact is often difficult for outside observers to grasp as they watch process and results rather than motivations. And it is all too obvious that bureaucratic eagerness to free the individual from worry and pain may end in choking him with paternalistic red tape.

Pure individualism is of course anarchy, in which every individual's freedom is at the mercy of the most rapacious elements. At the other extreme a society completely controlled by Big Brother deprives the individual of purpose and choice, and he might as well be an animal in a zoo. Somewhere between lies the social organization that encourages self-realization without destroying the rights of others, that protects the person but does not smother him, that balances and reconciles the interests of the one and the rights of all. The question then is, are the Scandinavian countries, in the thoroughness of their social programs, establishing the golden mean or are they edging too far in the direction of stultifying control?

Government: Institutions and Attitudes

Orderly government seems to be one of the talents of the Scandinavians. They have tensions and conflicts but few disruptions, and corruption is all but unknown. Government is a "common concern" and is regarded as the agent of the citizenry, not its enemy or its master.

From the time of the establishment of national states the king stood as the center and head of government. The crown was often the organ through which the common people sought relief from the more immediate exactions of the nobility. Gradually, through the nonviolent evolution of democracy, monarchial power has been reduced to the faintest shadow. In Finland and Iceland, the two most recent state creations, the king has vanished from the scene. In the three older states, however, kingship remains as a hallowed institution, lacking authority but retaining respect and serving as a potent stabilizer. The king stands above party and personifies the nation. In time of crisis he may be a comforting and unifying influence, as exemplified strongly during World War II in Norway and Denmark. The poet Kaj Munk epitomized popular sentiment in that time of Danish despair as he hailed King Christian X for his morning horseback ride through the streets of Copenhagen, a symbol to prove that "Denmark keeps her saddle as before."

No longer does a Gustav Adolf lead a nation to conquest and feats of valor, or a Gustav III inspire a flowering of art and literature. Rather, royalty has shown a remarkable adaptability to the changing demands of society. Carl XVI Gustaf gave proof as he ascended the throne in 1973; he took as his motto "For Sweden— with the times." And he assumed the simple title "King of Sweden" instead of the high-sounding but obsolete "King of the Swedes, the Goths, and the Wends." Over in Norway Carl Gustaf's cousin King Olav had been allowed to marry a commoner, and their son might someday be king—blue blood did not seem as vital as at one time. In Denmark the law had been changed in 1953 so that Margrethe, another grandchild of Gustaf V of Sweden, could become queen—no longer was male succession essential.

With all this relaxation of the rules for royalty was it possible that kingship might be abolished? Republican agitation had been vocal for decades. But it was low key and small scale. In 1972 a proposal to make Norway a republic after Olav's death received only five votes in the Storting. In Sweden the issue became critical in the revision of the constitution in 1972–1974, yet polls indicated continuing favor both for highly admired Gustav VI Adolf and for monarchy as an institution; Carl Gustaf's succession came without incident in 1973. The king was stripped of the last vestiges of authority; he no longer must preside over the council or even appoint prime ministers; with the change of a word or two in the constitution the office can be abolished. But it stays.

In Iceland the president has at least as much power as the modern king. In Finland the president has greater authority than any other head of state in the North. He has broad powers in foreign policy, a temporary veto in legislation (for neighboring kings the veto atrophied long ago), powers of appointment in church, army, and government, and a limited power to issue decrees. The close balance of political forces and the personal strength of Urho Kekkonen, prime minister five times and three times elected president for six-year terms, have enhanced the powers of the presidency even beyond the intent of the constitution. And in 1973 Kekkonen was voted by the parliament an additional extraordinary four-year term.

The judiciary is of course important but not equal to the executive or the legislative branches. In Norway the constitution of 1814 established a system of separation of powers and the judges have attempted to tread the path of judicial review à la John Marshall. Since 1818 the courts have practiced "the right and duty to determine the question whether an administrative act was lawful"; and throughout the North the citizen is protected carefully against possible injustice by officials. Nowhere else, however, have the judges attained as much power as in Norway. The claims they made to power irritated some of their fellow citizens as early as 1827 when a Norwegian professor wrote to a Danish friend, complaining that the judges "are considered, God knows why, as the patron saints of the idolized constitution." The courts asserted themselves still more after the victory of parliamentarism in the 1880s. In general, however, the legislative bodies of Scandinavia are unchallenged in authority, as in England. The job of the courts is to interpret and apply the law, not to question its constitutionality.

Special courts are often set up to deal with special problems such as water power and administrative law. Labor courts are established which utilize a combination of adjudication and conciliation, and which bring together on the same bench trained judges and lay representatives of the parties to dispute.

In each country the basic law is simple and clear, and is available to the public in condensed and codified form. An American is constantly amazed at how few lawyers he sees in courts or parliaments or business. The ancient right of a freeman to plead his own case persists and is practiced. Lay experts are used regularly as assistant judges, as for example in the local courts of Finland and Sweden and in special courts like the Danish maritime and commercial court.

In each country one finds a pragmatic attitude toward law and courts—as toward life in general. Capital punishment was abolished long ago in Norway because it did not deter crime, but wartime treason was something that called for stern measures, so the government simply legislated capital punishment. Means are adapted to the need. Another illustration of this is the way in which labor courts, where the letter of the law seldom has much significance, have become in fact and in name courts of arbitration. This is the practical approach. Of course the basic supremacy of the parliament over the courts is likewise practical, a recognition of the authority of the electorate. It is, for better or for worse, a more flexible system than that in the United States, less flexible than that in Britain.

The parliament is the real power in each country, and in the parliament the will of the people can express itself quickly and effectively. There has been a tendency to unicameralism, also, as in other countries with the ministerial system—for it is difficult for a cabinet to be responsible to two different houses. Finland's Eduskunta or parliament is composed of only one 200-member chamber. This body, elected on July 1 for a three-year term, chooses a Grand Committee of forty-five which serves as a steering committee and names the standing committees. Iceland elects fifty members to the Althing, and then these fifty choose seventeen of their number to sit in an "upper house." This is somewhat like the system in Norway.

Norway's parliamentary organization is unusual, a compromise between the bicameral and the unicameral. The Storting is elected as one body, but when the 155 members meet, they divide themselves into the small Lagting and the larger Odelsting. Both the Storting as a whole and also each house elect a president and a vice-president, and these six officers form the influential steering committee. Fifteen of the seventeen standing committees are chosen from the Storting as a whole, and each reflects the proportional strength of the parties. Bills originating in one house or *ting* commonly pass there first, then go on to the other for approval. If agreement is not reached the whole Storting meets and a two-thirds vote is then required for passage. Budget legislation and certain other classes of laws are handled in the first instance by the entire Storting, and in these cases a majority vote is sufficient. The Storting can best be conceived as a one-chamber body with two semi-independent committees.

Denmark had a two-chamber Rigsdag until 1953, with a conservative and slow-changing upper house. Despite some cooperative features it came to be felt that a straight unicameral system would be more responsive to the popular will. Folketing was taken as the name of the new parliament, elected by universal male and female suffrage of all over twenty-three years of age (reduced to twenty-one in 1961). The 179 members include 2 from Greenland and 2 from the Faroes.

Sweden abandoned her ancient system of the four estates in 1865 for a bicameral Riksdag, and it was during the life of this body that parliamentary authority established itself. The two houses had joint committees and cooperated closely, but the differing bases of election made the First Chamber slower to change, less representative. As early as 1954 a committee was established to investigate the need for a new constitution. The antiquity of the 1809 Form of Government with its many revisions produced inconsistencies between law and practice. The revision committee's first major proposal was for the restructuring of the Riksdag, which after January 1971 consisted of one house with 350 members to 1974, thereafter 349, elected by general suffrage for a term of three years. The proposal was specific in stating that since all power in the Swedish state emanates from the people, and since the Riksdag represents the people, it should be the foremost organ in the state. This was no change from practice, yet it was a far cry from the corresponding declaration out of ancient law (retained in the 1809 constitution) that "the king alone shall govern the realm." Now he is the "symbol of the country."

Thus, all five states of the North now have parliaments that are elected by universal suffrage, that operate essentially as unicameral bodies, and that enjoy the final authority in the state.

Proportional representation, the established electoral pattern throughout Scandinavia, attempts to keep both parties and geographical districts properly balanced in the parliaments. In Sweden the population and the numbers of representatives are large enough that it comes out rather fairly. Denmark has the most highly refined system, mathematically perfect for distribution of delegates according to votes, but amazingly complicated. Iceland, with scattered districts and small population, sets up for the Althing three classes: (1) twenty-one representatives chosen from single-member districts; (2) twenty chosen from party lists; (3) up to eleven compensating seats parceled out to balance the whole as well as may be. Proportional representation encourages people to vote for principles and/or their own special interests, lessens the importance of political personalities, and helps to maintain the stability of parties. Major fluctuations are rare. Another effect is to encourage people to vote, for every vote counts in the reckoning, and the result is a turnout of 80 to 90 percent of the eligibles.

A very important side effect is that within parliaments proportional representation facilitates strict party discipline, for the delegate is there not as an individual but as a representative of his party.

Partly owing to proportional representation the party system is fundamentally different in the North from that in the United States. Instead of two parties vying for office the basic pattern is of five parties: conservatives, liberals, centrists, social democrats, communists. In ideology the first three tend to emphasize the rights of the individual and to question the propriety of all-encompassing government. They are the parties of the right, sometimes called the bourgeois parties, or the nonsocialists. The social democrats and the communists have in common a penchant for strong state oversight of society and the economy. But since it is often the little differences that divide men most sharply it is not surprising that the parties of the right find it almost impossible to agree on common action; and the parties of the left cooperate even less easily! It is therefore only the delicacy of the balance of strength that occasionally drives these parties of convictions into each others' arms.

Numerically the nonsocialist parties muster something like half the popular vote and the left parties the other half. However, there are many variations from country to country and from time to time; the situation is never static.

The conservative parties are heirs of the parliamentary groupings that dominated political life in the late nineteenth century. They represent an ideology and a class: they like things as they are—or as they were yesterday; the members often are men and women with large economic interests, influential position, and what remains of the landowning farmer class. No longer do they dare hope for power, but they have interests to protect and they want to check the excesses of the left. They favor strong defence and the protection of private property, and they support monarchy where it survives. In Iceland the conservatives have joined hands with the liberals to form the Independence party; in the other countries they remain distinct but perhaps with different names such as Union party in Finland and Moderates in Sweden. It needs emphasis that they are not reactionaries, but throughout the North they are really moderate and they seek to attract younger voters. They accept as a fact of life the social programs legislated by their political opponents; if they should come to office they would try to modify and restrain but they would not scrap the well-established "welfare state."

The liberals are the heirs of the reformers who struggled for suffrage rights and parliamentary responsibility. Having succeeded, they found themselves squeezed between the dwindling but vigorous conservatives on their right and the burgeoning social democrats on their left. They were torn between approval of the conservatives' emphasis on personal freedom and sympathy for the welfare programs of the social democrats. Within their own ranks they suffered from manifold differences of opinion of their diverse membership: prohibitionists, free-churchmen of various persuasions, pacifists, intelligentsia, labor, and others. They took strength from their intellectual leadership and from the fact that liberal newspapers (some party-affiliated and some not) were the most widely read newspapers in each country. The oddity might seem that the papers did not swing more votes, but we can see the same peculiarity in the United States.

The farmers' parties are difficult to place in the political spectrum. In their strong sense of nationalism and their concern with traditional culture and rural interests they lean to conservatism. They are especially concerned with their own material well-being, and they are cognizant of the weakening numerical position of agriculturalists. Hence they are opportunistic and often enter into political bargaining with the social democrats. In the 1960s they moved leftward, particularly in Finland where the party represents small farmers and farm workers. In Finland, Norway, and Sweden they took the name Center party and appealed for support from clerical workers and others in the cities. Shrewd leadership of men such as Gunnar Hedlund in Sweden (and now Thorbjörn Fälldin) increased their parliamentary strength while their original clientele was diminishing. In Finland they have led in several coalitions, and have elected several presidents, including Urho Kekkonen. But changes in nomenclature could only slowly erase the bucolic image.

These three individualistic and special-interest parties inevitably have difficulty to cooperate. Historical rivalries form a barrier, and the problems of reducing three sets of leaders to one is an obvious additional stumbling block. Together they may poll 50 to 55 percent of the vote, yet no one of these groups can hope to attain by itself a majority position. Their coalition governments (when excluding the social democrats) have been short-lived. Their small-group interests and connections are more important to them than the broad principles on which they agree with each other. To put it even more simply: they would rather be right than to hold shared power. The more workable coalitions, when coalitions are possible, seem to be between the pragmatic center and the social democrats.

The social democrats became the beneficiaries of the liberal reforms of the early twentieth century. Middle-class liberals and working-class socialists joined hands in the fight for the ballot. Once the principle of universal suffrage was established, the largest class could win the largest vote, and workers formed the largest class. In the Scandinavian countries, in the second quarter of the twentieth century, a remarkable parallelism occurred between acceptance of the democratic principle and the rapid growth of industry and an industrial working-class. A farsighted social democratic leadership rose at the same time, able to take full advantage of this combination of circumstances. Thorvald Stauning in Denmark (1873–1942) and Per Albin Hansson (1885–1946) and Tage Erlander (1901–) in Sweden were unusually capable, as were several of their lieutenants. More than any other of the party groupings, the social democrats of the five countries have developed similar programs and have regularly interchanged ideas with one another. They have pursued clear goals but they have followed Fabian tactics and have been willing to make progress slowly. Divided opposition and narrowness of view in both right and far-left (communist) groups opened a wide field for the purposeful politics of the moderate socialists. Since the early 1930s they held power for thirty years in Norway and for over forty years in Sweden, and at one time in mid-century all five countries had social democratic administrations.

They have achieved fundamental social change. But their gradualism has avoided violent disruption and has won acceptance of their reforms from the citizenry as a whole. In the countries where they are dominant theirs is no longer a working-class movement so much as it is an attempt to build a whole nation that is one happy family of workers. Yet in this hope the social democrats have been somewhat disillusioned, especially in Sweden. They have found that high wages and modern apartments and a month's vacation are not everything in life. To complete the democratization of society they began in the late 1960s an all-out demand for fuller equality (*jämlikhet*): meaning not just negotiations between labor and management but participation of labor on boards of directors of banks and businesses; not just central facilities open to all (schools, libraries, hospitals, theaters, recreation) but equality of access to such facilities, requiring the placement of such institutions within easy reach of people in remote and sparsely settled areas; not just education available to all, but recognition that vocational education is as worthy as classical; equalization of incomes; separation of the church from its long association with the state. Antimonarchic sentiment is strong among some social democrats, but there is also nostalgia and respect for this venerable institution. The rank and file of social democrats are less radical than their leaders, but the goal of all is an egalitarian society—a society in which solidarity is the keynote.

Except for Iceland, where the party system is rather different, the social democrats normally form the largest single party, but they have not been able anywhere to maintain a clear majority. Usually they must form coalitions with the centrists or the communists, and this makes for instability, especially in Finland.

The communists play a marginal but significant role. During World War II they were effective in underground activities and their prestige produced a burst of postwar support. But external events cut their strength. First, the United States quite unreasonably refused to collapse according to predictions; then desperate and ruthless moves by Soviet Russia in Czechoslovakia in 1948 and the militarization of the workers' society brought disillusionment and fear. In 1948 the Finnish communist representation in parliament fell from forty-nine to thirty-eight and in Sweden from fifteen to eight. In Norway in 1949 the communist vote was halved and the Storting delegation reduced from eleven to zero. The Danish communists lost half of their eighteen seats.

These setbacks in the welfare states caused some serious rethinking in communist ranks. They play the parliamentary game and occasionally hold the balance of power, or at least help on key votes to maintain the socialists in office. They appeal to youth and to left-wing sentiment even when it is not strictly communist. Their marginal position in the governmental system produces splits and name changing, for example, to "Socialist Peoples party" in Denmark, and "Left Party-Communists" in Sweden. In the three central countries they normally poll 4 to 5 percent of the vote but frequently lose out in parliamentary representation. In Finland the communists were legally banned from 1930 to 1944, but since 1945 they dominate the Finnish Peoples Democratic Union which musters almost a quarter of the seats in the Eduskunta. Sometimes they participate in ministries. Their strength is based on a combination of "industrial communism" and "backwoods communism." In Iceland the communists have absorbed dissatisfied social democrats into their Labor Union or Popular Alliance which is one of the major parties and sometimes is included in coalition governments.

Now for the exceptions. The basic division into five groups is worth keeping in mind, but it is being challenged in the 1970s and it has been shattered in Denmark. Temporary split-offs occur in these countries as they do everywhere, but the fragments resulting from personal quarrels or small-group special interests tend either to melt away, like chips off an iceberg, or to be reassimilated. However, deeper forces appeared in this new decade, and no one could foresee what the ultimate effect might be.

In Sweden the 1973 election, projected to be a bourgeois victory, ended in a stalemate, the three parties of the right gaining 175 seats and the two parties on the left 175. The five-party structure survived, but with some startling shifts in party strength: the liberal Folk party dropped from 58 seats to 34, and the Center jumped from 71 to 90; the Social Democrats lost only one seat, but were left increasingly dependent on the Communists.

In the Norwegian elections of 1973 the liberals (Venstre) lost even more dramatically, falling from thirteen seats to two, while another liberal minded group, the Christian Peoples party, rose from fourteen seats to twenty. Labor (social democratic) lost twelve seats, but the eye-openers were the sudden appearance of the far-left Socialist Alliance with sixteen seats, and the maverick protest followers of Anders Lange with four seats.

Denmark, forced into an unexpected election early in De-

Party patterns in Scandinavia (number of parliamentary seats and percentages in recent elections).

Denmark 1975	Finland 1972	Iceland 1974	Norway 1973	Sweden 1973
Conservatives	Union	Independence	The Right	Moderates
10 6%	(Democratic	25 42.7%	(Høyre)	51 14%
Liberals	League)	Progressive	29 19%	Liberals
(Venstre)	37 18.5%	17 24.9%	Liberal	(Folk)
42 23.5%	Swedish	Social Demo-	(Venstre)	34 10%
Radical	Peoples	crats (Labor)	2 1.5%	Center
Venstre	10 5%	5 9.1%	New Peoples	90 26%
13 7%	Peoples	Union of	1 0.7%	Social
Christian	7 3.5%	Liberals and	Christian	Democrats
Peoples	Smallholders	Leftists	Peoples	162 46%
9 5%	18 9%	3 4.6%	20 13%	Left Party-
Progress	Center	Labor Union	Center	Communists
24 13.4%	35 17.5%	(Popular	21 13.3%	13 4%
Center	Social	Alliance)	Anders	
Democrats	Democrats	10 18.3%	Lange's	Total seats
4 2%	55 27.5%		4 3%	350
Social	Christian	Total seats	Labor	
Democrats	Federalists	60	62 40%	
53 30%	4 2%		Socialist	
Left	Peoples Demo-		Alliance	
Socialists	crats (National		16 10%	
4 2%	Coalition)			
Socialist	34 17%		Total seats	
Peoples			155	
9 5%	Total seats			
Communists	200			
7 4%				
Total seats				
179 [a]				

[a] Includes 2 seats for the Faroes and 2 for Greenland.

cember 1973, revealed a chaos of political thinking. Every one of the five parties in the Folketing of 1971–1973 lost seats—the Conservatives from thirty-one down to sixteen, the Social Democrats from seventy dropping to forty-six. Three smaller existing parties, Christian Peoples, Justice (the single tax followers of Henry George), and Communist now polled enough votes to gain the representation that they could not win in 1971. A rebel group left the Social Democratic party and under the name Center Democrats was able to win fourteen places. But the shocker was the eruption of the antitax, antibureaucracy, all-out protest "Progress party" led by Mogens Glistrup. From nothing it grew in less than a year to be the second largest party in the country with twenty-eight seats. Could the state be governed with ten parties, bitterly divided, and with a prime minister who had behind him only twenty-two party members in the Folketing?

The answer was no. After another year of political bickering and economic recession Prime Minister Poul Hartling called for new elections, and they were held in January 1975. The machinery of democracy continued to function but produced no decision. Hartling's Liberals were encouraged when they almost doubled their seats from 22 to 42. But they were far from a majority, and their new seats were won from their most natural collaborators, the Conservatives and the Radical Liberals. On the other side the Social Democrats increased their strength, too, to 53 seats, and they did this by reducing or eliminating smaller parties of the left. And Glistrup's negativists lost only four seats. The immediate result was therefore only a stiffening of political opposition, with both Liberals and Social Democrats claiming victory and the leadership role. Hartling's economic reform program, a wage and price freeze, would now meet hardened antagonism from labor. There was no clear mandate, no natural coalition, only rejection of a proferred solution.

The significance of this chronicle of chaos is of course the wide permeation of dissidence, and it applies not only to Denmark. It was reminiscent of the Poujadist movement in France of the 1950s, with Glistrup in the role of Poujad as catalyst of discontent. To greater or lesser degree throughout the North the traditional calm politics of consensus was gone. Parties were becoming fractionalized. Interest in the older party organizations weakened, perhaps partly because national television lessened the importance of local party leaders. Proportional representation made it easy for new groups (such as Glistrup's) to gain a foothold quickly. Frustrated and angered voters were no longer held to former allegiances through fear of reprisals. For people thought they could depend on the guarantees of the social welfare system.

But now the social welfare system itself was threatened by economic disaster and taxpayer revolt. The Danish economy was the most vulnerable, but the burdens of constantly expanding social welfare were keenly felt also in Finland and Sweden and even in oil-hopeful Norway. Did the Danish dilemma of the mid-1970s portend new and radically different political alignments and programs both in Denmark and throughout Norden?

Obviously the segmenting of political opinions could no longer be contained within the five-party framework. In the United States the two-party system functions, under normal conditions, by providing for compromises and adjustments of divergent interests within the parties themselves; in the Scandinavian and most other European systems "parties of principle" develop more or less consistent programs, and the ultimate political compromises are made at the parliamentary level. Ministries must often be formed by coalitions of two or more parties, or if agreement is impossible a minority or caretaker government must be appointed and controversial issues postponed. Finland frequently has had to resort to this solution, unsatisfactory though it is. The Balkanization of politics owing to irreconcilable economic and social tensions and the resulting multiplicity of parties produces in the end a stagnation of government—which is exactly what Mogens Glistrup demanded.

Yet the structure of government built up through centuries is a power in itself. Parties and parliaments are policy-making organs, and the everyday activities of government can proceed without them for an indeterminate time. The real government may be the bureaucracy.

The finger of government that reaches out to the individual is the administration, the functioning agencies, and officials and clerks. The vast bureaucracy spawned by the welfare state touches the individual dozens of times a day—through the postman, the policeman, the tax assessor and the collector, the food inspector, the teacher, the train conductor, the telephone operator, and more and more. All these are instruments of the gargantuan structure that guides and controls the lives of people. They make the decisions that matter. In Sweden they number one in every five of the work force, and the proportion is similar in the other states, and not too different wherever one looks in twentieth-century industrialized societies. The way these functionaries apply the law may often be more important than the laws themselves.

Generally speaking this horde of diverse civil servants is directed by some twelve to twenty executive departments or by provincial or communal governments. Openings are advertised and applicants carefully selected on the basis of merit, although without the American system of separate civil service examinations. Political patronage as it is known in the United States is virtually nonexistent; only the policy-making positions at the highest level are filled on a political basis. Employees retain their various party affiliations and are often active politically. In some of the countries they are forbidden to strike, but they occasionally do so anyway. The civil servant in the North enjoys a secure and prestigious position.

The Swedish system differs somewhat from the norm. In the seventeenth century the top administrative posts were reserved for the nobility and only gradually did this aristocratic preference disappear; remnants of it linger still in the Foreign Office. The most significant difference in the Swedish structure is the separation between the twelve ministerial departments and the 170 administrative agencies. In Sweden, uniquely, the agencies usually operate in autonomous fashion and with responsibility not to any particular cabinet officer but to the ministry as a whole. The directors-general of the larger agencies hold posts comparable to cabinet status. In Norway the cabinet posts themselves are frequently held by experts rather than by political leaders.

A feature common to all but particularly notable in Sweden is the extensive use of investigative commissions for studying specific problems prior to the making of laws. The commissions are authorized by the parliament and include both members of the government and specialists from relevant segments of the community. They issue reports that are exemplary for thoroughness (the SOU, *Statens Offentliga Utredningar*); these are used as a basis for legislation and are studied appreciatively by the neighboring countries—as, for instance, the reports on school and university reform, on constitutional revision, on problems such as alcohol and drugs.

Elaborate methods are employed to tap the opinions of the people as a whole, especially through the widely organized interest groups and study circles. The Social Democratic party is adept in the use of these groups to learn grass roots thinking, also to influence that thinking, and to discover young leadership talent. At the highest level frequent conferences are held between government leaders and financial and business executives. In Finland the sauna provides a marvelous setting for relaxed weekend discussions, in Sweden the prime minister's estate at Harpsund is a favorite meeting place, the seat of the so-called "Harpsund democracy" (it corresponds in a way with Camp David, but is used for broader government purposes).

The place of government in society, the part it plays in making the national communities what they are, can best be seen through accounts of their activities in certain specific areas, though this must be but a sampling.

Planned Security: Health   ·

The health of its citizens is a primary concern of the welfare state. The new attitude is stated in a nutshell by David Hinshaw:

The dominant social welfare conception throughout the world has developed from (a) a growing humanitarianism, (b) an emerging sense of social justice, (c) depression-created insecurity, (d) a misconception that the state owes every citizen a living, (e) the assumption that the forces of science, engineering, industry, and commerce (which have magically created so much comfort and opportunity for so many people) can pro duce the wealth necessary to make realizable the welfare dreams of today's social and political leaders.[1]

This and following chapters are devoted to an attempt to explain the pragmatic Scandinavian application of these ideas. The northern peoples are building a new social structure, somewhat paternalistic or at least Big Brotherly, yet still far short of the regimentation of totalitarianism. The purpose is to free the individual, not to bind him, and is based on the concept that to free the many sometimes requires restraints on the few. Inevitably overeager legislators or bureaucrats sometimes lay restrictions on everyone and hinder both security and achievement.

In the old rural society of Scandinavia, as elsewhere, there was security within the family. The farm was a family enterprise, and

1. *Sweden: Champion of Peace* (New York: Putnam's, 1949), p. 208.

each family member contributed according to his ability and received according to his need. When a man's days of work were over he was cared for as a matter of right; had he not in his younger days produced more than he had eaten? When he was injured or ill he was cared for because he was a member of the family; no other reason was necessary. A destitute family or an individual alone was supported by neighbors. In Denmark a regular system survived into the nineteenth century which allowed the destitute to make the rounds of their neighbors' farms and receive a meal at each in turn. Similarly the fishing communities of Norway closed ranks and carried on when fathers were lost at sea. So too, when the nazis carried off to prison camp the breadwinner of a family he could be sure that his children would be housed and fed.

The shift from agriculture to industry and the movement from country to city weakened family ties and made it impossible for families to assure security to their members. On the European continent and to a lesser extent in the North the Christian church gradually assumed responsibility for relief of poverty and distress. Alms boxes in the churches collected contributions and the pastors dispensed charity. Such a system, however, was never quite satisfactory either psychologically or economically. With secularization and the growth of population and industry it became less and less satisfactory. Neither pleasant nor sufficient was the contemptuous charity tossed out by rugged individualists who had won their top hats. It was not even good business to produce a weak and bitter laboring proletariat. The problem was, how could the individual be protected and be made most productive? If neither the family nor the church could find the answer, then the job belonged to the state. Hence the secular government slowly assumed more responsibility. Local communities were required by law to care for their poor people, and the central government offered a helping hand.

In 1837 a committee of the Swedish Riksdag was appointed to investigate the problem of relief. The committee came to no definite conclusion as to whether aid should be centralized in Stockholm or left largely to the communities.[2] But it recognized that the

2. "Mostly it happens that the poorest people in greatest need are taken to the poorhouse. Others receive occasionally money or provisions. Children who are in need are dis-

simple personal methods of the past were no longer adequate. Not everyone could become the pensioner of a wealthy farmer. Nor could all beggars be deprived of legal protection and forced into the army or into "work houses" which threw the innocent poor into contact with criminals, had a degrading effect, prevented marriage, and threatened loss in the next generation. From 1840 many of the unemployed were put to work draining marshes, building roads, and later railroads. A law of 1847 began the cooperation between the state, the county, and the commune which has come to characterize the relief program.

The state at the same time gained two allies: emigration and industrial development. Emigration gained momentum in the 1840s and reached flood tide in the 1880s. Thousands of young men and women left to give their brain and brawn to the New World. Their places at home and the thousands of new places created by factories and railroads slowly built up an unprecedented demand for labor. Arthur Montgomery is probably right when he suggests that the building of railroads in the mid-nineteenth century meant more for social development in Sweden than did legislation.

Yet there remained famine and crime, unemployed and poor, the sick and the aged. Emigration and industrialism helped solve some problems; they created also many new ones through breaking up of families, the growth of cities, the increase in industrial accidents. The state had a job bigger than ever before. The tasks of government under a new social policy were similar throughout Europe. In countries such as Germany, England, and France the problems were often more acute than in the North. But the Scandinavian governments showed themselves peculiarly responsive to the needs of their people, and out of careful study of their own situation and of the methods used by their neighbors to the south and west they worked out their solutions.

The principle of state regulation of working conditions was es-

---

tributed among foster parents. In some places in the country where there are no poorhouses, the poor live for certain periods of time with the richer people and there they do as much work as is possible for them. Still there are only few places that do not have begging at all. Most communities take begging for granted." (Translated and slightly condensed from quotation in Arthur Montgomery, *Svensk socialpolitik under 1800-talet,* 2d ed. [Stockholm: Kooperativa Förbundet, 1951], p. 73.)

tablished in the eighteenth century both in Denmark-Norway and in Sweden-Finland. Denmark then operated under an autocratic monarch and Sweden under a paternalistic mercantilism. Many of the basic principles underlying programs for workers' welfare date from this period of "Enlightenment" in Europe. Control legislation on such items as child labor and hours of work in mines continued into the early nineteenth century.

In Norway, for example, mercantilists and liberals in the Storting agreed on an act making arrangements for the management of the Röros copper works (1818): The laborer was entitled to a pension at age sixty-five, the amount to depend on family responsibilities and former wages; in case of illness caused by his work he was to get full wages for one month and one-half in the next month; he might work only eight hours underground in winter and nine in summer; he could buy food from the company at cost plus 10 percent. In 1842 these rules were extended to all mines in Norway. Similar acts were passed for shopmen, cotters, and seamen. Attempts to enforce such laws and additional rules requiring safety devices led inevitably to "inspection acts" and supervision.

Steadily there grew a broadening of government interest in the workingman. The state was concerned with national production. Then too, its interest was enhanced because the workingman was playing an increasing role in politics. Mass education, universal suffrage, and social legislation were born of this union of economic and humanitarian motives. The problem of the workers' security came to be seen as a problem of the whole society.

Thus it was that the Scandinavian states began in the late nineteenth century to build up bodies of social legislation that have become models for much of the rest of the world. German and other experience were helpful, but these northerners were never slavish imitators. They examined their own needs and possibilities first, borrowed techniques from outside only insofar as these seemed to fit. In the careful thinking out of every step they improved and invented at many points, and ended with a unique pattern of government-individual relationships.

Insurance against the devastating results of accident, illness, and old age was the first major field of the new activity. S. A. Hedin in Sweden raised the question of social insurance in the

Riksdag of 1884, and by 1886 a law on accident insurance was passed. Sickness insurance came next, but haltingly. Norway too began, in 1894, with insurance against industrial accidents of factory workers and within the next twenty years had broadened the law to include fishermen and seamen. Finland in 1895 started in the same way with an act holding employers responsible for industrial accidents.

Since only the details differ in the different countries, Denmark may serve as an example of a carefully integrated scheme of social insurance. "Support for self-support" is the basic principle. It is partly voluntary, partly compulsory and involves an intricate pattern of cooperation between individuals, businesses, private societies, and government agencies both national and local. Except for old age insurance it requires at least some contribution from the individual. Regulation is national, administration is largely local. The Danish system is a typical Scandinavian blend of individual responsibility and social responsibility.

Health insurance evolved from the voluntary "sick clubs" that sprang up after the middle of the nineteenth century, these clubs being replacements for the self-help guilds that were abolished in 1860. Now they are widespread, usually one for each commune (several in the larger cities) and are managed by their own elected boards. They enroll all citizens—farmers, shopkeepers, and workers—who earn a skilled worker's top pay or less. Those who earn or have more than this income are required merely to belong to an "association" wherein they pay a nominal sum and get slight benefits, but they may be quickly transferred to the full insurance sick club in case need arises (if, for instance, they lose their high-income status). The associations are therefore passive organizations, a reserve for the sick clubs.

Funds for health insurance come 75 percent from the societies and 25 percent from the state. They provide not only for direct expenses from illness but also, for workers who lose income, a daily cash benefit. Beyond this, general public funds support the major expenses of the hospitals and thus keep the individual's costs very low. Actual amounts and services differ somewhat in different communes and clubs. For instance, some include dental work and some do not. The individual has a choice of doctors, but fees are regulated by the clubs according to a locally negotiated schedule. In the hospitals the practice in Denmark is different from that in the United States in that all attention is given by full-time staff physicians; being or not being a sick club member of course has no effect on that.

This system combines insurance and relief, or compensation and assistance, and has social-psychological advantages. The individual gets what he needs, and even though he may not pay for all of it he has the sense of contributing. He retains the status of an insured person; he is not classed as a pauper.

Many other kinds of insurance protect the person from the material effects of almost any disaster that may strike. Disability insurance (dating from 1921) is funded by contributions from the individual, employers, the commune, and the state. Compensation is adjustable according to the degree of disability and also to pensions, other income, and the cost of living. Exact amounts are determined by a special court. Insurance against industrial accidents is paid for 90 percent by the employer, on the theory that such costs are a proper charge against expense of production. The beneficiary gets financial recompense and is entitled if necessary to programs of rehabilitation and retraining. Widows' pensions vary according to need, especially the number of children.

Old age is reckoned as a special kind of invalidity, but "Old Age Pensions" come as a right and without payment of any special contribution. This has been true since the act of 1891. These pensions are financed out of general revenues and the costs divided: four-sevenths by the state, two-sevenths by the communes in general, and one-seventh by the commune in which the recipient resides. Payments are in two categories: the basic pension of about $130 per month per couple, plus a fixed supplement of about $350 per year. The actual amount of the basic pension is raised up or down according to place of residence, other income, degree of incapacity—blind people, for instance, receiving an additional sum. Both the elderly and those on other forms of social security are entitled to remain in their own homes as long as desired and then to have care in an appropriate institution, of which there are many throughout the country.

Unemployment insurance is a different category, but operates on principles similar to the various forms of sickness insurance.

For unemployment, however, the employer pays only a token amount, the worker pays about half, the state one-third, and the commune one-sixth. The state contributions are based on a percentage of the contributions of the insured, but vary from an even matching of the payments of the lowest paid workers to only 15 percent of the payments of highly paid workers. Benefits are never paid for the first six days of unemployment and are paid for a maximum of 100 days in a year. Still further to discourage deliberate idleness a worker is required to accept a job even outside his special training and at the regular rate of pay for that job. In other words, pay is based on the work done, not on the worker's special training. Throughout the country the state operates labor exchanges to facilitate new employment. In case of strikes or other industrial conflict the worker must look to his union's funds. In short, the state will help the individual, but it will not be imposed upon, and the worker who is idle or on strike can never gain as much as the equivalent of his regular wage.

To the general scene here presented from a Danish stage we can add a few examples from Sweden, illustrating both the broad similarities and the differences in detail. In Sweden the Basic Pension is paid for by employees and taxpayers as a whole and on retirement is everyone's by right. The Supplementary Pension (ATP for the Swedish name *Allmän tillägspension*) is paid for by the employers as a percentage of wages and by self-employed persons for themselves. The two pensions together normally provide a person at age sixty-seven with an income about two-thirds of his earnings during his best years. The formula for determining the amount is complicated and contains provisions for adjustment based on the consumer price index. Further adjustments in this and other forms of benefit (such as disability insurance, illness, child care, rental supplements, widows' pensions) recognize the differences in cost of living between a city like Stockholm and a small town. The goal is to maintain for the recipient a constant purchasing power. However, the basis of the ATP pension is the individual's own input, and it becomes therefore less and less adequate for the elderly as inflation races on. The insurance aspects of the pension are emphasized in that the ATP payments are made after age sixty-seven whether a person is working or not; he is thus encouraged to continue at work, unlike the situation in the United States where social security benefits are curtailed (until age seventy-two) for those who continue to earn regular wages.

Many of the laws on social aid have been passed after conferences between the social ministers and experts from all the Scandinavian countries, so that some legislation is identical and administration is coordinated. A Danish worker employed in Sweden, for example, will pay his fees to the Swedish authorities and collect therefrom, too, if he lives there after retirement or disability. This system of reciprocity extends throughout the North. All people are cared for, whether through insurance or through grants: the blind, the ill, the mentally troubled, paupers; and the basis for all care is *right,* the right of the human being, the right of the member of society who is less fortunate than his fellows.

However, insurance or assistance against distress is ameliorative at best. Much is being done on a more positive basis. In Norway, for example, Public Health Boards were established by a law of 1860 and have steadily expanded their usefulness. The country has several hundred public health districts in cities, towns, and rural communities. The district health officer occupies a prominent place in his community, and serves on juvenile courts, factory inspection boards, building commissions, and health organizations. He is assisted in each case by a local board which must contain one woman, the public engineer when there is one, and a veterinary if possible. From two to four members are elected for four-year terms. These boards throughout the country have supervision over epidemic diseases, water, cemeteries, public halls, garbage, and housing conditions. Here again is the system of local democratic control, with national coordination and supervision through the Ministry of Health and Social Welfare. Preventive medicine is strongly emphasized, as in the continuing fight against tuberculosis.

The quality of health and health services in the northern countries is exceptionally high and belies the complaints about "socialized medicine." Flaws there are, indeed, such as too few doctors in the isolated areas, too few nurses everywhere. Certain diseases rank comparatively high as causes of death: arteriosclerosis and heart disease, lung disease, cancer, and ulcers, while the various contagious diseases have been brought remarkably well under

control. In four of the countries the suicide rate is high, but unusually low in Norway, and nowhere as high as the reputation
with which they have been tagged. The murder rate is infinites-
imal by American standards—these people may kill themselves
but not each other! Medical research is on a high level. Hospitals
are among the best in the world and Sweden, for instance, has 16
beds per thousand people as compared with 11 for the USSR and
8.5 for the United States. If the acid test of the effectiveness of
health measures is length of life, the Scandinavians pass with flying colors.

Life expectancy at birth.

Country	Male	Female
Denmark	70.1	74.7
Finland	65.43	72.57
Iceland	70.8	76.2
Norway	71.03	75.97
Sweden	71.72	76.13
France	68.2	75.4
Great Britain	68.7	74.9
Japan	68.35	73.61
Switzerland	68.72	74.13
West Germany	67.62	73.57
United States	67.0	74.2

Source: *Statistisk årsbok för Sverige, 1970,* table 460. Figures are for the mid-1960s.

An incidental item that has nothing to do with longevity but
only with statistical ingenuity: when a baby is born in Sweden the
first thing he gets, along with the slap from the doctor, is the identification number that will be his through his lifetime and forever.
It is made up of the year, month, day, and the numerical sequence
of his place in that day's baby crop. Thus Knut Knutsson, born on
the fourth of July, 1975, as the one hundred tenth baby of the day
would get 75 07 04 0110. This is his social security number, his
army serial number, his police identification—almost everything
except his telephone number.

Special problems of health and sanitation arise in these lands of
long winters and heavy clothing. The bath is not necessarily a

daily exercise. Yet when the Finns, for example, go to the sauna they get gloriously clean. The sauna is a family and sometimes a social event, and prudery is at a minimum; the bath is often the occasion for a weekend outing. The rural bathhouse is a special building of logs with shelves around the sidewalls, a fireplace covered over with a pyramid of stones, and in the roof a small outlet for smoke and steam. When the stones are heated, water is thrown over them, and the bathers bask in the steam. They are stripped clean and lie first on the lower shelves. As they begin to warm up, a girl or an older woman comes in and beats and scrubs their perspiring bodies with birch twigs; as they can bear it they crawl up to higher shelves and more intense steam as fresh water is dashed on the hot stones. When their pink bodies can stand no more they jump into the snow outside or perhaps through the thin ice of a nearby lake. Then a rubdown and an evening by the fireplace. The sauna is a highly effective way to sweat out either business problems or political tangles.

In the cities modern electrified saunas are built into new houses or apartments. The public bathhouse also remains an important institution, though slowly disappearing. Men and women carry their little suitcases with change of clothes and make special appointments for the "Class A bath" and perhaps a massage, much as American women make their dates with the beauty parlor. There is no longer any excuse for the filthiness of the nineteenth century, of which a famous doctor said: "Most people of the lower classes in Stockholm get their bodies clean only twice—when they are born and when they die."

Child Welfare

The fear of population decline and the social interest in children, particularly in Sweden, have led to much legislation in recent years. The first Swedish child welfare legislation dates from the twelfth century and an institution for orphans was established in 1633. Children are regarded as a social asset and a community responsibility regardless of the accidents of parenthood.

The birthrate in Scandinavia tends to be low. However, once a child is born he could hardly find a spot on earth where he would have a better chance to grow to maturity. The accompanying table on infant mortality indicates that only the Netherlands, Japan, and Switzerland come into close competition; the United States ranks rather low among the supposedly "advanced" nations. Sweden takes a world first, and it is also in Sweden that a girl baby has the longest life expectancy—approximately seventy-seven years. Such statistics are not accidental.

Highly interesting developments in the health field have come since the legislation of 1937. In this program state aid and regula-

Infant mortality during the first year of life.

Country	Year	Male	Female
Denmark	1967	19.0 [a]	12.4 [a]
Finland	1968	15.9	12.7
Iceland	1968	19.1	8.1
Norway	1968	15.0	12.3
Sweden	1969	13.9	9.4
France	1966	20.8	15.5
Great Britain	1966	20.4	16.4
West Germany	1967	26.0	19.8
Netherlands	1968	15.8	11.6
Switzerland	1968	19.3	14.8
Greece	1967	35.8	32.4
Italy	1967	36.3	29.1
Rumania	1968	58.6	47.6
Japan	1967	17.6	13.7
China	1968	22.1	20.2
United States	1967	25.2	19.4

Source: International tables in *Statistisk årsbok för Sverige, 1971,* table 475.

[a] Per 1000 births.

tion limits itself to preventive medicine and is therefore somewhat different from the socialized medical system in England. Every prospective mother in Sweden is entitled to free prophylactic treatment, examination, and advice on prenatal care. More than 68 percent take advantage of the opportunity. Every infant is entitled to free examination and preventive treatment, and over 85 percent receive it. Vitamins and medicines are available free for both mother and child. Later in life vaccination for tuberculosis is compulsory and free.

All this and more is organized through local Child Welfare Boards, established in every community according to the law of 1924, charged to "follow attentively the prevailing conditions in the commune with reference to the care and training of children and youth" and to help them. These Boards have supervision of matters affecting juvenile delinquency and have introduced many reforms in procedures of dealing with such cases. They also have oversight in the whole broad realm of health facilities.

The state gives subventions for equipment and pays part of the salary of doctors and nurses; the community pays the remainder. The total cost is in practice divided about equally between state and locality. Dental clinics are established on a similar pattern, and with a similar distribution of cost. However, the individual child pays a small fee, the second child in a family still smaller, and the third less than that. Where these dental clinics exist the participation is practically 100 percent of the children. These services, dental and medical, emphasize prevention strongly and use regular private physicians and dentists on a part-time basis in clinics and schools. The result is both improved general health and increased work for the private practitioner. The services provided for children include day nurseries, playgrounds, summer camps, and careful legal protection.

The other Nordic countries operate their child welfare systems on much the same plan, and each has contributed its own innovations. For instance, it was in Norway that the "Oslo breakfast" originated, and it has spread to many countries in Europe. At school any child may obtain an invigorating morning meal: orange (when possible), milk, biscuit or bread, cheese, raw carrot or apple. This breakfast or lunch furnishes not only vitamin quality but the social significance of training in cleanliness and manners.

Concern for the child in society goes so far as to recognize that for him psychological atmosphere is as important as food, and this thought lies behind much of the social legislation. Sweden, for instance, has recently made provision for a "social salary" for a mother whose man, unmarried but father of her children, has disappeared from the scene. She gets a weekly cash payment, free rent, and the annual child allowance.

How Sinful Is Sex?

Distortion and misinformation have been widely spread about sex in Scandinavia, with a focus especially on Sweden and the sinfulness of sex. Sex is a universal phenomenon, and middle-class mores throughout the so-called Christian western world are basically similar. Yet sin is redefined from generation to generation and customs do vary in different societies. Throughout the West attitudes toward sex have changed considerably from the nineteenth century to the era of Hollywood and the hippies (though practices may have changed less than attitudes). In all eras practices have varied between the social classes, for example, with male nobility and royalty being allowed special privileges, with little attention being paid to what "the lower classes" did, and with the middle class calling for rigid standards.

Sweden (and Scandinavia in general) present variations which popularizers have magnified beyond the bounds of reason or truth. These variations may stem partly from that distant time when polygamy was accepted; Christianity never completely overcame this background. Long distances from church and priest were permitted to excuse delay in the sanction of marriage. And anyway, it was asked by this practical rural folk, why was marriage necessary unless a child was born or at least on the way? Promiscuity was rare, prostitution was minimal, but a couple might live together for months or years without priestly or legal blessing. The law recognized this custom by providing that the child of an engaged couple was legitimate. Hence, statistics were rather meaningless when they categorized as "illegitimate" babies born within less than seven months after the marriage of their parents. Probably 30 to 40 percent of Swedish babies still come within this category; pregnant brides are common. Within recent years both the term and the concept of illegitimacy have been abolished. Sometimes one or both parents prefer not to marry at all and there is practically no social ostracism of unwed mothers or of children born out of wedlock. The old "double standard" has all but vanished, and much hypocrisy too. Social insurance benefits may be paid to whichever parent cares for the children.

Under these conditions the situation for the child became about the same with unwed parents as with divorced parents. The divorce rate increased throughout Scandinavia during the 1960s, until in Sweden and Denmark it was about one out of four marriages, in Finland and Iceland one out of each six or seven, in Norway one of each eight. Marital fidelity, incidentally, appears to be about the same in these as in other European countries. Premarital sex is regarded as something quite different, and a Swedish survey of adults indicates that 90 percent of them had experienced sexual relations before marriage.

Abortion regulations are cited as another example of sexual sinfulness, and the abortion rate is indeed high. However, the law on this is clear and abortions must be sanctioned by the National Medical Board. The long-standing prohibition of abortion (once under penalty of death) was abandoned in 1939 largely because of the number of deaths due to illegal abortions. The liberalization of the law and the new controls have reduced deaths from abortion to less than half of the former figure. As justification for abortion, social reasons as well as physical and psychological are valid. Only about 4 percent of pregnant women apply for abortions, and only some two-thirds of these are allowed. (Women from abroad can seldom get permission because the necessary background information cannot be obtained in time.) It would be impossible to say whether the actual rate of abortion is greater in this comparatively permissive system than in countries where the operation remains illegal but is nevertheless practiced surreptitiously.

Birth control information is easily obtainable. The private National Association for Sex Education maintains clinics and laboratories and has forty-odd stores throughout the country handling prophylactics and contraceptives. Posters and books remind both sexes of the risks and responsibilities involved in sexual intercourse: Both of you are responsible. Can she depend on you? Can you depend on yourself? Equality of responsibility toward children is also stressed. Much as Sweden wants to see the birthrate increased, a strong emphasis is placed on health and the idea that "every mother ought to enjoy the suns of two summers between each childbirth." "Children, yes. But when we want them." Undoubtedly these policies have played a part in the fact that Sweden now has the lowest infant mortality in the world.

Sex education in the schools is frank and thorough—and controversial. It was put into the curriculum in 1940 and made compulsory in 1956. Beginning in the first year of school, children learn about the difference in the sexes and problems of home life, then on to facts about the sex organs and their functions, to contraception and the birth and care of babies. All is supposedly taught within an ethical framework. TV programs continue the process of education on similar subjects, particularly in their social and moral aspects. One would not think this could leave much interest in commercial pornography, though this is often flaunted in the newsstands (perhaps especially for the foreigner?). Since 1971 public displays of pornography have been prohibited in Sweden, and the still greater permissiveness of Denmark has been curtailed.

In essence the Swedes and their Scandinavian brethren emphasize the naturalness of sex as opposed to the Victorian emphasis on the sinfulness of it. In the United States, however, a social revolution has occurred in the last generation profoundly altering the sex habits of youth—witness among other things the changes in college housing patterns and in the disciplinary tasks of deans of women. Perhaps sexual freedom has come to be rather similar on both sides of the Atlantic, which is still far from saying that license is condoned on either side.

As to the status of women in society it still cannot be said that complete equality has been attained. Denmark has a queen (the first since 1412); Finland was the first country in Europe to have full suffrage for women (1906); in parts of Iceland an actual feminine superiority was enjoyed in the Middle Ages. Now women drive taxis and work on the assembly line, but only recently has the principle of equal pay been accepted (and practice has not fully caught up with principle). In all the northern countries, as in Europe and America, men predominate in legislative halls, in the courts, on boards of directors. Equality of opportunity is legally established for education and for jobs, but Woman still floats vaguely somewhere between the pedestal on which she once was stood and the committee table around which she may one day sit as a partner. Fredrika Bremer in the nineteenth century and Eva Moberg in the twentieth have been effective protagonists of women's rights. Alva Myrdal has achieved influence and high political position. But, while Ibsen's Nora has been relegated to the past, Alva Myrdal cannot be regarded as typical.

Housing as a Social Concern

Closely related to questions of health and child welfare is housing. Actually, housing is a central factor in social welfare as a whole, influencing family life, children, religion, and the stability of the community.

The Stockholm housing exhibition of 1930 was a pioneering and an eye-opening illustration of modern design. The influence of German functionalism was evident and also the philosophy of Frank Lloyd Wright. The Swedes proceeded, though, to make something of their own, to create new designs in houses and in furniture for Swedish living. They have shown themselves clever in planning apartments for comfortable living in small quarters. Both apartment houses and "villa" homes were constructed to take advantage of all available sunshine and of views across water or valleys. An illustration of this earlier twentieth-century architectural planning is a group of octagonal apartment buildings, eight stories high, built on an irregular rocky height in Stockholm; each small apartment has a balcony large enough for two people—three if necessary, and an open view.

The cities of Scandinavia are keenly aware of the need for open space. Stockholm allots about half of its land development to streets, playgrounds, and parks. The law requires of individual subdividers that they turn over to the city at least 40 percent of the tract for such purposes. Most cities in the North have extensive colony gardens, where closed-in apartment dwellers can have cottages and little patches of land for flower or vegetable gardens and for sitting in the sun.

Copenhagen has a tradition of municipal landownership dating from 1100 when unfenced farm lands became public property. Once the city purchased an entire adjoining village. Such land was held by the city but rented to individuals. In 1795 a government commission wanted to sell some of the lands to help pay costs of restoration after the great fire, but the city objected in strong terms: "The property and ground of Copenhagen belong to the city and its inhabitants, those of the future no less than of the present; therefore, any attempt to take away from future generations the opportunity to utilize this property . . . is positively deplorable." [3]

This philosophy so strongly expressed almost 200 years ago is still the guiding principle of the Danish authorities. As the growth of Copenhagen has spread out and threatened to overwhelm nearby towns the trend is being controlled by national and regional planning. The basic scheme is to direct urban development along a series of "fingers" reaching out from Copenhagen, carefully preserving open country between the fingers. Zoning regulations and housing standards are coordinated so as to provide the best possible housing for the current generation and the future also. Denmark was fortunate enough to lose little housing in World War II, and building boomed thereafter.

Half of all Danish housing, and since 1958 two-thirds of new construction, has been in single-family homes, for the Dane loves his garden plot. Quality of construction and building design is enforced by government rules and induced by subsidies and tax adjustments. Grants are made in relation to the number of family members and in inverse relation to income. Thus the large family is encouraged to build with ample space, while the small family can obtain no assistance for building beyond a few rooms. The new housing is equipped with modern bathrooms, automatic dishwashers, and other conveniences, plus a view to garden or countryside.

Multiple family units comprise about one-third of new construction, and in this field the Danes have made imaginative innovations. Self-contained communities have been built, such as Albertslund west of Copenhagen—with white houses and black fences, pedestrian traffic separated from vehicular, enclosed garden squares, markets, and so on. Another recent venture is the collective house, an apartment house with hotel facilities such as restaurant, nurses, child care, shops. On the west coast of Jutland, near Hanstholm, a new city for 35,000 people may become the ocean port of tomorrow, built on the site of an eleventh-century Viking stronghold. Much of the new construction is in prefabri-

3. See J. Graham, *Housing in Scandinavia* (Chapel Hill: University of North Carolina Press, 1940), p. 8.

cated modules, and these form the basis for an active export business to twenty or more countries, involving about 150,000 housing units per year.

Despite the social purposes and controls behind Danish housing, two-thirds of the construction is done by private contractors and most of the financing is also private. In addition, some 600 social housing associations or cooperatives build sometimes very extensively.

Government is concerned for the welfare of the elderly and handicapped, and many of the new developments provide ramps for wheelchairs and other facilities. Building plans are recognized as important for the realization of social goals, for instance, the living together of old and young, of healthy and disabled, rather than the segregation of special groups that produces monotony and often despair.

Throughout Scandinavia housing construction has been vigorous since World War II. Outside Helsinki the pleasant suburb of Tapiola is a model of a planned and balanced community: families of all income levels live together in a natural setting of woods and paths and swamp, with single houses and large apartments, schools, shopping center, restaurants, sports arena, almost everything except factories and big business. Kivenlahti is another and more recent community built for pleasant family living and full appreciation of nature.

Iceland faced unusual problems in converting from the sod houses of the nineteenth century and has invested in housing more per capita than any other of the Nordic lands in recent years. Iceland lacked building materials and has had to import them, up to 12 percent of her total imports. However, the country now produces her own cement and most new housing is concrete, spacious, and up-to-date. Reykjavik has grown rapidly but still has "all outdoors" for expansion.

Oslo, cradled among the mountains at the head of Oslo fjord, had to plan expansion with care. In the years just before World War II the city did a Herculean work in cleaning out slums in the central city. In this area along the waterfront the city erected its impressive City Hall. Out beyond the center the city built large apartment houses with modern facilities inside, playgrounds outside, and set a scale of low rents which private enterprise had to match. The biggest problem for both Norway and Finland came to be postwar construction in the far north, where the retreating Germans had left vast areas devastated. Over 100,000 people had to be evacuated from Finnish Lapland. Both Finland and Norway had to curtail building elsewhere in order to help the citizens of the northerly areas to reestablish their homes and common facilities. Subsidies were granted and controls were maintained so that people in their haste would not build shacks. The result of this great national effort was slower and more expensive rebuilding, but improvement of living conditions on a permanent basis.

Swedish authorities have been proud of the clean and convenient apartments constructed in cities and suburbs, and they have supported building in massive quantity. Among the residents, however, dissatisfaction has grown toward these concrete utopias. The layout is carefully planned, and the engineering is excellent, often including refinements such as vacuum disposal of garbage and trash. Objections are to monotony of style, lack of individuality, absence of trees and birds. In a community like Vällingby, a normal commuting distance from Stockholm, the stores are conveniently located, the walkways are smooth and clean, the traffic pattern is well regulated, the train to Stockholm is fast and comfortable, the rents are reasonable—and life is dull. Some of the newer planned communities are even colder and more monotonous in appearance, counterparts in concrete of the company towns of the nineteenth century. Farther out it is sometimes startling to find a group of gray skyscrapers in the midst of a landscape that still has wide open space and beautiful woods and lakes. Swedish officials who once thought of the relationship of home to nature as vital seem to be taking it into consideration less and less. Thousands of new apartments stood empty.

In palliation it must be said that the cost of building in the North is a restrictive factor, because homes must be solid. Furthermore, perhaps half of the families have cottages for summer or weekend use in the country or by the shore and get their contact with nature during periods of leisure. The fact remains that in urban and suburban housing the achievement is efficiency, not sociability or geniality. At least the slums of the past have been eliminated.

In all the Nordic countries ownership of house or apartment is made easy. Contractors may obtain generous subsidies, and the head of a family may borrow from government funds or government-guaranteed funds most of the cost of a home. He may even postpone payments until his youngest child has reached earning age. If he rents, he may have his rent reduced 30 percent if he has three children, up to 70 percent if he has eight (this in Sweden).

Municipalities occasionally do the building themselves. Most construction is carried on by various kinds of cooperative organizations backed by government money. Details vary in complex fashion, but the methods always provide for aid to either single or multiple dwellings. Mortgage allowances may run from as low as 25 percent to as high as 97 percent, and the period of amortization may be as much as sixty years. Housing cooperatives are a standard form of organization. In Sweden, for instance, the Tenants' Savings and Building Society (HSB) is one of the largest operators. It has a central office in Stockholm that furnishes architectural and financial guidance, local "parent societies" that manage the building enterprises, and "daughter societies" of tenants in the particular building or development. Another popular method of organization is the building association set up as a joint stock company, a system widely used in Finland. Community housing associations are also established by local government bodies. And large firms assist in housing for their employees. Only a nonprofit system with long-term, low-cost financing can assure the ideal of good housing for all, and this is the common goal.

Labor and Socialization

Erik Brofoss, Minister of Finance and later head of the Bank of Norway, has stated Labor's attitude well: "Labor's views on economic democracy are based upon what can be called the 'social concept of capital.' The owner of a private enterprise does not merely exercise exclusive private legal rights and does not administer his private property only. He is entrusted with the management of the productive capital of our society upon which economic progress, social prosperity and the economic future of the workers depend . . . Among the fundamental principles of democracy should also be the recognition of the workers as partakers in the organization of economic life." [4]

4. Quoted in Herbert Dorfman, *Labor Relations in Norway* (Oslo: Tanum, 1966), pp. 145–146.

Throughout Scandinavia this is the philosophy on which the policies of government are based. In Sweden Gunnar Adler-Karlsson calls it "functional socialism." It assumes that the worker as well as the owner or manager wants to make a contribution to the society of which he is a part. It does not deny selfish motives but counts on the fact that the individual realizes that his selfish purposes cannot be realized apart from society. As Ragnar Frisch puts it: "The real problem is to find an economic and political system that will put in the center of things the individual's freedom and his moral and ethical values . . . and *simultaneously* make it possible to utilize material advantages—natural resources and human intelligence—in a really rational way." [5]

If this sounds like a too idealistic program—well, it probably is. No one would claim that it is implemented to the point of perfection. But the ideals that men profess, the goals with which they identify, are vitally important. The materialistic emphasis is strong, though it might be difficult to establish that it is stronger in Scandinavia than in other societies. Insofar as there is a difference it lies in how material advantages are distributed. In Scandinavia, working on the basis of the "social concept of capital," and in collaboration with government labor has achieved a socio-economic revolution in the twentieth century. As it has been well put by Robert Dahl, "Some of the most profound changes in the world take place in a quiet country like Denmark where hardly anyone raises his voice and the rhetoric of revolution finds few admirers." [6] Great wealth has not been eliminated but it has been curtailed; poverty has been all but wiped out; a high degree of economic equality has been achieved. How has it been done?

The first relevant factor is that these societies are small and comparatively homogeneous in race and religion and language (the Finns representing the chief variant). Second is that they have never been societies of easy abundance; conditions of climate and isolation have demanded hard work and cooperation, as in the fishing industry, for instance. Third, the tradition of education, of reading and thinking and discussing, is ancient and deep-seated. The study circles of the labor movement are only a mod-

5. In his essay "Det uopplyste pengevelde" [That unenlightened money power], in Torild Skard's *Nyradikalisme i Norge* (Oslo: Gyldendal Norsk Forlag, 1967), p. 110.

6. *After the Revolution? Authority in a Good Society* (New Haven: Yale University Press, 1971), as quoted by S. M. Lipset in *Saturday Review,* March 20, 1971, p. 27.

ern adaptation of well-established practices. Fourth, and closely associated with the other factors mentioned, is the social conscience embedded in every class. The aristocracy felt it in older times, partly because of the intimate relationships of owners and workers in the decentralized rural industries of farming and the *bruk* (timber mills, iron foundries, for example). In recent times, as labor has won a dominant position it has accepted the burdens of responsibility. Labor did not come to power through violence and a program of destruction but through the workings of a democratic system. Labor unionists have no desire to bulldoze their way to disaster. They realize that the know-how of management is essential for the functioning of a complicated economic system and they are willing to cooperate. The interlocking relationships of labor and the Social Democratic party accentuate and facilitate the exercise of political power. For labor realizes that the Social Democratic party is its party, and that its power must be exercised responsibly. If the party is discredited by extremism or scandal or malfunctioning, labor is itself weakened. Caution is reinforced by the fifth of our basic facts: that the balance of forces in each country is rather even between the socialist and the nonsocialist parties—in fact, if the bourgeois groups can unite they can outvote the socialists (that is, labor). Labor's power rests upon its unity and its moderation—which, admittedly, is occasionally forgotten!

Certain aspects of the history of the modern labor movement help to explain its attitude and the position it has attained throughout the North. The movement is essentially indigenous although it has been influenced at various points from outside, especially by Marxism and German social reform in the late nineteenth century, and by Russian communism in the period after World War I. Marcus Thrane, of a middle-class Norwegian family, was converted to socialism during travel on the continent, and in 1849–1851 was momentarily successful in organizing a workers' association in Norway. August Palm, a Swedish tailor, learned his socialism in Germany and agitated long and effectively in Denmark and Sweden. But pragmatic politics soon overshadowed doctrinaire ideologies. Communism won wide popularity during World War II as an effective resistance movement against the Nazis (in Denmark and Norway), but soon after the war it clashed with national feelings and dropped into a minor position numerically. Even in Finland where communism is strongest the Finnish Communists are more Finnish than communist. Communism has gone national in each country and has adapted its methods to the parliamentary system.

National federations of labor organizations developed early in each of the Scandinavian countries and these gave strength and continuity to the movement. The old guilds had been abolished in the 1860s, and unions began to be organized in the 1870s and 1880s. Before the middle of the twentieth century they enrolled better than 90 percent of the industrial workers in each country and from half to two-thirds of the entire workforce. In Denmark the employers formed their Employers' Association in 1896, and the unions built their Amalgamated Trade Unions in 1898. Within the next year these two inclusive associations defined their relations and the relations of employers and employees in general in what is known as the September Agreement. This agreement recognized the rights of each party to "decree and approve labor stoppages"; declared that a strike or lockout must be voted by at least three-fourths of a "competent assembly"; required two notices to be given, fourteen days and seven days before a stoppage; and specified a three-month notice for cancellation of a labor agreement. The right to organize was stated, as was the right of an individual to refrain from being organized. The employer was specifically recognized to have the right to allocate work. One notable passage in the Agreement deserves to be read beyond Denmark's borders:

It is taken for granted that the Amalgamated Trade Unions will be willing to work with all its might together with the Employers' Association for peaceable, stable and good working conditions, first and foremost by ensuring that nothing be done by any organization whatever under any circumstances to prevent any worker from making use of his natural right to do so much and such good work as his abilities and training permit.

Featherbedding is frowned upon by labor as well as by employers.

Under this September Agreement, which is still in force, a Permanent Court of Arbitration was set up in 1900 and was given legal prerogatives. In 1910 it became the Fixed Court of Arbitration. One of its far-reaching decisions was that if an organization remains passive when it should step in to halt an illegal action, then the organization is liable as an accessory. The emphasis in labor relations, however, is not on legal processes but on agreement. Conciliators were set up in 1910 to aid organizations to come to a settlement.

In Sweden labor has come a long way from 1770, when an ordinance stated, "If journeymen or other workers unite for the purpose of causing a rise in wages be each one fined . . ." By 1864 the guilds were abolished, and in 1872 the first trade union was formed. But labor's position was pitifully weak as was illustrated by the famous Sundsvall strike of 1879. That affair, however, dramatized to labor its weakness. By vigorous action based on the right of the individual to form associations, labor's right to organize was established. In 1899 *Landsorganisationen* (LO) was founded through the Social Democratic party; and in Sweden it was labor which first built a comprehensive national organization of organizations. LO has since that time made itself one of the great powers in the state, perhaps the greatest power.

In 1902 the counterpart to LO was established, the Swedish Employer's Association (SAF), and soon, as James J. Robbins concisely puts it:

The associational structure in the labor market had matured into a powerful instrument of *private government* by voluntary groups . . . to the State was reserved but a fraction of disciplinary power in the relations between the organized adversaries, and one of the most important official State organs dealing with labor relations, the Labor Court, was composed of judges, a majority of whom were outright representatives of these organized interests.[7]

The major pattern of organization in Sweden is the industrial union. The closed shop has not been an issue any more than in Denmark. By a careful statement agreed upon in 1907 between LO and the Employers' Association the employer's right to allot work and to discharge was recognized, also the right to hire regardless of union affiliation. The barbers are the only major group who maintain the closed-shop principle. Yet practically all

7. *Government of Labor Relations in Sweden* (Chapel Hill: University of North Carolina Press, 1942), p. 11.

Swedish industrial and craft labor is unionized; the unaffiliated worker is regarded as a parasite, a man refusing to shoulder common responsibilities; labor is so strong that it does not need artificial compulsions.

The Basic Agreement (or the Saltsjöbaden Agreement) of 1938 is the parallel in Sweden to the September Agreement in Denmark. It is an "instrument of functional self-government." It establishes a Labor Market board of six members (three representing each group) to provide for settlement of disputes without state interference, limits conflicts affecting essential service, affirms principles and methods of labor-employer relationships, and protects individual rights. It "rests upon the assumption that while the interests of both sides are likely to conflict in many instances, it is to the advantage of each, without attempting to destroy the other, to compromise those interests peaceably." [8]

Much the same spirit, and even much the same history, characterize the labor movements in Iceland, Norway, and Finland. The Norwegian LO was organized in 1899 and an employers' association in 1900; there is the same privilege of either employer or employee to affiliate or not, and also the same attitude toward the individual who will not join hands with his fellows; and there is the basic agreement and the Labor Court. In Finland development was somewhat later. The typesetters formed the first union in 1894, then a generation afterwards the rights of labor were spelled out in the constitution, both the right to organize and the liberty of the individual to abstain from joining.

The centralization of authority in the national federations is an outstanding characteristic of the labor relations scene in Scandinavia, and so is the Basic Agreement. This results in repeated and often strenuous negotiations between representatives of the two inclusive organizations of workers and employers. They battle vigorously for advantages, but they seldom attack each other. One observer, in his denunciatory book about Sweden,[9] expresses horror at the degree of understanding between the employer representatives and their labor opposite numbers, and thinks much of the rhetoric of conflict is merely shadow boxing. He fails to understand that men can have divergent interests and yet not hate

8. Ibid., p. 137.
9. Roland Huntford, *The New Totalitarians* (New York: Stein and Day, 1972).

each other as human beings. Most of all he seems unaware that a generation or more ago employers and employees recognized that they had not only differences but also common interests; and that once they had come to terms in the Basic Agreement they did not have to fight over the same issues in each successive bargaining session. Each "side" is fully aware that it is only through the cooperation of management and labor that either party or the country as a whole can prosper.

The party affiliations of labor are unusually strong, and in Sweden the Social Democratic party is really the political arm of the labor movement. Many unions hold group memberships in the party, and the chairman of LO (Arne Geijer, 1956–1973) was one of the most powerful figures in government, though technically he had no government position. At lower levels many of those who prove their capacity in the labor organization are tapped for government positions; both official and personal relationships are so close that the term "interlocking directorates" is not too strong. The flow of personnel between labor and government in Sweden is surprisingly like that between business and government in the United States. In Norway the position of labor in government is only slightly less solid, while in Denmark, Finland, and Iceland labor's affiliations are rather more diffuse.

Relations between state and labor are illustrated in labor's 27-point program for postwar Sweden. Chairman of the drafting committee was Ernst Wigforss, Minister of Finance, and the outstanding ideologist and intellectual of the labor movement. The first item was full employment: "That is the principal objective of our economic policy. To achieve this end, our monetary system, state finance, price and wage policy, and private and public undertakings must all combine to provide full employment for labor and material resources." The state is expected to regulate prices so as to prevent depression; to assure steady employment through coordinating plans with industry through "a joint public body"; to grant credits to obtain markets and raw materials abroad; to increase housing and cheap consumer goods; and to improve the system of labor exchanges and job training.

On the foundation of this full employment the state must next assure higher wages, higher living standards, and fair distribution of income. It must bring about a leveling of the differences in income between agricultural and industrial workers and between men and women; expand insurance and unemployment benefits; shorten hours; improve public health; equalize educational opportunities; and (in the long run) abolish class distinctions.

The third major category of goals is "greater productive efficiency and increased economic democracy." These are to be attained by national planning of investments; government supervision of foreign trade; rebuilding of crowded areas and gradual transfer of apartment houses to municipal ownership; "rationalization" of agricultural and domestic work; "government support for nonprofit production or socialization where private enterprise entails abuses or monopolization"; publication of price agreements; greater support for research; control of the quality of goods; and last but not least "greater influence on the part of workers over the administration of industry."

In pursuance of these goals much has been accomplished. When a factory is closed down or workers are laid off they are given opportunities for retraining and are paid regular wages during the training period. Progress has been made in housing, health, education, in other areas. Most interesting in the 1960s and seventies is the government's two-pronged drive for equality (*jämlikhet*) and participation. The opening section of chapter 2 of the constitutional proposal of 1973 reads: "The community shall look for justice and equality among the citizens. Each citizen shall have the right to education, work, and social security." The next section reads: "The worker should through law or agreement be assured influence over direction and division of work and other questions which concern him in his employment. He should by law be protected against removal for inadequate cause."

As to participation in management, one wonders a little how much Sven Svensson and Ole Oleson really want it. They seem interested but vague. A few years ago I asked two workers in a pulp mill, after they brought up the subject, if they thought sharing in the responsibilities of management should bring with it sharing of the risks, such as sharing either profits or losses. They were dumbfounded that anyone could raise such a question. They wanted a larger share in profits, they wanted to help make decisions, but they had not the faintest notion of sharing in any resultant loss. They and their fellows thought of themselves as laborers, employees. Changes in attitude have come with the younger generation, but it is still true that labor accepts political responsibility more readily than management responsibility.

For labor itself is a career. The laborer's son can become a law-yer or a teacher or a banker as he can in the United States, but he is less likely to do so. He is more likely to accept the status if not the occupation of his father, and to do so with a feeling of self-respect. Such attitudes differ in the various parts of Scandinavia, and they differ only in degree between Scandinavia and the United States. But the difference exists. Scandinavian society is less fluid than that of the United States, labor is less mobile. In-dustries and cities are growing, however, and new winds are blow-ing; the degree of difference is smaller than it was a generation ago.

Production methods are efficient, but they depend somewhat more on the man, somewhat less on the machine than in the United States. The proportion of handicraft work is considerably greater. This is partly owing to deliberate policy, and it results in preservation of skills and in a sense of pride in workmanship. The laborer respects the managerial skill and general economic knowl-edge of the employer; he expects the employer to respect the skill-ful eyes and hands which guide a pail of molten metal or construct a table or shape a vase. The laborer therefore can sit down in a wage conference with his employer with a sense of his own dignity and worth. There is little of either humility or resentment. The la-borer is simply representing one set of interests, the employer or manager another set of interests. Labor as a whole is a clear-cut functional group, and it has political and social power. But it remains labor. As labor representatives join boards of directors they are expected really to represent labor. Shareholding by labor leaders is frowned upon, for labor hesitates to compromise its position. In the spring of 1973, the Danish Social Democratic gov-ernment nevertheless proposed, and then withdrew, a scheme for a large central fund for share purchases, the fund to be contrib-uted by employers and managed by government, employers, and labor, to be paid out at long intervals to employees. In Sweden government itself is moving toward share-owning participation in private business.

Violence and bloodshed have had their day, and disastrous

strikes have tested the strength of both management and men. The Sundsvall strike in Sweden has been mentioned, and in 1909 labor tried and failed in a great general strike. In Finland strikes and strike threats have often made the air tense. Denmark used a general strike during World War II as a most effective weapon against the nazis. Worker demonstrations in Iceland have sought to bring pressure on the government. The general spirit of recent times is represented more accurately, however, by the no-strike pledge taken by Norwegian labor after World War II. With this was coupled a wage-stop act in 1947, for the socialist government and the worker-citizen recognized that the upward movement of wages as well as prices must be stopped to avoid runaway inflation.

As to the setting of wages, details differ from country to country but the general pattern is similar to the Swedish: the government determines what should be the total wage bill for the nation for a period of one to three years; LO and SAF (the employers' association) negotiate allocations in large categories; local committees of managers and workers iron out the details for their particular jobs. It is this three-way cooperation between state, industry, and labor that has so significantly slowed the process of nationalization in these essentially socialist societies.

An essential element is labor's political power. Because of its position of responsibility labor recognizes national interest as well as its own class interest. The more far-sighted leadership of both labor and capital seem sometimes close to discovering where the functions and the advantages of each are balanced and intermeshed. A degree of mutual confidence, at least on the personal level, has resulted. A story told me years ago and confirmed by one of the participants will illustrate the prevailing attitude.

In France labor and capital were cutting each other's throats with strikes and lockouts and physical violence. They heard that in Sweden labor and employers had learned how to make agreements for mutual advantage. So the French invited a delegation of Swedish employers and employees to come to Paris to discuss the problem of industrial relations with French employer and employee representatives. At a long table the French employers sat together toward one end, laborers at the other; across the table sat the two Swedish groups. Before the discussion began a French labor delegate asked where was the interpreter. The Swedish workers did not know French, but the employers did. The Frenchman's question was translated by an employer, and the Swedish employees answered that the employers would be their interpreters. The astonished Frenchman said, "What, can you trust them to translate fairly?" When this question in turn was translated, the response of the Swedish labor delegates was to get up and throw their arms around their employer-opponents and to shake their fists at the distrustful French workers.

However, although each side knows that it can count on the integrity of the other, labor relations are not all sweetness and light. Sometimes a strike may be waged by discontented labor against its own higher officials, as in the "illegal" 1970 strike in Kiruna; sometimes it may be a protest against the government-labor combine as when in 1971 the Swedish salaried workers refused to yield to the wage-leveling decreed in the name of equality. Upward mobility of labor's wages can be accepted as good, but when this is accompanied by stagnation in the incomes of the better-educated and better-paid there is bound to be opposition; when the avowed purpose is elimination of income differentials, the opposition on economic grounds is going to be exacerbated by resentment based on wounded prestiges. The happy egalitarian society has not yet arrived.

Education and the Media

"No one may marry or enjoy civic rights until he can read"—so prescribed a Swedish-Finnish law of 1686. The rule was enforced by a confirmation examination in Luther's Catechism. The sanctions have changed with time, but to this day the Scandinavian countries rank at the top in literacy.

Cathedral schools in the North date from the twelfth century, but they touched only a few, chiefly trainees for the priesthood. Yet even in sparsely settled Iceland such schools and also pastors in their homes taught the rudiments and nourished a lasting literary tradition. The sagas instead of television enlivened the long winter evenings. Gradually education has broadened in content, has moved into well-equipped buildings with carefully trained teachers, and enrolls practically everyone from seven to fifteen (or sixteen) years of age. Religion is still part of the curriculum, but now it is likely to be analyzed and dissected rather than being taught as faith. Schools are all but universally state and community controlled, with only a few private schools remaining out of the past.

Not only have the schools become public but the elite selectivity of the earlier twentieth century has also disappeared. As recently as 1950 the great majority of students at the University of Uppsala belonged to Social Group I, which comprised only 5 to 6 percent of the population. Only a small percentage of youth from Social Group III, comprising a majority of the population, even took the student examination qualifying them for university admission. Swedish universities were as exclusive as aristocratic Coimbra in Portugal or the Oxford of "the good old days." In Scandinavian universities a true cross section of the population could be found, probably, only in Iceland and Finland, with Norway and Denmark somewhere in between. However, within the last generation a revolution has been brought about in the whole structure of education, with the Swedes leading the way.

Swedish Social Democratic politicians at last, in the mid-twentieth century, woke up to the fact that the only trained corps of leaders for business, manufacturing, diplomacy, or domestic politics was coming from the social elite. Their own social democratic leadership represented a unique few who had deserted their social class or who had risen by their own bootstraps. Such leadership could not be expected in the next generation. As the ominous prospects became clear the leaders looked at school systems abroad, in Russia, and especially in the United States. After thorough investigation they legislated drastic changes for the democratization of education. Instead of dividing pupils at an early age between an academic life and a practical or vocational life they set up a comprehensive school to hold together pupils of all social classes until age sixteen. Segregation by social class was the "integration problem" in Scandinavia. The reforms provided for a common curriculum, diverging only slowly in the later years. They abolished the student cap which had become a symbol of the elite, the special examination that had been its prerequisite, and the romanticized ceremonies that went along with it. The content of studies was made less important, and the concepts of social adjustment were made more important. The teachings of John

Dewey had something to do with this, and the political needs of the social democrats had much to do with it. Conservatives, both political and academic, protested vigorously but were overruled. One of the protesters complained bitterly that these destructive ideas had come on polluted winds from across the Atlantic.

The investigation had been thorough, and there was far more to the school reform than the obvious political aspects. Sweden's Nordic neighbors followed developments closely and in more moderate ways adopted similar reforms. Norway, for instance, began moving from its seven-year elementary school system to a nine-year school much like the Swedish. It will be topped by a three-year *gymnas,* and then the university. In Norway, too, the private schools are dwindling and are expected soon to disappear. Norway has a particularly varied pattern of post-*gymnas* schools— vocational, commercial, arts and crafts, fisheries, marine engineering, and marine cooking, and on and on for almost every thinkable occupational preparation. The trend is to make fundamental education more general and leave specialization to the end.

In each of these countries the university level institutions have been of exceptionally high quality, whether in the humanities, the sciences, medicine, or technology. Until recently the number of such institutions remained small: Uppsala (founded 1477), Copenhagen (1479), Lund (1686), Åbo (1640, transferred to Helsinki, 1827), Oslo (1811). In the twentieth century, to meet the explosive demand for higher education have been added Reykjavik; Turku, Åbo, and Jyväskylä; Stockholm, Gothenburg and Umeå; Århus, and in the 1970s a new one at Ålborg; Bergen and one started in Tromsö; plus a number of university colleges and branches in order to make higher education more accessible. Only the older institutions have schools of theology, and the newer ones tend to emphasize science and technology plus the social sciences. University-level technological institutes have long been of high grade and, like the Norwegian one in Trondheim, have attracted far more students than could be absorbed at home— hence Nordic engineers have emigrated and helped to build cities and factories and bridges in the United States and around the world. In all branches of higher studies a straining for perfection has tended to raise requirements higher and higher. In Sweden this resulted in the 1960s in a deliberate deflation of the doctoral degree, which had become a superdegree demanding long years of research; the idea was to make it more nearly comparable with the American Ph.D.

The extraordinary pressures on universities in the 1950s and 1960s led also to fundamental reexamination of the place of the university in the community. Most exhaustive was the Swedish government investigation which after five years of study issued its 1400-page report, the "U 68," in 1973. By this time more humanists and social scientists had been trained than could be absorbed in the job market, and in any case the social democrats had always favored practical over theoretical education. Hence one thrust of "U 68" was to emphasize the importance of career-oriented subjects. Another was the proposal for a central administration of all universities, along with a widespread diffusion of new university locales. There should be a total of nineteen university centers, carefully distributed geographically; higher education must be brought to the people. Teaching and research were to be administered separately, which deeply worried those who realized the values of the association of these two functions. While debate on the report raged in educational and political circles and in the press, the demand for university admission suddenly slacked off. The new university "filials" already established had few students, and some of the older universities had more teachers and facilities than they could use—a phenomenon not unique to Sweden. Liberals and conservatives who had abhorred the proposals from the beginning saw some hope to slow down and modify their impact. The changing situation and the strength of protest delayed implementation, and only two things were sure: politicization and democratization of education would continue, and so would debate.

The unique institution of the Scandinavian educational system is its folk high school—"the talk high schools for adults" as an American student described them. The institutions of adult education are as uninhibited and as varied as are the multiple facets of modern civilization. They take "unacademic" youth and older citizens up to any age and they give cultural appreciation to wide segments of the population, as well as an understanding of social problems. Beyond that they give inspiration, training, and self-confidence to many of the present and future social democratic leaders in political and economic life.

The modern renaissance began with Bishop N. F. S. Grundtvig (1783–1872), the Prophet of the North, who in a period of national disaster and discouragement showed Denmark how to make from "outward loss, inward gain." He was a Christian reformer in a modern society, and his medium was education; through it he redirected the mind of Denmark. He visited England and felt the heroic spirit of the nineteenth century; he sensed in the great factories the "sound of Thor's mighty victorious hammer." God meant man to achieve. Through poems, hymns, and personal inspiration Grundtvig helped Danes to feel that nothing was impossible. But man must know, and he must work. Knowledge must be born not so much through books as through speech, through "the living word." "Dead are letters even if they be written with the fingers of angels, and dead is all knowledge which does not find response in the life of the reader." Knowledge must be in the people, not just in leaders of government and business offices. How achieve such goals?

Grundtvig emphasized small schools for youth in the upper teens, schools where personal contact would be influential, and preferably with a farm attached. "The conscious fellowship of a people" made the school as well as the nation. The man to implement the Grundtvigian idea was Kristen Kold (1816–1870), a "rustic blend of Socrates and Pestalozzi," who, as Peter Manniche describes him, as a boy "was so awkward with cobbler's tools that his parents in despair sent him to a teachers' training college." From seminal schools for peasant boys at Ryslinge and Askov an idea spread from Denmark to Scandinavia and to the world. The emphasis was not on job training, not on educating for a different status in life; it was on development of mind and personality. Farming was taught, and economics, but the major subjects were history and the Danish language. The terms were usually short and mostly in the winter season of slack work on the farms. Both young and old learned to know themselves and to understand their culture. They learned to think, to discuss, and to cooperate.

Norway, Finland, and Sweden established similar institutions which have flourished like those in Denmark, and some have been made into Scandinavian rather than national institutions. In a beautiful location at Elsinore in Denmark is the international folk high school long directed by Peter Manniche and attended by students from around the planet. The schools in other countries have moved away somewhat from the ethical purposes of Grundtvig. Some, such as Brunnsvik in Sweden, have become workers' institutes, emphasizing studies in unionism and economics.

But in all of Norden the folk high school has been no sterile institution ending in itself; it has led on to an infinite variety of adult education projects. Many of the veterans of the folk high schools became the nuclei of study circles in their own communities or factories. The study circles of the Workers' Education Association in Sweden register hundreds of thousands of participants, and they have become the training grounds for labor leadership.

Widespread systems of public lectures reach not only women's clubs but cross sections of the population. Four- to six-week institutes in remote places reach thousands more. Municipal libraries have mushroomed, to serve both study circles and individual borrowers. Norway, under the leadership of American-trained Arne Kildal, has done a particularly notable work in library extension, under difficult conditions of distance and population sparseness. Traveling libraries, like traveling hospitals, have been put on special book-boats sailing in and out of the fjords of the west coast.

Another of the unusual phenomena of adult education is the "peoples' university" inaugurated by students of the university in Stockholm. During the depression in 1933 they wanted to do something useful and offered themselves as teachers or discussion leaders. It became an extension university with neither grades nor credits, and the idea spread to other cities in Sweden and throughout Scandinavia. When the students of Copenhagen became interested they went to Stockholm to study the problems, then adapted the idea to their own situation. They held registration in the city hall, and 300 queued-up at the opening hour. Within three days 7000 had registered. Every class but one was filled to overflowing. The last class was entitled "Jesus as seen from the documents." With several hundred left in line that filled up too, and the instructor was hurriedly telephoned—could he repeat the class for another 200? That he could not do. The secretary handled the situation in a typically Danish way: standing on the city hall steps he called out to the waiting line, "We are sorry, but Jesus cannot be duplicated."

Much of the work in these institutions is begun as foreign language teaching, but expands from language to a study of the foreign country concerned and often to travel in that country—and to group tours and classes in Paris, Rome, or London, even tours to America. Education in all its forms opens windows to the world, and the smallness of these countries demands special emphasis on languages and the study of other cultures. Long before American students began their "junior year abroad" young people from the North spent summers or years in England or on the continent, often working in families to pay their way and to get the more intimate touch. English is the language first required, and the second foreign language is usually German or French. Beyond English, which is regarded as essential, the authorities want a good spread of linguistic skills, hence they provide the choice between French and German. Jonas Orring, director of the school administration, has stated this policy in a way which emphasizes not only the importance of foreign languages but the attitude toward education: it is for the benefit of the community as much as for the individual who gets instruction.

Educational institutions go far beyond home and school to include the press, radio, and television.

The only real public debate comes in the press, and even this is more and more muted. On the most vital issues of politics the press of Scandinavia has come to a point of either consensus or acceptance (or is it resignation?). In foreign policy Denmark, Norway, and Iceland accept their alliance with the West and only Iceland seems uncomfortable about it. In Finland the policy of neutrality with careful adjustment to Russia's tender feelings arouses no serious opposition—it is recognized as necessary to survival. In Sweden neutrality has become a shibboleth universally accepted; occasional complaints are oblique, not direct. One cannot say that such widely held beliefs are enforced by government; they are a common heritage, results of the historic experience of each country.

Nevertheless there are many issues on which conservatives, liberals, social democrats, and communists have basic differences of outlook. Such attitudinal variations are reflected in the press, which is in each of these countries as free as a press can ever be. Ownership may be individual, corporate, or party, though in Denmark there is no party-owned paper. Affiliation with at least the point of view of a party is common. A striking fact is that despite the strength of the social democrats their newspapers rank low in circulation; everywhere the liberal and independent conservative papers attract the most readers, as the accompanying table shows. Is it because of their advertisements and features, or do people want to read opinions different from the official line? Papers in the capital cities are always the most important although the "provincial" press is often vigorous and respected, as with *Jyllands Posten* in Denmark, *Uppsala Nya Tidning* and *Sydsvenska Dagbladet* in Sweden.

Aside from the evening tabloids the most widely distributed daily in the North is Stockholm's *Dagens Nyheter* (liberal), with better than 400,000 copies, with almost 600,000 on Sunday. Like its rival *Svenska Dagbladet* (conservative) and the leading papers in the other capitals, it carries strong editorials, good general cultural coverage, and world news. Many people buy two or more papers in order to get the differing points of view and the special features. Norway has about 80 dailies; Sweden has about 165 with a circulation of 4,200,000 in a population of 8,100,000.

The smaller papers everywhere have difficulties with rising costs and competition with the urban monsters that can now reach even distant points quickly. In an attempt to save a pluralistic press, the parliament of Sweden has introduced a special state support to papers with economic problems. The subsidy is financed by a tax on advertising, much disliked by the nonsocialists, but all parties approve the support program. Perhaps the tax will have an additional effect desired by the government, namely to reduce what it regards as the economic waste of advertising.

Weekly and monthly magazines are somewhat less important in Scandinavia than in the United States, while the newspapers are relatively more important. Nevertheless there are significant magazines of news and opinion such as the vigorously liberal *Farmand* in Norway, the widely circulated *Vi* (We) in Sweden, a popular weekly published by the cooperatives, the conservative *Svensk Tidskrift*, and many others.

Newspapers with their political leanings or affiliations and approximate circulation, 1970.

Newspaper	Affiliation	Circulation
DENMARK		
BT (evening)	Conservative	186,000
Berlingske Tidende	Conservative	176,000
		325,000 Sunday
Politiken	Radical Liberal	140,000
		240,000 Sunday
Aktuellt	Social Democratic	100,000
		115,000 Sunday
Land og Folk	Communist	5,800
		9,300 Sunday
Jyllands Posten	Independent Conservative	76,000
(Århus)		160,000 Sunday
FINLAND		
Helsingin Sanomat	Independent	265,000
Aamulehti (Tampere)	Conservative	128,000
Uusi Suomi	Conservative	93,000
Hufvudstadsbladet	Swedish (Conservative)	71,000
Suomen Sosialidemokraati	Social Democrat	41,000
Three communist papers with from 33,000 to 57,000 each		
ICELAND		
Morgunbladid	Independence	35,000
Timinn	Progressive	16,000
Visir	Independence	13,000
	Social Democratic	6,000
	Communist	6,000
NORWAY		
Aftenposten	Conservative	191,000 morning
		157,000 evening
		215,000 Saturday
Dagbladet	Independent	103,000
		131,000 Saturday
Arbeiderbladet	Labor	71,000
		79,000 Saturday
Friheten	Communist	8,500
SWEDEN		
Expressen (evening)	Liberal	623,000
		684,000 Sunday
Aftonbladet (evening)	Social Democratic	507,000
		531,000 Sunday
Dagens Nyheter	Liberal	455,000
		557,000 Sunday

Newspaper	Affiliation	Circulation
Svenska Dagbladet	Conservative	162,000
		165,000 Sunday
Sydsvenska Dagbladet	Conservative	120,000
		158,000 Sunday
Göteborgs Posten	Liberal	285,000
Arbetet (Malmö)	Social Democratic	103,000
Ny Dag (biweekly since 1965)	Communist	15,000

Source: Nordisk statistisk årsbok, 1971.

Newspapers have maintained the independence in which they were born, but the situation is quite different with the other mass media. All of the radio and television systems are either owned by the state or operated under state license. A listener-viewer misses the commercial breaks when he can get up and stretch or speak to his wife, and he must pay a license fee for the privilege of listening. He must accept the programming of a state monopoly, and sometimes he wonders if this produces duller programs than those in countries where competition rules. (Many American programs are rebroadcast.) He also suspects that instead of being browbeaten by advertisers he is being more or less subtly propagandized by government.

In Sweden the national telecommunications system provides the network facilities, and the government licenses the corporation and appoints half of the board that programs radio and television. Harsh charges have been directed at the corporation for television's one-sided treatment of the Vietnam war, its strong anti-American bias, and its leftist outlook. Certainly the government is pleased with these attitudes, but there is no evidence or probability that it ordered anything of the kind. It didn't have to—the reporters and actors were already, if anything, leftward of the government. On the other hand, despite the commands in the law requiring impartiality, objectivity, and "extensive freedom of speech," and providing an overseeing Radio Council, no provision is made for enforcement. Television supplements the school program in many ways, among others in extending sex education. The Broadcasting Corporation wields enormous influence, emphasized by the fact that Sweden in 1972 had 332 *licensed* television sets per 1000 population, while Denmark had 284, Finland

256, and Norway 241. The United States had 399, but of course
not licensed. As of two years earlier Great Britain had 284, West
Germany 262, and the USSR 127.

By whatever tests one can apply—literacy, book publishing,
newspaper distribution, schools and universities and adult education, radio and television—clearly the Scandinavians are among
the best educated and most informed peoples to be found anywhere.

The Ombudsman

The office of ombudsman is a Scandinavian institution that has
received much attention in recent years. New Zealand and Canada and several states in the United States and some of the new
countries of Africa have adopted the idea, and the name at least
has been applied to officials in business concerns and on college
campuses. It originated in its present form with the Swedish constitution of 1809 and it has been adopted and even extended in
the other Scandinavian countries (Finland, 1919; Denmark, 1953;
Norway, 1962).

Bureaucracy sometimes rides brutally over the rights of the individual, either because of careless disregard, or because regulations cannot cover exceptional cases, or for other reasons having
to do with the fallibility of laws or officials. Any society that seeks
justice must provide channels for appeal and correction of mistakes, but too often the procedures of complaint go through the
same governmental structure as the thing objected to. Hence it
was that the Swedes provided for a judicial agent (*Justitie Ombudsman,* or JO) acting under the authority of parliament to be a
watchdog over administrative officials and acts.

With the expansion of bureaucracy the JO's task has grown in
both complexity and importance. Out of the thousand or more
complaints filed each year from 75 to 90 percent are rejected as
petty or unjustified, but even in these cases the aggrieved party
has had the psychological satisfaction of a means of protest, and
probably also a needed explanation of *why* he was treated as he
was. In scores of cases real errors are found or derelictions of
duty. In these instances the JO ordinarily discusses the matter
with the official concerned and tries by persuasion to get the
wrong righted. If necessary he can take the official to court, but

this happens rarely. Such recourse is rare because the prestige of his position is usually sufficient to obtain compliance.

Actual power to change a law or a ruling he does not have, but, for example, if he finds that a murder is committed because the law did not permit the police to detain an insane suspect he can recommend a change in the law—and he will be heard. He can publicly criticize a police chief who exceeds his authority by prohibiting an unsavory town character from appearing on a public street—and get a reversal of the ruling. He can castigate a priest for tearing down a poster announcing a Salvation Army meeting, and thus prevent a recurrence. He can investigate (on his own) the case of the editor of a school paper who was given a bad conduct mark for failure to show an article to the principal—and get the faculty to rescind its action.

The ombudsman is in the first place a man respected in the community, with salary and position comparable to that of a Supreme Court judge. He has the right to see all relevant documents and access to whomever he wishes to consult. The press checks with him each day, and the power of publicity is at his disposal. He is empowered not only to accept complaints from individuals but he can and does initiate proceedings whenever he senses there may be injustice. Occasionally he makes inspection trips, visiting courts, hospitals, schools, smelling out little and big cases of wrongdoing, suggesting remedies. He makes an annual report to parliament (up to several hundred pages), but he is never ordered by parliament to undertake a case or to desist from prosecution. He is a free agent, appointed for a several-year period and frequently reappointed. Both Stephan Hurwitz in Denmark and Alfred Bexelius in Sweden have been kept at their posts for many years. The ombudsman has, of course, a deputy and a staff of lawyers, but has difficulty in handling the workload. His office gives people confidence that there is someone concerned not only with the welfare of society as a whole but with their own rights as individuals. In addition to the JO, a military ombudsman is a long-established official, and recently a consumers' ombudsman and an "economic freedom" ombudsman have been added.

In brief, the ombudsman is an officially sanctioned watchdog over Big Brother. It must be emphasized that he is an agent of the legislative, not of the executive branch. His existence as a permanent official makes unnecessary the ad hoc appointment of a "special prosecutor," and may indeed, because of his watchdog role, help to avert the situations that require special action.

The Cooperative Movement

The cooperative societies are private organizations, but their activities and leadership are closely connected with social democratic ideals and institutions. They mean much to the material progress of Scandinavia and are an integral part of the "Middle Way."

Soon after the Rochdale cooperative was founded in England in 1844 the idea took root in Scandinavia, but growth was feeble for the first half century. Around 1900 several societies began to flourish, and soon came phenomenal development. The scheme seemed to fit these close-knit communities of the North, where the people were homogeneous and intelligent and accustomed to working together. Resources were too meager to waste, and any opportunity to save was welcomed.

The cooperative movement became intertwined with the social program and with economics. In each northern country it grew to be supported by 25 to 50 percent of the population. The consumers' cooperatives handled from 10 to 40 percent of the retail trade. Connected wholesale organizations did a large volume of business in import and export and influenced the entire productive system. Farmers' cooperatives sometimes had monopoly control within their limited fields. The movement was voluntary, but was usually supported by enabling legislation. It existed side by side with private enterprise and in open competition with it.

The movement in Finland was unique in character and extent. There the first cooperatives joined farmers and urban workers in a common organization. The farmers, however, were independent operators, imbued with the philosophy of individualistic capitalism. They built their cooperatives solely for the purpose of saving themselves money on the goods they purchased (or sold). The industrial workers of the cities, on the other hand, saw in the cooperative movement a lever by which the whole social and economic structure might be transformed. This fundamental divergence in point of view led to a split in the movement in 1916 and to the organization by the "reformist" group of Kulutusosuuskuntien Keskuliitto (KK), and its wholesale society (OTK), while the older groups, dominated by farmers and bourgeois, continued as the Yleinen Osuuskauppojen Liitto (YOL), with its wholesale society (SOK). Both groups grew by leaps and bounds.

By the end of World War II the two organizations, commonly known as KK and SOK, together enrolled about 850,000 members and did an annual business of about $14,000,000. They were the two leading business concerns in the country. The membership represented at least 50 percent of the families of Finland, and the two companies counted 40 percent of the national trade. These cooperatives ran life insurance companies, hotels, restaurants, bakeries, mills, fish-curing establishments, dairies, sausage factories, shops, and farms. Their stores were well-planned, often handsome modernistic structures, and their main office buildings in Helsinki utilized the finest of materials and architectural skills.

In Norway the consumers' cooperative movement went through many vicissitudes, but in the twentieth century became firmly established, with now one central organization and several hundred local societies. Each individual member pays for his capital share, and he receives usually a 5 percent return on the investment. Sales are made at regular market prices, and the member then receives rebates on the goods he buys. Reductions are first made for reserves and for administrative costs. Since there is no profit on the purchases of members there is also no tax on that business; but the Norwegian cooperatives also sell to nonmembers, and such sales are taxed. Reserve funds, and the factories owned by the Cooperative Union for making cheese, chocolate, flour, shoes, and so on, are taxed the same as any business enterprise.

Additional local cooperative societies, not affiliated with the central association, follow a different principle in sales. They sell not at market prices, but as low as possible, and thus let the purchaser "take his rebate home in his basket." All together the members of the various consumers' societies, with their families, number in Norway more than one-quarter of the population.

In Denmark the cooperative movement and the folk high schools have been intimately interrelated. The pioneer leaders of cooperative organization came to a considerable extent from folk high school students, and the folk high schools for many years carried on the educational work which is part of the cooperative movement. In town after town, village after village, small groups of workers and farmers came together to buy their foodstuffs, then their clothing and their household goods, attempting to evade the high prices caused by the profits of middlemen and retailers. They fought tense economic battles with the entrepreneurial interests, but slowly they established themselves on firm footing. The system they built is highly decentralized, yet the 200 local distributive societies are now all members of the cooperative wholesale.

The story of Swedish cooperation has been well told and widely read in Marquis Childs' *Sweden, The Middle Way,* although most of his readers gain an exaggerated impression of the bigness and the goodness of Swedish cooperation. In its essentials it was the same kind of development as in the other Scandinavian lands; conditions were similar, ideas were interchangeable. Price advantages of large-scale buying and distribution were brought to Sweden by the cooperatives as they were brought to the United States by the chain stores. In the relatively small market of each of these countries organized buying was particularly significant. Social advantages were secured by the working together of people in a great common enterprise. The Swedish consumer cooperatives have grown to about 700 societies and 880,000 members, representing almost one-half of the population. Their field is retail trade, where they handle about 18 percent of the total (as of 1970). In groceries they do over 35 percent of the business. And they are coordinated in a great national federation, Kooperativa Förbundet (KF), which is Sweden's largest commercial concern, with sales in 1971 of $1,376,000,000. The Domus department stores have grown and spread spectacularly in recent years and appeal not just to members but to the general public.

These various consumers' cooperatives have extended their activities far beyond mere local buying and selling. Their factories, production, and techniques have been influential in a realm wider than figures can indicate. For example, it was in the folk high school cooperative society milieu in Denmark that Mrs. Anine Hansen in 1894 proposed the milk recording societies: farmers began to keep records of production from their different cows.

They soon discovered that with a poor cow it might cost 585 øre to produce a kilo of butter, whereas with a good cow it cost only 112 øre. Milk-recording societies spread through Denmark, Scandinavia, Europe, and to the United States. Rapidly the quality of cows improved, and the quality of butter too.

Price dictation by private concerns was broken down by the establishment of cooperative factories for margarine, overshoes, bread, and rubber tires. Capitalist operators learned the hard way that if they did not keep their prices reasonable the cooperatives would take their markets from them; they learned too that if they managed efficiently and sold at fair prices the cooperatives would not attempt to supplant them.

Just as the cooperatives grew from local to national organizations, so they developed also a larger Scandinavian organization, not for overall control but for servicing the national societies. The Scandinavian Wholesale Society was organized shortly after World War I and is now the chief foreign purchaser for the societies of Finland, Denmark, Sweden, and Norway. From its central office in Copenhagen it buys (for the national societies) coffee by the thousands of tons, sugar, cottonseed, grain—varied products from all over the world, gaining the advantages of a single large-scale dealer.

It is in connection with an all-Scandinavian venture that there occurred one of the most illuminating examples of cooperative activity. The European electric lamp trust maintained high and irrationally different prices in various countries: the price on the same 25-watt bulb in Sweden was 37 cents (1928), in Denmark 27 cents, England 52 cents, Hungary 18 cents! Anders Hedberg of Sweden's KF thought this way of charging what the market would bear had gone to a ridiculous extreme. Saving 12 cents a lamp on Sweden's use of 12,000,000 per year would mean $1,500,000. That was worthwhile.

Just then it became possible to hire the dissatisfied manager of the trust's Stockholm factory. KF had the funds and decided to build a new lamp factory. The trust invited Hedberg down to Geneva and told him what a foolish venture this was and how the trust could cut prices ruinously in Sweden. Hedberg was not in the least impressed. For one thing, he knew he had a loyal buying group. More important, as he told the trust people, they were interested in high prices, while his organization was one of consumers interested in low prices. If the trust wished to lower prices or even to give away lamps in Sweden that was good; it was the people's saving that counted.

When the factory began production its base had been widened. The cooperative organizations of Finland, Norway, Denmark, and Sweden united for ownership and sales in the North European Luma Cooperative Society. While the plant was still under construction the trust dropped its Swedish price to 27 cents. The Luma lamps were then placed on the market at 22 cents, and the trust had to meet that figure. The resultant savings were shared by the clientele of the five cooperating cooperatives in the four countries. They were shared also by the nonmembers who bought Luma bulbs, and they were shared by the entire consuming public: one factory had forced down the price of all bulbs, no matter who made them. The other side of the picture was that the shareholders in the trust had to look forward to reduced dividends. Repercussions spread to England where the first talk of a cooperative factory tumbled the price 10 cents. Here was a farsighted and daring venture in consumers' production, and a pilot experiment in international cooperation. And the Luma, much expanded, continues to operate with profit and now has plants in Oslo and Glasgow.

The story of margarine is similar to that of lamp bulbs—and the stories of overshoes and bread and rubber tires. This is why Sweden has been slow to pass direct antimonopoly legislation. The cooperatives have taken over the job of putting the brakes on capitalistic excess in the domestic market.

There is still another side to the picture of cooperatives in Scandinavia, for the consumers (even when they produce) represent only half of the economic interest. People must make money even before they can save it by wise purchasing. Producers' cooperatives are therefore also vitally important; they are for the most part separate from the consumers' cooperatives, though of course a man can belong both to a producers' and to a consumers' society.

In Norway, for instance, the price of milk kept dropping lower and lower, owing to unorganized production and selling. The farmer-producers were in danger of being ruined. Instead, most of them got together in eight district milk pools or "centrals." Membership represented from 80 percent to 97 percent of production, and the eight pools made agreements not to compete with each other and for the more successful pools to share profits with the less. They brought prices back and maintained them at a profitable level. But is not this itself a dangerous monopoly?

It could be, indeed. To check such a tendency there is called in that peculiar blending of private and government activity. A Marketing Board has been established, composed of representatives of this milk pool and of similar pools for meat and pork, and for eggs; other representatives are from the cooperative organization, the merchants' association, and the three agricultural societies. This Board guides in regulation of market and prices and is itself responsible to the Minister of Agriculture. Funds are obtained by small fees levied by the Board on the various products and by government fees on margarine and certain feedstuffs used on farms. Operation includes among other things a mixing of butter (up to 20 percent) in the manufacture of margarine; the actual amount is regulated and shifted by the Board so as to absorb butter surplus, yet maintain margarine manufacture.

In Denmark agriculture and producers' cooperatives are inseparable: "92 percent of all Danish farmers were members of cooperative dairies," which produced 94 percent of the butter; cooperative butter export societies handled about 50 percent of foreign sales. This is particularly significant because Denmark accounts for a large share of international trade in butter, as well as of that in bacon and hams and in eggs. Cooperative bacon factories do 88 percent of the killings of Danish pigs. Large proportions of the business in eggs and meat are handled through cooperative societies and likewise the farmers' purchasing of fertilizers and feedstuffs.

The cooperative societies, therefore, as well as the farmers individually, have a large stake in the government agreements for trade with Great Britain, Russia, and other countries. One can almost say that individuals, cooperative societies, and government are in business together, and this of course binds the community together in bonds of common interest for the maintenance of quality, fair price, and sustained production.

This common interest is activated by various forms of state aid for farm finance. In Denmark in the depression years of the 1930s a moratorium on farm mortgages was granted, and a fund of 100,000,000 kroner set up by the state for loans to farmers in distress. The interest rate was made to fluctuate with changes in the business cycle. Similarly in Norway a Loan Bank for Farmers was set up by the Storting to adjust debts and if necessary to force adjustment when the mortgage on a farm became higher than the actual value of the farm (by the deflationary process). Foreclosures under such circumstances obviously meant loss to creditors as well as to farmers; the Loan Bank tried to save both by forcing new appraisals, reducing mortgages, and by then granting new small loans to help the farmer on the road to recovery. "Support for self-support." In another branch of financial management, insurance, the cooperative movement has been remarkably successful, as with *Folksam* in Sweden.

The relationship of the cooperatives with the trade unions on the one hand and with the government on the other implies almost an interlocking directorate. Trade union members and their families are active in the consumers' cooperative movement, and there is a strong ideological sympathy tying unions, cooperatives, and social democrats together. Cooperative officials, like Axel Gjöres in Sweden, occasionally move over into high government positions. Both consumers' and producers' cooperatives are "big business" in each of these countries, and therefore they play a part, sometimes alongside large private interests, in trade agreements made by government with other governments, as, for example, the Danish trade agreements with England and the agreements of each of these countries with Russia. But they themselves become vested economic interests, and in that capacity sometimes find themselves allied with private business in opposition to state policy. They are likely to be as much against nationalization as any big capitalist; in Sweden Albin Johanson, then head of the KF, was credited with blocking the government desire to nationalize the oil industry after World War II.

In Iceland the totality of consumers' cooperatives in the villages, the fishermen's cooperatives, the cooperative insurance business, and others make this small country on a per capita basis the most cooperatively organized in the world.

Obviously the cooperative movement cuts a wide swath

throughout Scandinavia. Fully to round out the picture would require chapter upon chapter on production, sales, architecture, employment policy, reserves, correspondence courses, lecture series, schools, cooperative housing, publishing, and other matters too numerous to list. The movement is vast and almost all-embracing, a semiself-sufficient economic structure operating within a still larger economic order.

As a saga of business the story of cooperative expansion is dramatic; it rivals that of Andrew Carnegie or the dreams of Horatio Alger. Here is not one person combining chance and skill in the creation of a great economic structure. Nor is it the use and expansion of invested capital in gambling or the accidental discovery of a new gold mine. Here is the phenomenon of the little people, people without money or credit, strong only in the idea which unites them, acting together and building capital slowly out of savings made from this working together. They gain gradually in financial strength, but their real strength lies in their cohesion as a mass buying force. The great trusts could break small private interlopers by price wars; when challenged by the united cooperators they were fortunate if they could hold what they had. Again and again the cooperators determined the prices at which trusts (such as the electric light and the margarine) could sell their products.

In a way the cooperatives provide the means for spreading the base of investment and in providing an outlet for the savings of the small investor, as is done in the United States by the investment trusts or, in different fashion, by widespread popular shareholding (as for instance in American Telephone and Telegraph and similar corporations). The significant difference is that democratic control comes much closer to realization in the cooperative meetings—general meetings locally, delegate meetings nationally. The purpose of the cooperatives is economic, but the underlying ideal is economic democracy. The broad base of participation is their strength.

The cooperative societies cannot be scared, cannot be driven into financial debacle, cannot be lured away from their basic principles. The societies hold and increase both membership and customers because they offer good goods at cheaper prices. They do not rely upon appeals to moral or social idealism. Their appeal is economic, sometimes long-run rather than immediate, but the canny northerners are intelligent enough to understand the "long-run." The leaders have been shrewd enough to venture into only worthwhile enterprises, and their management of those enterprises is as able as the membership support is loyal.

The local cooperatives are able to cooperate in large national organizations, and the national organizations are able to cooperate with each other in one great organization to buy on the world market. The success of the movement is due fundamentally to two factors: (1) the economic factor, money savings actually achieved, and (2) the psychological factor, the satisfaction to people without individual economic power of controlling their own business. For such satisfactions the baker, the railway worker, and the housewife may spend as many hours planning for a grocery store as does a board of directors in managing a large manufacturing concern.

The success of the cooperative movement has worried many advocates of private business, yet there is surprisingly little outright opposition. It may be that the movement has now attained its full growth. Expansion appears to have leveled off, for the pace of growth is slower than a few years ago.

The cooperative movement has made a place for itself in a mixed economic system; it has not killed off private enterprise. It might or it might not function equally well in another environment; it has gone far in England and comparatively made less progress in the United States. In Scandinavia it is a triumph of economic democracy. This must be said by any fair-minded viewer of the scene whether he personally favors the cooperative idea or condemns it—just as anyone must recognize the success, for example, of John D. Rockefeller.

A General View

Many Northerners think social reform has gone too far. A banker in Gothenburg told me, "The Swedes are living beyond their means, and a sad day of reckoning is coming" and that was twenty-five years ago. An American ECA report of 1949 said the same thing. The *Chicago Tribune* has been reiterating it year after year ever since. The Swedes have had their troubles, but they are still afloat and have achieved a standard of living reckoned in the mid-1970s to be probably the highest in the world. Other Nordic countries have lacked the reserves of wealth and the productive capacities of the Swedes, but their social programs and economic patterns have been similar, and all of them rank high on any yard stick of civilization. The demoralization so often predicted for the welfare societies simply has not occurred—as yet. The question of the effects of extensive social legislation is nevertheless a vital one, and I have kept it in mind on successive visits to Scandinavia.

A persuasive explanation of the principles underlying the social welfare system was made by Erik Brofoss, Norwegian minister of finance, to a group of American students in Oslo in 1948. The state and society, said Brofoss, are perpetually revaluing old concepts, seeking the consummation of a better society. Twentieth-century private business has come to be characterized by trusts and cartels; production is organized for private advantage. But the state desires to gain advantage for all consumers. Private inheritance or wealth by itself should not entitle one to a privileged position. Wealth is really a possession of society, a social inheritance or a social product, and the proprietor is only entrusted with its administration. Workers should be treated as equals in a common productive effort; they should participate in management and share in the responsibility for the national economy. They deserve that incentive. Workers must feel the meaning of their work.

The need for initiative applies to workers as much as to capitalist entrepreneurs; the efficiency of workers depends upon their conviction that efficiency redounds to their advantage as well as to that of the capitalists. But the interest of small industrial groups and the interest of the country as a whole are not always synonymous.

Brofoss reminded his attentive listeners from west of the Atlantic that universal suffrage was once regarded as revolutionary but that it came to be looked upon as a fundamental right. Similarly the right of worker participation should now be regarded as fundamental. Society should determine what is to happen, not merely adjust to what does happen. The difficulties of any economic system are due not to nature but to man, so man should attempt to make himself the master . . . Brofoss was giving voice to the attitude of Scandinavian social democracy as a whole. His basic philosophy was in complete accord with the program of Swedish labor, of Danish, Finnish, and Icelandic practice.

How revolutionary is such a program? Is it a "middle way," a separate path between the right-hand path of capitalism, democracy, and individual freedom, and the left-hand path of communism, dictatorship, and mass thinking? Or is the so-called middle way merely a diagonal lane beginning in the right-hand lane, but veering irresistibly across into the left-hand lane?

The final answer to these questions we do not know. Now one can say only that the planners in Scandinavia intend to pursue a definitely practical line. They believe in principles, but they are not ideologues; they are intensely pragmatic.

That there are negative aspects in the concepts and practices of the welfare state cannot be denied. The psychological effect on the individual of being watched over and cared for may counterbalance the values of health and security. It may in the long run reduce efficiency, inventiveness, initiative, and productivity. It is almost certain to do so unless social motivations can be enhanced to equal the fundamental individual drives. The expense of Big Brother's bureaucracy is a burden that increases every year. More dangerous still is the growth of power in that bureaucracy, and the arrogance that comes with power. In housing programs and agricultural policy there is already evidence that officialdom can be blind to the interests of the citizenry. Control of vast sums in the pension funds is a threat to the continuance of free investment and to the existence of large private industry. The emphasis on material things and the standardization of architecture are ominous warnings for the values that peoples hold dear. The momentum of the all-encompassing state may, if unchecked, bring "1984" even before its time.

The essential difference between the socioeconomic policies of Scandinavia and of the United States is in the professed role of government. Notice that it is the "professed role of government," for in actuality Uncle Sam can become very avuncular: he may prohibit strikes, he may bail out key industries in distress, he may restrict imports, he may distribute largesse . . . but he acts uncomfortable about it. He knows that the American people tend to regard government as something external to themselves, if not actually as an enemy. Among the Scandinavian peoples the attitude is more that government is their agent, the natural executive of the common will. This is the basic difference that critics such as Huntford neither understand nor accept. There is a resultant limitation on freedom, certainly. To a large extent this restriction of freedom is a function of an industrialized technological society, of "progress." No American now enjoys the life of a Daniel Boone or even of a Theodore Roosevelt; no Scandinavian can be any more a Viking rover.

To look at it from a changed perspective we could say that the differences between Scandinavia and the United States are of two kinds: differences of degree, and differences of attitude.

Differences of degree are difficult to measure. It is unfair, for example, to compare specific kinds of taxes, for one may balance out another. If we take total taxes per capita, including social security payments, in relation to GNP (the gross national product) Sweden has probably the highest tax burden in the world. However, sometimes Israel claims the honor, and so does Denmark. Changes from year to year, different statisticians using different bases for figuring, and other factors make exact comparisons impossible. The accompanying table ranks fourteen industrial nations as of 1969–70 and gives approximate and suggestive comparisons.

Sweden, Norway, and Denmark all rank high in taxation and also in GNP, and all give extensive social services; the United States, highest in GNP, is lower in taxation because it leaves much of medical services and other services to be paid by the individual. Another comparison may seem even more surprising: Albert Rosenthal reckoned that as of the mid-1960s 3.5 percent of Swedes received welfare, and 4.1 percent of Americans; also, that Sweden's social programs cost 32.4 percent of GNP, while United States programs cost 28.9 percent of her GNP.[10] Americans got less and paid less, and they had somewhat greater decision-making power over how their income was spent, but the differences were clearly not as great as people are inclined to think.

As to the difference in attitude, the Scandinavian acceptance of government as a friendly power is most relevant. Perhaps this is

10. *The Social Programs of Sweden* (Minneapolis: University of Minnesota Press, 1967), pp. 152, 163.

changing somewhat as increased restraints become galling, but it is still true. The citizen knows that his government wants him to have a job and to be healthy. He is amenable to having government assume responsibility for his material welfare, assuring that hewn forests are reforested and that beaches are kept open and clean for everyone. With this in mind I once asked a young Norwegian social scientist how he could claim to be an individualist and at the same time be an avowed socialist. "Oh, of course," he said, "I'm for letting the Labor Government manage the material

Comparative taxation, 1969–70, in percent of GNP.

Rank	Country	% of GNP in taxes per capita	Rank	GNP per capita (US $)
1	Sweden	46.6	2	3230
2	France	45.7	6	2530
3	Norway	42.6	7	2360
4	Austria	42.2	12	1550
5	Netherlands	41.2	10	1980
6	Germany	40.9	8	2200
7	United Kingdom	37.7	11	1850
8	Denmark	37.3	5	2540
9	Belgium	35.8	9	2160
10	Canada	34.8	3	3010
11	Italy	34.8	14	1390
12	United States	30.8	1	4380
13	Switzerland	23.6	4	2790
14	Japan	20.3	13	1400

Source: Rearranged from table compiled by T. E. Chester for National Westminster Bank's *Quarterly Review,* May 1970.

things that don't matter so that I can be completely free to think the things and do the things that really do matter."

There are of course complaints, especially from business interests that object to being shackled, that dislike the obligation to register their business agreements. They warn of the dangers of paternalism and a weakening of the individual's "lust for work." Occasionally a professional man, a doctor, for example, will "goof off" and quit in his prime years because taxes take too large a share of his income. Yet such cases are oddly rare. In Swedish factories, in Finnish forests, on Danish farms—everywhere, men work conscientiously, effectively. There is little leaning on shovels. It reminds one of the illogical Presbyterians who profess to believe in predestination but who strive to be saved just as hard as if they really had to. There is a social ethic among the Nordics and a realization that if they don't work none of them will have anything; bananas don't drop off their trees.

Youth growing up under the educational influences of the social democratic regimes may push formal socialization farther. There is evidence that governments are feeling such pressures. But so far the idea of mass revolution is as repugnant as it is unnecessary. Every Viking was a chieftain and the heritage of individualism is still strong.

Based on this kind of attitude the several countries of Norden have developed remarkably similar programs, modifications of Western democratic capitalism, pragmatic and moderate rather than doctrinaire or extreme. Democratic processes are intact so that changes of personnel or program can be made if desired. "Control of the few—freedom for the many" is the essence. It is a mixed system which retains individualistic and capitalistic forms yet is directed by governments imbued with a socialist philosophy. Or it can be called a capitalist system of production paired with a socialist system of distribution. If it can hold to its course it is a real middle way, a central lane down the twentieth-century highway of an engineered society.

4 *Twentieth-Century Economies*

No longer do the starving and thwarted youth of Scandinavia emigrate across the Atlantic for opportunity in America. Migration continues but it is migration from the sparsely settled forest lands of the northern North to the cities of the south, from inland areas to the coast, from farms to industries. In the decades of the mid-twentieth century the urban-industrial magnet has also attracted several hundreds of thousands of immigrants from southern and eastern Europe. For Sweden the turning point from emigration to immigration was in 1930. In all of Norden the economic development of the twentieth century has been spectacular. The title of a recent collection of essays, "From Poverty to Affluence," catches the essence of what has happened.

Critics can be found in abundance, and each of the northern countries has its problems—social, economic, political, psychological. The solid fact remains that they have practically eliminated poverty, that their cultural level is extraordinarily high, their inventiveness and their productivity exceptional. They have created standards of living among the highest in the world. They have accomplished these things on a foundation of meager material resources and small populations. They are trying to apply intelligence to the development of their internal potential and their adjustments to changing conditions in the world. They borrow freely from the world's storehouse of ideas and instruments, and they adapt and invent. They argue and experiment, and they are a long way from the perfect society. Perhaps they have put too much emphasis on material progress, but at least they have achieved much of what they have sought.

For centuries the economies of the northern lands were simple and similar: agriculture, fishing, forestry, complemented with a small sea-borne commerce. Trade among themselves was slight, for each produced much the same kinds of commodities as did the others. But now differentiation has come, and many varieties of new industrial products. As a result of this economic revolution roughly one-fourth of the trade of these countries is with each other. A poetic historian could once generalize about three guidelines for the economic history of the North: the furrow of the farmer in the valley, the wake of the ship at sea, and the trail of the skis in the snowy mountains. The transformation from this primitive condition is almost complete, and now diversity is more important than similarity among the five states. Hence it is best to look at the highlights of the five economies individually, and then assess those elements, such as planning, that have more in common.

Denmark

The chief determining factors in Denmark's economy have been her agricultural potential and her insular position between the North Sea and the Baltic. Almost as important as these two shaping influences has been the ability of the people to adjust to changing external circumstances.

Farming is a cooperative business. Traditionally, Denmark is the country of intensive agriculture and quality production. Sixty-three percent of her land is cultivated, which is comparable with Hungary, but within Scandinavia that figure can be matched only by the southern part of Skåne in Sweden. The most important characteristic of Danish agriculture is its adaptability to change.

Changes took place in the late eighteenth and early nineteenth centuries in the pattern of landholding, when Christian Revent-low led the movement to emancipate the peasants and consolidate the village strip farms into separate holdings. Another major change came in the later nineteenth century, when cheap grain from the American plains flooded the European markets. Denmark met the challenge by shifting from raising grain for export to the feeding and export of livestock and animal products. Before World War II Denmark was the world's largest exporter of butter and eggs, with a strong concentration on the British market: Great Britain took 96 percent of Denmark's butter exports, and the Danes themselves used margarine. Then New Zealand took the lead in butter, and the egg market did a Humpty Dumpty: from 9 percent of Denmark's export value in 1938 eggs fell to 0.3 percent. The adaptable Danes turned their attention to pigs, perfected a breed that provided bacon precisely to the Englishman's taste, until three-quarters of British bacon imports came from Denmark. Canned hams gained in importance, half going to the United States and one-fourth to Britain. Milk and butter and cheese were somewhat interchangeable and flexible and played a large part in export, while the skimmed milk could be fed to the pigs. Adjustability assured survival of Danish agriculture.

War and depression and economic nationalism (abroad first and then at home) forced the Danes not only to do shifty footwork in planning exports but also to minimize imports. To slogans such as "Buy British" and "Buy American" the Danes responded "Køb Dansk." They made themselves almost self-sufficient in the breadgrains, wheat and rye. By careful analysis they discovered that barley was one of the best feeds for pigs. Therefore barley, which had occupied 15 percent of the acreage in 1938, was given 45 percent of acreage in 1970. The use of animal fertilizers and their own manufacture of fertilizers greatly reduced the former dependence on imports in this area. The Danes studied which ones of their "Danish Red" and "Black and White" cows produced the most milk and then eliminated the poor producers; their annual production per cow was in the late 1960s exceeded only in the Netherlands. Since horses eat more than do tractors 85 percent of the farms went to the use of tractors (1970) and agriculture became unhorsed (the number of horses declined to about 6 percent of the 1938 population).

Mechanization and scientific progress in agriculture generated social repercussions. Productivity more than doubled; whereas one farm worker could produce food for thirty-five persons in 1950 he could supply eighty-five persons in 1970. Since farms were small and most (90 percent) were individual freeholds, this meant a drastic diminution in the number of hired workers; farm work came to be done by owner families and their machines. The tendency was also toward larger farms, as it developed that farms of less than 75 acres lost money. Hence the number of holdings decreased from 200,000 to 136,000 (1970), and the consolidation trend continued. Roads and automobiles and the increased size of farms made it often convenient for the farmer to move his home into a village or town, and this led to a partial reestablishment of the village pattern of life.

Cooperative associations dominate both buying and selling. Ninety percent of the milk is handled through cooperative processing, and large cooperative cow sheds are making their appearance. Forty percent of the eggs and 50 percent of the chickens are sold through cooperatives, and "pig factories" handle most of the pork and by-products.

Even if, in the 1970s, Danish agriculture was down to one-quarter of total export value (as compared with one-half just before mid-century), this was still important. EFTA (European Free Trade Association) made it possible for Denmark to retain her primary market in England, but agricultural export to West Germany was a high second; Sweden came third. The vital importance of British and German demand for her food products meant that Britain's entry into EEC (European Economic Community) practically forced Denmark to follow. The domestic economy remained as vital as it had always been. Its high efficiency was maintained by the cooperative societies' attention to scientific evaluation and control, mechanization and the increasing size of producing units, attention to foreign market demands (especially the changing needs of Great Britain), and the ability to shift crop emphases with the changing times.

Fishing and the uses of the sea. Fishing has been important for the Danes since their early ancestors left their piles of fishbones and oyster shells in the ancient kitchen middens. In these modern days some 12,000 fishermen bring in a catch that not only provides food at home, and meal and fertilizers, but that is also significant in export value. Cod, herring, eels, lobster, shrimp are taken from the North Sea and beyond in modern diesel-driven steel vessels. Export facilities to the continent in refrigerated trucks are used both by the Danes themselves and by Norwegian and Swedish fishermen who often bring their catch into Danish ports. Plaice (*rödspätta*) is the most tasty and valuable fish for eating, but it is rivaled by the rare hornfish with its jade-green bones. Cod is the main catch and export from both Denmark and Greenland. In all areas the government carefully attempts to control quality, and much of the export from Greenland is handled by the Royal Trade Department. In Denmark itself about half the catch is sold at auction. The ancient custom survives of the crews sharing in both expense and profits, while the vessels are usually owned by their skippers. Fishing is both an individualistic and a cooperative occupation.

Denmark's insular position in the center of northern Europe determines many aspects of her economy, as of her entire life. Easy access by sea to the British market led to the export orientation of Denmark's agriculture, and the all-surrounding waters encouraged fishing. The country's gateway position at the entrance to the Baltic enabled her for centuries to collect tolls and to exercise a certain control over other peoples' shipping, and it stimulated her own commerce. Today the significance of the location is illustrated in the crowded Kastrup airport, and in Copenhagen's Free Port where 5000 ships annually exchange cargoes without the formalities and expense of customs clearance. The situation even tempts both Danes and Swedes to dream of an expanded metropolitan area spreading across the Sound into southern Sweden, with connections by bridges or tunnels. (It would be the Scandinavian counterpart of the bridging of the Bosporus and the tunneling under the English Channel.)

Exports of products and skills. Quite naturally, Denmark's geographic position led to shipbuilding—several of her streamlined Viking boats from the Middle Ages have recently been discovered and raised. In modern times Burmeister and Wain (founded 1846) became the largest manufacturing establishment in Denmark and one of the world's leading shipbuilders. This is the firm that bought and developed the diesel motor; the 1912 voyage of its motor-driven *Selandia* to the Orient inaugurated a new era— the trip might be compared in significance with the Atlantic crossing by the *Savannah* in 1819, or even with the voyage of the *Clermont* up the Hudson in 1807. In its own plants and through licensees around the world, Burmeister and Wain provides the world's most widely used marine engines. It helps Denmark to rank as ninth nation in shipbuilding.

But shipbuilders in Denmark and Sweden, and Burmeister and Wain in particular, are in serious trouble in the 1970s. Management, methods, and machinery have become encrusted with age. Among workers the lust for work lagged: machinery was started only late in the day, allowed to run down early before the end of the day. Rejuvenated blood and updated equipment were sorely needed.

Industry as a whole has displaced agriculture as the most important sector of the economy since the middle of the twentieth century. It occupies 40 percent of the labor force and makes 40 percent of the national product. The shifting balance between different sectors of the economy is highlighted by statistics of foreign trade as pictured in Chart 1. In 1912 industrial products made up 12 percent of export value; in 1938, 27 percent; in 1968, 66 percent; while agricultural exports sank in proportion in the same years from 88 percent to 71 percent, to 27 percent. Even industry is linked with the sea. For Denmark has no coal, no iron, no oil (though eager searching continues), no water power. Industry is concentrated in the ports, mostly in Copenhagen, because it is the sea that makes it possible and cheap for Denmark to import the essential coal and oil. Additional energy can be brought by cable under the Cattegat and the Sound from Sweden, and sometimes Denmark actually exports electrical power.

Almost one-third of Denmark's industrial workers are in the manufacturing and mechanical sector, one-sixth in food processing. One of the most important products is beer, for the Danes drink 92 liters per capita each year (double the Swedish consumption), and Carlsberg and Tuborg are luxury beers in restaurants around the world. Since 1876 the profits from Carlsberg have gone into a fund to support science and the arts—museums and expeditions and publication; recently Tuborg and Carlsberg merged and still larger funds are available.

Cement production is large, favored by lime and chalk deposits. This has stimulated inventions in cement processing machinery;

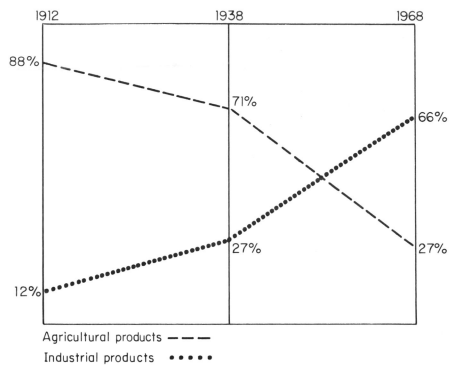

The shifting balance of Danish foreign trade (in percent of export value).

Danish engineers build cement plants abroad as well as at home. In fact, they produce "building systems" of other kinds as well: Turnkey houses and hotels, "finished and furnished," and they have exported thousands of tons of such units to Uganda, Tunisia, and other countries. Machinery of various kinds is a major export, but no automobiles.

Textiles and clothing are more imported than exported, but 5 percent of all exports nevertheless fall in this category. Another item that is small in the overall balance, but high in visibility and appreciation, is the porcelain from Royal Copenhagen and Bing and Grøndahl (such as Christmas plates, Mother's Day plates, and figurines). These and other special products such as silver craft, cheese, canned ham go in goodly quantities to the United States, but about three-fourths of all Danish foreign trade is with her neighbors in the North including England and West Germany.

The East Asiatic Company (founded 1897) is Denmark's largest concern, with 100 branch offices and 35,000 employees around the world. It has a fleet of thirty-odd ships, tin mines, rubber plantations, and rice mills; it operates in Australia with industry and timber importing; in Africa with timber and auto imports, cocoa and coffee exports; in Canada where it owns forests and sawmills and paper factories; in Brazil in the coffee trade; in London on the rubber market.

Denmark exports skills as much as products. Metals and textiles and many other raw materials must be imported, and it is the artistic and inventive skill with which they are processed that gives them salability and value. Trade is in quality products, and trade is extensive for a small country with limited resources. None of these small modern lands can have that magnificent variety of climate and soil that enables the United States to exchange within her own borders the oranges of Florida for the maple syrup of Vermont, or the cotton of Alabama for the pork of Iowa, or the oil of Texas for the cars from Michigan. The Nordic countries must produce each its own specialized items and trade them across international boundaries for the other things needed. The process is costly and for its optimum advantage demands diminution of tariff barriers. Hence the spectacular growth in the 1960s of trade within EFTA and the hopes for a larger area of free exchange within EEC.

Finland

The Finns, like the Danes and all peoples in small countries, must adapt their economy to external forces—or else remain stagnant in low-grade self-sufficiency. The people of the farthest north country in the world have developed a viable economy, an enviably high standard of living, and have produced art and music and literature of world renown.

The Finns face some of the same problems in their economy as do the Danes but also others that are different in both degree and kind. Both peoples have made spectacular advances in agriculture and in industry, but whereas the Danes have adjusted to the shifting demands of West European markets the Finns have been pushed by their eastern neighbor into sudden revamping of their economic structure. Climatic conditions too pose special problems: for instance, while Denmark enjoys about 250 growing days per year, southern Finland has but 200, and the northern parts only 150. How the Finns meet their problems is a fascinating study in man's adaptation to his natural and human environment.

An economy built of wood. Finnish social and economic life has been built, historically, on the inseparability of farm and forest. Two-thirds of the land area is green with pines and spruce, except when covered with a white blanket. In hard times wood has been eaten, and "coffee" has been brewed from the bark of trees. The Finn cultivates his small fields in the brief but brilliant summer, in the winter he goes with his ax into his forest plot when his horse can pull logs over the snow to the roadside. The average farmer (if there is such) has twenty-two acres of arable and eighty-five acres of forest. His farm has remained small, contrary to the consolidation trend among his northern neighbors, largely because of the disastrous territorial dissection of 1944. Finland then lost about one-tenth of her land but had to absorb the population off that land. It meant making room within her shrunken boundaries for more than 400,000 Karelians. The country managed the feat by redividing farms and by reclaiming land from forest, that great saving reservoir. Now the program of the state envisages retiring one-sixteenth of the land in the smallest farms and putting it into pasture or forest, but this reform must come gradually. A careful balance must be maintained between the food-producing farms and the income-producing woodlands.

In the meantime 35 percent of the cultivated area (65 percent of the farms) remains in farms of less than twenty-five acres. The great majority of these are worked by family members. One big plus for the Finnish farmer is that he has a wild card to play: when he needs money for a new roof or a tractor he can go to his woodland and cut some timber (to the specifications of a lumber company), haul it to the roadside and stack it to be picked up by company trucks. The price he gets may well be enough to persuade him to abandon his fireplace and buy oil to heat his house. The forest and various side occupations net him about one-third of his annual income.

Farm ownership resides with the operator of the farm—as of 1960 only 2 percent of farm land was rented. Reforms inaugurated in 1918, immediately after independence, enabled crofters and tenants to gain title to their lands, and even the influx of Karelian refugees did not destroy the new ownership pattern. Two-thirds of the forest land is also owned by farmers and other individuals; a small amount is in the hands of the lumber companies, and about one-quarter (mostly in the far north) is government owned. Cutting and reforestation are guided by trained foresters, and this expanding profession entices many farm sons from plowing and harvesting. The annual growth of the forests is reckoned at 43,000,000 cubic meters, and in some years the use is even greater than the growth.

When one turns to agriculture proper, it may seem surprising that Finland has under cultivation almost exactly the same acreage as Denmark—6,670,000 acres for Finland, 6,734,000 acres for Denmark. But distribution of ownership is different: Finland has 260,000 holdings, Denmark 136,000. Use differs greatly, too, for Denmark utilizes two-thirds of her acreage for grain, Finland less than one-half. And of course the big difference is that of her total land area, Finland being eight times as large.

Although productivity is low Finland has done more than any of the other Nordic countries within recent years to increase her agricultural output. The Finnish farmer produces between one-half and two-thirds of what his Swedish counterpart does, per acre, much more in the fertile southwest than in the more frigid north. Whereas Danish agriculture feeds Danes and also Englishmen, Germans, and others, Finnish farming falls short of supplying domestic needs. In certain crops, such as wheat and rye, Finland has attained almost self-sufficiency, and potatoes are raised throughout the country; barley is being pushed farther and farther north. Sugar beets are difficult to raise and provide only one-fifth of the domestic need. Almost half of the cultivated area is used for fodder crops, especially hay. Along with this goes the large number of cows (2,000,000) and export production of milk, butter, and cheese, plus eggs, meat, and hides. But neither cowhides nor even butter and cheese can equal in export value the little mink. Finland boasts the world's largest mink farm, growing 250,000; altogether 2,700 mink farmers produce this luxury fur, which is one of the few ways in which the northern cold can be turned to advantage.

Despite the obvious difficulties of mechanization for small

farms the Finn uses tractors for 90 percent of his plowing and harrowing and has almost as many machines as the Danish farmer. He uses milking machines for a third of that chore. As elsewhere in the North the use of machines is made possible by group agreements among neighbors and through cooperative societies. Cooperatives handle a large proportion of the buying of equipment and fertilizers and also the selling of products. But although in Denmark and other countries the horse has almost disappeared as a farm animal, in Finland large numbers are still in use, especially for the winter work in the forests.

Finland imports about one-third of her fish consumption, which already puts her in a category different from her northern neighbors. The Baltic Sea is not sufficiently salty for most ocean fish, and the Gulf of Bothnia is even less so. In the far northern interior river and lake fishing may be inhibited by long winters and by vicious mosquitoes in the summer; but the salmon and trout from cold, clear streams are rich rewards for the hardy sportsman, gourmet eating for his friends.

Transportation by water, land, and air. Nature provides good means of transportation, freezing rivers and lakes smooth in winter and filling long water routes in summer. Eight percent of the country is covered by water. In 1856 the Saimaa Canal began to provide access to the Gulf of Finland from hundreds of miles of interior navigable routes; in 1944 the territorial dismemberment cut off the canal, and not until 1968 was agreement reached by which it could once more function. Formerly logs were floated on the rivers, and wood was so plentiful that railway engines burned beautiful birch. Now roadbuilding has increased and logs are transported from the roadside stacks by truck. For passenger traffic the railroads have gradually lost out to automobiles (750,000 in 1971), buses, and the excellent network of airways.

Industrial and trade revolution, post–World War II. Since 1945 Finnish industry has developed rapidly and in some unusual directions. Stimulus was exercised by the Russian requirements that Finland pay reparations in specific commodities—a minor portion in forest products, most of it in electric cable, ships, and machinery. These were the things that Russia needed, and it mattered not to the Soviets that Finland lacked production facilities.

Finland had to create the facilities, and with heroic effort she did. Once the reparations demands were fulfilled the country was left with the factories and had to find markets for the products. Partly with continuing purchases from Russia, partly with fresh markets elsewhere, Finland built on these foundations, literally pushed by reparations requirements into the industrial-technological age.

The change came with accelerating momentum. In 1960 Finland was still the only Nordic country in which the largest category of workers (715,000) was labeled "farmers, loggers, fishermen," but by 1970 these workers numbered only 425,000 and were surpassed by the 663,000 craftsmen and production workers. The workers in service, administrative, and professional jobs almost doubled in the decade. These figures indicate something of a mid-century industrial revolution but still cannot hide the fact that for many years growth was not sufficient to absorb the new crop of workers who matured since the "baby boom" of the 1940s. Wages remained low, and thousands of unemployed young men and women were siphoned off to better-paying jobs in the towns and factories of Sweden. There they were when, in the mid-1970s, vigorously expanding Finnish industry tried to lure them home again.

Industrial expansion was powered by a doubling every ten years of the supply of electricity. As of 1970 the economically available water power had been harnessed, but reserves can be brought into use if prices for oil rise higher. High voltage lines now carry power as far as 400 miles down from the north.

The best measure of Finland's economic success is probably her foreign trade. About one-fifth of Finland's total product is sold abroad, a vital matter not only for the industries concerned but for the national balance of payments. In the 1960s Finland found eager markets in Sweden and the United States for her textiles and designs, including the popular Marimekko fabrics. Items like glass and the prized ceramics from the Arabia factory in Helsinki are highly "visible" but do not weigh heavily in the financial scales. The bulk of export value comes directly or indirectly from the vast forests—wood, pulp, paper, plywood, and furniture amounting in 1970 to $1,300,000,000 in exports, 56 percent of Finland's total. Nevertheless, in number of men employed and total value of production the forest industries were surpassed by the metal and iron industries, though these accounted for only a quarter of exports.

Finnish economic life, to a degree unusual in the northern countries, is dominated by a few big concerns. Largest of the private metal manufacturing companies is Wärtsilä, with twelve plants and 13,000 workers, making machines for various kinds of paper, from newsprint and kraft to fine papers, which it sells to nearby markets and to the rest of the world. It has foundries and shipyards, owns the Arabia factory, Nötsjö glassworks, and a large wharf in Turku. Valmet is an engineering concern with nine plants, 10,000 workers; it exports complete mills for paper and pulp manufacture, to the Soviet Union, for example.

The directional flow of Finland's foreign trade illuminates her economic as well as her political situation. Nature dictates that she find markets for her forest products in the densely populated, industrial, forest-poor countries of the West. Politics and proximity demand that she maintain strong trade relations with her neighbors in the East.

While Finland was an archduchy of Russia, before 1917, about 40 percent of her external trade was with Russia. In the period of new independence between the wars of the twentieth century, trade with Russia fell to 2 percent. Since 1945 trade with the eastern bloc has climbed to 14–19 percent. Exports eastward consist of ships (especially icebreakers), and mechanical and electrical equipment, the items for which Finland tooled-up to meet Russian reparations demands (there remains a question as to just how deliberately farsighted was this forced restructuring of the Finnish economy). Since the USSR is itself the world's largest exporter of wood products, and since such products constitute over half of Finland's exports, it is obvious that Russo-Finnish interchange must be limited. But Russia is a natural supplier of coal and oil and fills the lion's (or shall we say the bear's?) share of Finland's needs, and for this Finland has northern Europe's largest refinery. Russia also supplies many automobiles and other manufactured products.

Finland's forest products, of which paper and mechanical and chemical pulp comprise the largest share, go primarily westward. During the 1960s when EFTA helped Finland to expand her exports the countries of "The Outer 7" took about one quarter of Finland's export (Great Britain alone buying almost 20 percent). Trade with EEC countries amounted to about half of the total. Finland was thus profoundly concerned with the curtailment of EFTA and the expansion of EEC. With Great Britain, Finland sold more than she bought, as she did with the Benelux lands; she bought more from Sweden than she sold, and the same was true with West Germany. But with the large groupings her trade balances were surprisingly well evened out. Especially was this the case with Russia and other communist countries with whom Finland was involved in balancing agreements. With countries across the Atlantic, Canada and the United States, trade was understandably small. Yet this far northern producer of plywood and prefabricated units like window frames, and of machines and water tanks, found markets in far places such as South Africa, Asia, and Latin America. In 1970 total trade almost balanced at $2,600,000,000 of imports and $2,300,000,000 of exports.

For this far-flung commerce a merchant marine was important, and Finland was developing a good motorized fleet. It was still, however, smallest on a per capita basis of the merchant fleets of the North, despite the large increase in the 1960s.

The dramatic changes in Finnish economy are perhaps best illustrated by employment statistics: workers engaged in agriculture declined from 75 percent of the total in 1880 to 20 percent in 1970. In the same period those employed in commerce and transportation increased from 3 percent to about 20 percent, and industrial workers from 8 percent to 35 percent. Towns of 1,000 people in 1850 grew to 25,000 and even 80,000; Helsinki had 21,000 inhabitants in 1850, and its metropolitan area counted over 800,000 in 1972. These developments were associated with the "population explosion" stimulated by the war in the decade 1940–1950.

On the economic front Finland fights a perpetual struggle, as closely contested as the persistent political struggle. In the deep cold of the north the trees that are the green gold of Finland grow slowly. Distances in the sparsely settled land make communications long and costly; even electricity must be carried by cables for hundreds of miles to the more populous south. Investment funds are desperately needed for industry, power, transportation, schools, housing; although investment rose in the postwar years to almost one-third of national income it was still not enough. The overshadowing nearness of Soviet power adds an element of doubt to every major decision, be it economic or political, and forces the country, for better and worse, into unnatural economic enterprises. Wood, the one basic resource both in its natural state and in its multivaried processed forms, makes Finland dependent on the ups and downs of the world market in this one commodity—her Achilles heel is made of paper. Her natural markets are in the West; her powerful and watchful neighbor is in the East. Finland was permitted to be only an associate member in EFTA; she felt it impossible to join her Scandinavian brethren in the commercial cooperation of Nordek; it is unthinkable for her to consider regular membership in EEC and she has to settle for a commercial agreement. Treaty-bound restraints imposed by Russia restrict Finland's military spending, which is of course a boon to the economy. However hard the pressures, and whether advantageous or disadvantageous, Finland continues boldly to maintain the stance of independence. She shifts and adjusts within a restricted range of maneuverability but she refuses to knuckle under.

Iceland

Finland's is a national economy based on wood; Iceland's is based on lack of wood. Perhaps there were a few forests in the Middle Ages, but they were quickly used or destroyed by sheep grazing; since then there is hardly a tree in the island more than three feet high. Houses were long built of turf, now increasingly of concrete. Materials for motor fuel and heating (except for hot water) must be imported, and paid for by other exports. Iceland's small size and big problems have led government to play an exceptionally large directing role in the economy.

Fish, an unpredictable economic base. Like Finland, Iceland has one rich resource, in this case fish. In the middle years of the twentieth century fish accounted for 90–95 percent of Iceland's export value, and 24 percent of her total national income. Ten percent of her workforce were fishermen, and another 10 percent were employed in land-based fish processing. But the notorious undependability of fishing, the inherent unpredictability of the seasons, the incursion into the country's traditional fishing waters by foreign trawlers, with depletion of supply, and long disputes over territorial limits—all these made the Icelanders ponder the advisability of diversification. More and more the state attempted to guide economic development in new channels, and the result was a drastic economic reorientation.

Around this island in the northern mid-Atlantic warm and cold currents of the ocean meet and blend and provide a strong attraction for fish of many varieties. The continental shelf surrounding the land, and roughly paralleling the coastline some fifty miles out, furnishes good spawning grounds. It is so good for cod and herring, plaice, capelin, and others that the Icelanders have not been left alone to harvest their vitamin-rich wealth. Fishing vessels have increased in size from small motor-driven boats to large trawlers of 600–1000 tons. Although Iceland has many of her own trawlers, others come from Norway, England, Germany, and Russia. The purse seine for herring, the long lines (up to ten miles and with as much as 20,000 hooks), and additional modern gear threaten to destroy the fishing beds. Iceland tried to protect her vital industry by extending the three-mile limit to four, by prescribing a ten-mile limit in the bays, by drawing the baseline from headland to headland (thus closing off bays and inlets), then in 1958 by declaring a twelve-mile limit. This unilateral action led to a long and disastrous boycott of Icelandic fish by Great Britain, but finally Iceland won her point (1961).

Overfishing nevertheless continued and some species were exhausted in the nearby waters. Pollution from ship wastes added to the problem. Iceland determined to assert her right to control the entire seabed of her continental shelf as far as fifty miles from shore. On September 1, 1972, she moved to enforcement with gunboats (each with the name of one of the gods of the Vikings). A few months later Icelandic patrols began cutting trawler lines and British naval escorts shot at the patrol boats. The "Cod War" was calmed by a truce late in 1973, but issues remained unresolved and rumblings were heard suggesting a 200-mile limit. Iceland refused to submit the dispute to the International Court or to make bilateral agreement with the British. Perhaps eventually world agreements on the Law of the Sea will find a solution, for similar conflicts involved many coastal countries. For Iceland the issue is vital for her economy and sensitive for national feeling.

Some fish are consumed or sold directly; some are sundried on huge racks in the barren interior; some are salted; an increasing proportion are filleted and frozen and sent to markets in the United States and Europe. Unfortunately the herring, most valuable and most fickle of the fish crop, is becoming more and more difficult to locate. Fishmeal is an important export item and also fish oil—especially the codliver oil that keeps so many youngsters unhappy but healthy. Canned seafoods are of increasing importance for export: caviar, fishballs, shrimp, herring sardines, brook trout, and salmon. Marketing is a problem and is being handled by combinations of producers and even by joint agreements between producers in Iceland and in the Faroes. One strong selling point is the relatively pollution-free seas from which the fish are caught.

The vagaries of the fishing business were well illustrated in the early 1970s. There had been some bad years in the 1960s, and in 1971 the unpredictable herring could hardly be found; cod grew scarcer and scarcer. But the take of shrimp, scallops, and lobster increased. Most spectacular of all was the enormous increase in the catch of capelin, 1973 and 1974 being record years. Thirty thousand tons of frozen capelin were sold to Japan, and the Icelanders hoped that smoked and canned capelin might compete with sardines. The rapid increase in world prices gave the Iceland industry rich dividends: the value of fish exports in 1970 was $60,000,000; in 1973 it was up to $215,000,000. The total catch was 894,000 tons. Interestingly, the diversification of Iceland's industry was at the same time lowering the proportion of fish in the export value to about 80 percent instead of the earlier 90–95 percent.

Sheep the best crop. Agriculture in Iceland struggles against heavy odds. The raising of grain was abandoned in the sixteenth century because of deterioration of climate and shortage of labor, and only recently have new techniques brought some success with barley and oats. What does grow luxuriantly is grass, and this has led to the overwhelming emphasis on animal husbandry, especially sheep raising. The grasslands are naturally swampy and covered with rough hummocks. Draining and leveling, especially since 1942, have vastly extended the usable pasture and hay producing acreage, and ditching tractors are constantly making more land available. The erosion which destroyed much of the old grassland is thus being checked.

Sheep are scattered widely over the Icelandic landscape, numbering from 800,000 in the winter to as much as 1,600,000 in the summer. It is sheep that provide mutton for the table, skin jackets and wool for clothing the family, rugs for the floor, and a very significant export item. The climate helps the sheep to grow thick coats of long-fibered wool. The number of cattle has increased two and one-half fold since 1920, and the yield per cow has almost doubled. Thus has been established the basis for butter and cheese export. Horses were for generations the sole means of transport in Iceland, and their numbers grew to over 60,000; in the course of a century some 160,000 "Iceland ponies" were exported. Within recent years tractors have replaced the draft animals, autos and airplanes have replaced the carriage and saddle horses. The 30,000 workhorses now left stand unemployed among the hummocks.

The farm labor force has experienced a decline even more dramatic than that in continental European countries, from 80 percent in 1860 to about 15 percent in the 1960s (although this latter figure does not include workers engaged in industrial processing of agricultural products). Agriculture is of course favored in government policy. For example, since 1936 a state monopoly or state control has curtailed importation of potatoes, and on several products domestic prices have been guaranteed. When certain items such as mutton are exported the government pays a subsidy to make up for the lower price on the outside market, and the subsidy in the 1960s rose to half the domestic price. On dairy products subsidies were often even greater. The price base is determined by a committee of six, three from the Farmer's Union, three representing the three labor unions. General control of production, prices, and marketing is in the hands of the Agricultural Production Board of nine members, five of whom are elected by the Farmer's Union, four chosen by the big marketing organizations. Two fundamental principles underlie the price and subsidy system: (1) the farmer should be allowed an income comparable to that of the city industrial worker; (2) normal production should leave a surplus for export, so that in times of poor crops the country may still have enough to be self-sufficient.

Jumping on the industrial bandwagon. The development of industry is most spectacularly illustrated by the increase of its proportion in the labor force from 1.1 percent in 1860 to 37 percent in 1970. Expansion of industry began to be significant about 1900; it was stimulated by the depression of the 1930s that curtailed exports and thus prevented purchase of imports—things *had* to be made at home; and it was given the big boost by World War II, with its demand for products and the consequent infusion of money into the Icelandic economy. Despite the obvious potential of hydropower, its development was slow because of the sparsity of population and the lack of capital. A small public electric power plant was built in 1904 and the first major hydroelectric plant in 1937 on the Sog River, beginning to use the vast potential of the melting glaciers. A freezing plant was built in 1930 in Reykjavik, forerunner of a highly profitable method of fish processing.

As of 1960, of the total manufacturing output 60 percent were food products—particularly processed fish. Manufacture of ships and fishing equipment was almost nonexistent, these things essential for production being traditionally imported. However, new brisk winds of contact and communication swept over the land. The government took stronger leadership in the economy. Exports, even if they had to be subsidized, brought in capital. A sense of self-confidence grew, a feeling of "I can do." Small factories were started, and natural resources were put to use.

Underlying Iceland are both water and heat in stupendous quantity. The land has been built by volcanic action; as recently as 1963 men could watch the creation of the island of Surtsey in a mighty clash of fire, lava, and water; ten years later they could see the destruction of the chief town in the Westmann Islands. Hot water and steam have poured from the geysers (and here the word was born) since long before man came to Iceland. Gradually the hot water has been piped to reservoir tanks and on into the towns; it heats the houses and flows in the water mains of three-quarters of the homes of Reykjavik. Electricity for the whole country is provided almost entirely by hydropower and reaches even distant farms and is important for power supply and for lighting through the long nights of winter. Estimates say that the total harnessable water power is from 31 to 35 billion kwh, and only a little over 2 percent has yet been used. Nature provided neither coal nor oil, but it gave alternatives.

From deep in the earth can be tapped also great power in steam. This natural steam is being used to dry the water from diatomite deposits in the bottom of Lake Mývatn in northern Iceland. The Diatomite Filter-Aids Plant is owned 51 percent by the state and the rest by the Johns-Manville Company which sells the filter-aids.

The largest project directed by government action in the 1970s, and by far the largest industrial enterprise in Iceland, is the aluminum plant at Straumsvik near Reykjavik and its power supplier, the Búrfell plant. Búrfell, on the river Thjórsá, was built by the National Power Company, which in turn is owned jointly by the state and by the city of Reykjavik, and supplies power not only for the aluminum plant on the coast but for Reykjavik and all southwest Iceland. Major shares in development costs came from the World Bank and from American institutions.

The aluminum plant at Straumsvik is financed by Alusuisse of Switzerland and represents the first major acceptance of foreign capital. Vigorous objection was raised to the proposal, for Icelanders are acutely aware of threats to their economic and cultural autonomy. Not only the capital but the raw materials come from abroad, and the finished product is re-exported (as is the case with plants elsewhere, such as in Norway and on the coast of Africa). But the clear advantages were enough to outweigh the objections. Operations began in 1969 and by 1970 the income was already significant. To this must be added the wages paid to labor. Careful provisions were made to guard against pollution and waste disposal, not too difficult because of the surrounding lava fields. Already plans were being discussed for a similar plant in northern Iceland.

A land that skipped the railroad era. Transportation and communication were long dependent on ships or horses. The land was both too poor and too sparsely settled to justify investment in railroads, and there are none. Roads are still inadequate but are being built. The last treacherous twenty-mile section of the road around the island was made safe in 1974. Bus lines extend for considerable distances, and the number of private cars is growing rapidly: at the end of 1970 Reykjavik had over 20,000 and the country about 47,000. The airplane early became Iceland's answer for distance travel, and the country has two international carriers—Loftleidir flies to North America and Europe; Icelandair to Europe and domestically (in 1974 these lines merged in a holding company, Flugleidir).

A little country with world-wide trade. On March 1, 1970, Iceland belatedly became a member of EFTA, and the immediate effects were electrifying. EFTA countries admitted Iceland products duty free, and Iceland's exports to these countries jumped 42 percent in the first year, and imports from them by 34 percent. Iceland was allowed ten years to abolish her tariffs against EFTA members, but these duties were reduced already 30 percent in the first year. Iceland's tariff revenues actually increased, because of the increase in trade. Lamb went to the Nordic countries; whale products, cod meal, fish fillets and oil to the United Kingdom; canned herring to Sweden; aluminum to Switzerland. Woolen goods and skins went to varied markets, and their export value rose from 13,000,000 kronúr in 1969 to 85,000,000 kronúr in 1970. All this was a tremendous boost to the diversification policy, but was it only a temporary thing? EFTA seemed about to disintegrate with the admission of Britain, Norway, and Denmark to the EEC. Iceland did not join EEC but she did obtain a favorable trade agreement with this European Community.

Foreign trade, the interchange of goods, is what makes it possible for the people of a small one-product country to live balanced and civilized lives. Icelanders live well because they can exchange their fish, and other items in increasing quantity, for the necessities and luxuries of modern living. For example, they need oil for the rapidly increasing automobiles, and they buy it from Russia in return for fish. This exchange arrangement proved a considerable boon when the oil crisis struck in the fall of 1973, for the fishing fleet could thus get most of the oil that it needed.

The most astonishing aspect of trade of this little country is the breadth of its distribution and the high degree of specialization in different markets. Year by year fluctuations are great, so let us take a sample from the year 1964: 80 percent of the dried salted fish went to Brazil; 66 percent of the stock fish to Nigeria and 30 percent to Sweden; about half of the iced fish to West Germany and the other half to Great Britain; 54 percent of the frozen fish to the United States; 27 percent of the codliver oil to Norway, but the total was distributed among forty-seven countries; 53 percent of the herring oil to Norway; 39 percent of the exported roe to Sweden and 40 percent of the sheepskins; 56 percent of the mutton to Great Britain; 40 percent of the wool to Hungary. The characteristics of trade that emerge from the tables are, in first place, this worldwide scattering and, in second place, the permanent importance of Great Britain and the increasing importance of the United States. In broad proportions, about two-fifths of Icelandic trade was with the EFTA countries, one-fifth with EEC countries, and one-fifth with the United States.

The Icelandic economy is lilliputian in comparison with that of a big country. This factor of size, plus the overwhelming dependence on fish in foreign trade, make necessary a most careful management, a kind of guidance that can hardly be provided by any other institution than the state. As early as 1885 the government started a bank, the first in Iceland, and through many shifts and changes has maintained direct action in financial affairs. In the twentieth century the state has assumed an increasing position of positive leadership in the economy, not always with success. In the 1950s the government attempted an elaborate system of export subsidies and import duties aimed to aid agriculture and balance the economy. The results were nearly disastrous, with rapid inflation, price distortion, and economic slowdown. In 1960 much of the old program was abandoned for a new emphasis on stabilization, investment, and diversification.

Worldwide inflation helped to ease Iceland's own chronic inflationary problem, and her situation was aided, too, by the fact that she had no military establishment to maintain nor any previous wars to pay for. The deeply ingrown fear of foreign investment was overcome sufficiently to permit the Alusuisse aluminum plant at Straumsvik. Central government combined with local government (especially that of Reykjavik) in harnessing the immense power potential of the rivers, even when this too required the assistance of foreign capital. The results have been a steady increase in the standard of living, so that in the 1960s Iceland had approximately the same per capita number as Denmark of telephones and automobiles, a slightly higher gross national product and caloric consumption. This was accomplished without an extraordinary tax burden because import duties paid 50 to 60 percent of national revenue and the state monopolies in alcohol and tobacco another 15 percent. The achievements of recent decades have encouraged national growth not only in economic but in social and cultural areas. At the same time rapid development has led to heavy expenditures and in the mid 1970s close to the brink of economic disaster.

Norway

Of all the unexpected economic revolutions in northern Europe the Norwegian is probably the most unexpected and the most spectacular. This sparsely populated, rugged, and poor land of the far north has abandoned whaling, is rapidly becoming industrialized and urbanized, produces a higher per capita income than Great Britain, and has struck oil in the North Sea. Except for the continuing importance of the merchant fleet and the magnificence of her mountains, the old generalizations about Norway are no longer true. What has happened?

One of the world's great merchant fleets. Even the fleet, one of the strongest elements in the economy, has experienced dramatic change and growth. In the nineteenth century Norway had one of the world's largest fleets of sailing ships. She adapted slowly but successfully to steam and then to motorized vessels. In World War I half her fleet was lost, but she made money, and by the end of the "long armistice" period she had doubled the tonnage of 1914. Again in World War II half of this new fleet was destroyed and Norway's position on the seas was threatened. But Norwegian shipowners moved boldly to rebuild and adapt to the changing demands of ocean transportation. The need was for more and larger tankers to carry the increasing flow of oil. By 1969 over half of Norway's merchant fleet consisted of tankers, including a few giants of 100,000 tons and up. They traveled the routes of world trade, many of them never appearing in Norwegian ports. Actually the Norwegian ships were so busy running errands for other countries that two-thirds of her own imports were brought by the vessels of Germany, Sweden, Denmark, and other countries. Norwegian operators kept their vessels up-to-date by selling off the older ships and buying new ones; they kept half of Norway's tonnage at less than four years of age. Furthermore, they were equipping their vessels with computerized systems for loading, navigating, and unloading, with extreme minimizing of human labor. About one-fourth of the new ships were built in Norway's own shipyards, more in Sweden, Japan, and West Germany, and contracts for future deliveries were huge.

As of 1971 the world's largest registered fleet was Liberian— 38,500,000 tons (but this registration was only a matter of legal convenience for owners in various countries); Great Britain had 27,000,000 tons and Japan about 30,000,000 tons; Norway had 22,000,000 tons, sailing slightly ahead of the United States and the USSR with about 16,000,000 tons each. And the Norwegian fleet continued to grow, with another 22,000,000 tons on order. On a per capita basis Norway had by far the largest tonnage (except for Liberia). This country of 4,000,000 people operated almost 10 percent of the world's shipping.

The significance of this great merchant marine for the national economy can hardly be overestimated. The earnings of the fleet in foreign currencies care for about two-thirds of the costs of Norway's unusually large import. The fleet employs almost 50,000 men and women (of whom about one-fifth are foreigners). Related shipbuilding and outfitting give employment to many more. Despite labor governments and socialist policies the ships remain in private hands, partly because, unlike the fleets of some other countries, Norway's does not require subsidies. It makes money and it pays high taxes. Norway's most famous ship company is Wilhelmsen, founded in 1861 in Tönsberg, now one of three firms with over 1,000,000 tons each. The various shipping companies cooperate but do not combine.

A subtle by-product of this fleet that sails the seven seas is the international-mindedness of a people who could otherwise easily feel isolated. Ultima Thule is more closely integrated with world society than are many countries lying nearer the geographic center. Norwegian merchants and engineers have established themselves in ports all around the earth. Explorers like Roald Amundsen and Fridtjof Nansen have reached into the far corners of the planet, and eight of them have been memorialized with place-names on the moon. Trygve Lie, Edvard Hambro, and many more have played significant roles in international organizations, and Norway is an active member of NATO. Outlying possessions stretch from Queen Maud Land at the South Pole to Svalbard in the far north. The sea and seamanship are the prime causes of this interrelatedness.

Fishing, a way of life. The sea is good for more than sailing. From time immemorial fish have been important in the diet of the people and in their economy. For years Norway was the chief whaling country, and only recently has the drama and the rich productivity of whaling vanished. Even now there is some hunting of certain kinds of whale in nearby waters although the great days of Moby Dick are gone. Sealing in the waters off Newfoundland is still an annual event, though recently subject to an American protest campaign.

Although in relation to the total national economy fishing is most important for Iceland, Norway is far in the lead among the northern countries in absolute statistics: As of 1970 Norway had a total of 43,000 fishermen (down from over 60,000 in 1960). The catch varies considerably from year to year, but mackerel and capelin usually rival each other in quantity while the lesser tonnage of cod is the most valuable. Despite its importance for the diet and the economy, fishing amounts to only about 2 percent of the gross national product, 10 percent of export value.

Fishing is far more significant for Norway than can be indicated by statistics of weight and value, and of number of boats and fishermen. Fishing is a way of life and the very raison d'être of the coastal villages that for millennia have lived by and from the sea, and whose social and economic structure is based on the cooperative ownership and activity of the fishing boats. Of the total of 36,000 fishing vessels 32,000 are craft with less than 30 h.p. motors. They belong, usually on a profit-sharing basis, to the men of the fishing villages along the fjords of the western coast, of Lofoten and the island shield all the way from Rogaland in the southwest up to Finnmark in the north. Seasonally they sail for herring or cod to the banks off Iceland, but the major catch is nearer home and north around Svalbard. Scientific cooperation enables the hundreds of small boats to learn from research vessels where and when the schools of fish are concentrated, and they converge by the hundreds. (Notice in the accompanying table that Denmark has but one-tenth as many boats as Norway yet hauls in half as much fish.)

For centuries beyond record both herring and cod have come in from the sea to spawn along the Norwegian coast. These and numerous local varieties provided nourishment for man from the Stone Age on to modern times. It was wealth in fish for sale to the continent that brought Hanseatic merchants to Bergen and fish long counted as the chief item of export. Instead of being salted as in the Middle Ages the cod is now filleted and frozen; herring is

Comparative fishing statistics, 1970, 1971.

Country	Year	Number of fishermen	Number of fishing craft	Catch (tons)	Value of catch (US $)
Denmark	1971	15,457	3,660	1,348,874	123,000,000
Finland	1970	6,341	308	82,100	19,300,000
Iceland	1971	5,888	812	684,285	65,000,000
Norway	1970	43,018	36,168	2,698,170	197,000,000
Sweden	1971	6,996	5,786	227,600	39,000,000
Japan	1970	—	—	9,308,500	—
Great Britain	1970	—	—	1,009,000	—
USSR	1970	—	—	7,252,200	—
US	1970	—	—	2,714,300	—
World total	1970	—	—	69,300,000	—

Sources: Nordisk statistisk årsbok, 1972 and Statistisk årsbok för Sverige, 1972.

filleted or ground into meal; all yield oil; and the tiny sprat (sardines) that do not travel far while alive are canned. Increasingly the best grade of fish are being fresh-frozen in the fishing ports and flown to Great Britain and continental markets.

All of this notwithstanding, few fishermen depend on the sea for their entire livelihood. They supplement their income with work in farming or forestry. But for many fishing is the basic occupation, and the fisherfolk of the west coast regard the offshore waters as their own, belonging to the national domain just as definitely as the fields and the hunting grounds in the high fjelds. Hence they demand the exclusion from these waters of the large foreign trawlers that would prodigally exhaust the fishing grounds and destroy the life structure of the villages. Further-more, during World War II the Norwegians lived on a diet of fish and potatoes and they do not forget the importance of fish for their self-sufficiency.

Farming on 3 percent of land area. The Norwegian farmers make the most they can of that meager 3 percent of their land that is arable. But the size of farms is severely limited by the rugged facts of geography, and the growing season is short, especially in north-ern Norway. Productivity cannot compare with that of more fa-vored lands. Practically all (95 percent) of the bread-grains must be imported. Farming units are small and, despite attempts at consolidation, 100,000 of the total of 164,000 holdings (1970) are still under twelve acres each. Many smaller farms are being aban-doned, and total tilled acreage is declining. The number of work-ers is also decreasing, and only 7 percent of these are hired; farm-ing in Norway as elsewhere in the North is almost entirely a family operation. The traditional transhumance system is dying out, and the picturesque *seter* in the mountains are falling into decay or are being taken over for vacation homes by city dwellers.

There is, nevertheless, a positive side of the agricultural scene. Scientific methods and the use of machinery counteract the loss of manpower and make possible an increased product. Because of the smallness of the farming units tractors must also be small, but since 1950 they have displaced horses (100,000 tractors and a reduction from 190,000 to 40,000 horses). Government subsidies and general political sensitivity for the rural population ame-liorate hardships. Self-sufficiency has been attained in a number of products, especially potatoes. As throughout the North, the cultivation of barley has spread rapidly. Certain fruits can also be grown successfully. Since the most satisfactory crop of all is hay, the meadows are carefully tended for hay and grazing, and em-phasis has been put on livestock. The Norwegians are great milk consumers (one and one-half times as much as the French or Ger-mans and almost three times as much as the Italians), and their own cattle and goats produce all of this and more too for export in the form of cheese. Animal products—milk, meat, eggs, and furs—amount to about $450,000,000 per year, two and one-half times the value of all field crops. Practically all sales, as well as purchases, are handled through cooperative associations, assuring the actual producer the maximum possible return.

Three areas are especially fertile because of ancient marine deposits and moderate climate: Jaeren, a small district in the extreme southwest; Östfold and Gudbrandsdal, inland from Oslofjord; and the land around Trondheims fjord. Farming, like fishing, is a tough economic struggle, but it too represents a hallowed way of life.

Forest growth is slow. Forestry is often a subordinate activity to farming, and sometimes it is vice versa. Nearly one-fourth of Norway is forested, and the ownership is held mostly by about 120,000 small producers. But growth is slow and harvesting conditions difficult. The total crop or forest removal for Norway in 1971 was less than 10 million cubic meters, without bark (compared with 43 million in Finland and 61 million in Sweden). Hence Norway must import large quantities of wood, much of it from Sweden, to support her woodworking and paper and pulp industries; exports of paper and pulp go primarily to EEC countries.

These three sectors of the economy, fishing, farming, and forestry, are intimately interrelated. Most fishermen are either farmers or foresters as well; most farmers are foresters, too, or fishermen; most foresters do some farming or fishing. All are an integral part of Norwegian life, and both fishing and forestry are significant elements in the country's foreign trade. Yet despite their profound historical and social importance these three sectors together account for only 6 percent of the gross national product. The shift of emphasis has been due largely to the development of Norway's unique energy resources.

Industry run by water. With water Norway has built major industries for aluminum and for nickel and ferro-alloys. Water foaming down from fjeld to fjord is interrupted in its flow to turn great turbines and create electricity. Having no coal except in Svalbard, Norway must use her abundant "white coal." Practically every home in the country has been electrified, and Norway leads the world in per capita consumption of electric power (13,000 kwh per year). About one-third of the power is used for general and domestic purposes and two-thirds for industry. Along the coast the aluminum processing plants take advantage not only of the water falling from within but of the vast expanse of water in the ocean providing cheap routes of transportation, transportation both for the incoming ore and for the finished product outgoing to world markets. For a generation this happy combination worked so well that it was used almost to the limit of its potential. Then, as demand increased, not even reservoirs could guarantee a sufficient and steady supply of water. Norway had to contemplate importation of fuel to produce electricity by thermal processes.

At this crucial point came the discovery of oil in the North Sea (1968). One find followed rapidly after another, and prospecting was eagerly pursued not only in the southern part of the North Sea but in the ocean as far north as Svalbard. International consortia (including Phillips, Shell, Petronord, altogether nine companies) were involved in varying shares in the operations in the different segments into which the North Sea was divided. These jurisdictional segments were precisely mapped and allocated to Norway, the Netherlands, and Great Britain. Each of these countries faced development problems similar to those of Norway. The British complications were exacerbated by Scottish nationalist hopes that oil might enable them to attain independence. From an economic point of view the impact of oil wealth was likely to be greatest on Norway with her small population and limited resource base.

Largest of the early finds was the Ekofisk field, 200 miles off the southwest coast of Norway. One of the country's industrial giants, Norsk Hydro, quickly began construction of a huge refinery near Bergen and looked forward to the development of major petrochemical enterprises. But the dominant role in drilling and exploitation was to be reserved to the state-owned company, Statoil, and in the region north of the 62nd parallel Statoil would have complete authority. Dangers of pollution and threats to fish life were much in the consciousness of the authorities. A great additional bonus was realized when natural gas was found to be part of the petroleum strike in the Frigg field; Sweden immediately expressed an interest in supply by pipeline.

Before the end of 1975 Norway expected to be a net exporter of oil, and by the early 1980s to see oil as a third or more of her

total exports. This whole economic bonanza spawned great hopes
of industrial expansion and social betterment. But problems had
yet to be overcome. The famous storms of the North Sea threatened both loading platforms and tankers, and the offshore
"deep" seemed effectively to block a seafloor pipeline from wells
to the Norwegian shore. Hence pipelines from Norwegian fields
were permitted to British and German coasts. Ingenuity of
various kinds was required, but it will certainly find a solution and
Norway's energy of the future will come from oil as well as from
water. These technical problems seemed to bother the Norwegians less than the potential financial and social difficulties.
These aspects of the sudden-wealth situation will be discussed in
connection with planning programs.

Invention sparks manufacturing. Much of Norway's success in
meeting the technological challenges of the twentieth century is
owing to her inventive engineers. They have perfected pumps,
loading devices, and other equipment for ships. They invented
the widely used Söderberg electrode technique for the electrolysis
of aluminum. Their Simrad fish-detecting equipment is used in
some 20,000 fishing vessels of fifty countries. Fishing, shipping,
and all forms of manufacture are being rapidly "rationalized"
(that is, adapted to technological processes and businesslike methods). Genius in invention and skill in manufacture have spread
Norwegian products around the world and even before the oil
strikes had transformed the national economy from its long dependence on the fishing-farming-forestry-shipping syndrome.
The engineering industry now reckons its share of export value at
11 percent.

Norsk Hydro furnishes a spectacular example of what is hap-
pening. It is one of the three largest industrial concerns in Norway, the largest electrochemical operation in northern Europe,
and is owned half by the government and half by private capital.
Founded in 1905, it grew out of the invention of the electric-arc
furnace. Nitrogen fertilizer was the original product that created
a large export business and led the company on into chemicals,
aluminum, resin for plastics, petroleum, and even the industrial
production of salmon. One of its recent undertakings for an international group of investors is the management of a fertilizer plant
in Qatar in Arabia to produce ammonia and urea for world mar-

kets, especially Asian. The plant utilizes the previously wasted gas from the Dukhan oil fields. Some forty Norwegian engineers and business people direct the plant and its 500 employees. Norsk Hydro also has interests in plants in Rumania, Hungary, and North Carolina.

Another evidence of the coming-of-age of Norway in this industrial and international century is the Viking Concern, Norway's largest manufacturer of rubber shoes. It is moving its production establishments to Malaysia where the rubber is and where labor costs are one-fifteenth of the costs in Norway. Financing is assisted through the Danish East Asiatic Company. The new factories will export the entire product, more than half of it directly back to Norway.

Norway, like Denmark, has been building ships since Viking times. In fifty yards, 24,000 men make fishing boats for Norway and for export, and build freighters and tankers for ocean traffic. In 1972 the Akers firm delivered the first of fourteen supertankers of 285,000 tons each. Ships head the list of export products, with 14 percent of the value.

A new challenge to inventiveness and construction capability was presented by the problems of oil drilling in the North Sea. The Norwegians developed drilling platforms so good for their purpose that they now build platforms not only for their own use but for prospectors in many seas.

From self-sufficiency to interdependence. With the development of manufacturing and shipping serving worldwide markets, Norwegians have had perforce to modify their older, more self-sufficient economy. Not many generations ago they exported timber and fish, now they process wood into pulp, paper, paperboard, furniture; and the fish they first make into meal or oil or freeze and fly to market. Their industry was once mainly the manufacture of such things as clothing and shoes for the domestic market. Now the Norwegians import large quantities of textiles, chemical products, fruits, vegetables, and even fuel, machinery, and raw materials. Whereas in the 1860s two-thirds of imports were for consumption, a hundred years later only about one-eighth are consumption goods; the largest shares are manufacturing and transportation equipment and materials for processing and resale. The exchange of goods has increased enormously.

Norway's trading partners are chiefly Sweden, West Germany, and the United Kingdom. During the EFTA period trade with her Nordic neighbors almost doubled and amounted to more than one-fourth of her trade turnover; another one-fourth was with the EEC countries. Trade with eastern Europe increased in amount during the 1960s but decreased in its proportion of the total to less than 4 percent.

The economic accomplishment of the mid-twentieth century is magnificent and is the result of many factors: engineering genius and manufacturing skill; rationalization of manufacturing processes; farsighted state investment (less than 10 percent of total and about the same as the amount of foreign investment, but carefully pinpointed to aid the less favored northern region and to stimulate industry); most important of all, the luxuriant wealth of "white coal" plus the swelling world demand for products that require electric power. State planning and control, especially in agriculture, was highly complicated, but happily this, plus world conditions, made possible a full employment situation. Yet the economy became increasingly vulnerable to shifts in world demand and was somewhat slowed in growth (perhaps fortunately so) by lack of capital. Growth was also hampered by geographic factors that forced most industry into small-scale operation. A factor difficult to measure but undoubtedly positive in effect was the stubborn nationalism that made Norwegians realize they could do things as well as anybody else and that made them resist stringently any outside pressures to restrain their technological development. For the future this spirit of independence and the lack of economic self-confidence that made Norwegians reject membership in the Common Market may become negative factors. To date the country has experienced a rapid yet measured move from rurality to industrialization and urbanism.

Sweden

Both the rate and the character of economic development in Sweden differ from the patterns in the other Nordic countries.

From passivity to aggressiveness. Passivity was the hallmark of the Swedish economy for generations and centuries, but it certainly is no longer.

Sweden has not only the largest land area among the Nordic countries (173,600 square miles) and the largest population (8,000,000 +) but she also has the greatest variety of natural resources—fertile fields in Skåne, forests all the way from Småland to the far north, a wealth of mineral deposits, flat lowlands and towering heights, sea routes open to the markets of the world, climate that is mild in the south and rugged in the north, within her own borders varied facilities for both recreation and production. Was it due to such natural advantages that self-satisfied Swedes played for generations and centuries only a passive role in international trade? With a few spectacular exceptions (especially the Viking period and the continental wars of Gustav II Adolf), the Swedes were long content to live within themselves. In the Middle Ages their commerce was conducted by Germans and Lowlanders; immigrant groups like the Scots and the Flemish have been allowed to play prominent roles in the industrial life of the country. Even in the twentieth century and despite a vigorous drive for markets by several sectors of the economy, the deep-seated attitude of being sufficient unto themselves is evident in the strong opposition to affiliation with the European Common Market. On the other hand the trend of the twentieth century has been toward a more and more aggressive world-oriented economy and a high standard of living.

Planned use of the resources of the land. The ancient population and food-producing centers of Sweden have continued to be the main agricultural areas: Uppland, where the land has been rising through the centuries, and where the pockets of fertility rest between outcroppings of rock; Västergötland and Östergötland in the south central part of the country; and above all Skåne in the south where fields stretch wide over a gently undulating landscape. As population increased in the nineteenth century attempts were made to enlarge the arable by draining marshes and biting into forest. Some of this reclaimed land has remained useful, but much of it never did yield proper returns.

Therefore the authorities have reversed the former program and in the Småland highlands, for example, are requiring that the poorer land be reforested. Farmers are not allowed to sell their land for agricultural use, and the small farms and gardens are being abandoned. The spruce and pine that grow so well are more profitable than the potatoes that grow so feebly, and now Sweden is half-covered with forest.

Throughout the North, as in all industrialized countries, the agricultural population has declined and in Sweden the acreage as well. The accompanying table shows in simplified statistics the trends, highlighted by the decline in the agricultural work force along with the increase in productivity. Machinery, fertilizers, and scientific agriculture have transformed this most fundamental

Statistical trends in Swedish agriculture, forestry, fishing.

Category	Year	Number	Year	Number
Men and women				
in work force	1940	790,000	1970	277,000
Farming units	1944	406,000	1972	144,000
Acreage of				
arable used	1932	9,250,000	1972	7,500,000
Crop return	1820	5-fold	1968	9 fold
Farm animals				
Horses	1919	716,000	1972	55,000
Cattle	1932	3,000,000	1972	1,830,000
Oxen	19th cent.	300,000	1948 [a]	1,600
Goats	1919	133,000	1950 [a]	7,000
Sheep	1919	1,500,000	1972	332,000
Hogs	1919	717,000	1972	2,430,000
Forest cut of wood				
(cubic meters, with bark)	1937	46,000,000	1971	77,000,000
Fish catch				
(salt sea, tons)	1935	107,000	1971	228,000

Source: Compiled from *Statistisk årsbok för Sverige,* various years.
[a] Thereafter not listed.

sector of the economy. Cooperative organizations have helped the process by enabling the individual farmer to mechanize his operations and to buy and sell collectively. Yet even with government subsidies and other "special handling," the farmer has not been able to keep abreast of the city worker in income.

The national plan for the 1970s envisages ongoing change. More and more farmers will be given early pensions or compensated and retrained if they are willing to change occupation. By 1980 another million acres will probably be withdrawn from cultivation, and the number of farms reduced to under 100,000. Only 5 percent of the Swedish land surface will be tilled. SR (Special Rationalized) farms will be established, each with 70 to 100 acres of arable and 250 to 400 acres of forest. A man and wife operating such a farm should have 25–30 head of cattle and should work about 3000 hours per year. Other SR farms are planned to be about twice as large and to be operated by a man and wife plus one hired hand, working a total of 5000 hours per year.[1] Part of the plan is deliberately to reduce self-sufficiency in foodstuffs to 80 percent. Sweden sees greater profit in industrial production.

In reemphasizing forestry Sweden is building on strength. Fifty-six percent of the country is covered with birch, spruce, and pine. For countless generations homes, fuel, tools, furniture, and toys all were made of wood. In the nineteenth century and down to 1925 forest products were Sweden's major export; as of 1970 they still amounted to one-quarter of total export. An interesting sidelight is that the quality of Swedish pulp is so valued that it is bought in Vermont to blend with American pulp in making the finest paper for checks.

Industries dependent on the forest employ about 15 percent of the country's workers and account for the same proportion of industrial production. Sweden is second only to Russia in Europe in total timber cut. In certain specialties such as paper pulp she has 8 percent of world production, newsprint 4.5 percent. In total paper consumption Sweden ranks second only to the United States (though Canada almost ties her).

Present policy is to expand forest production still further. The government controls development not only in the lands owned by the state and the municipalities but in the quarter owned by companies and the half in private hands. Cooperative societies handle much of the actual processing in pulp mills, sawmills, and paper factories. Marketing is of such vital importance that, unless improved arrangements can be made with the Common Market, a number of concerns will establish plants abroad, inside the EEC tariff wall.

1. See Tore Kellberg's article in *Financial Times* (London), April 10, 1972, and for more thorough treatment see *Svensk ekonomi, 1971–1975, med utblick mot 1990*, Statens Offentligan Utredningar [SOU], no. 71 (Stockholm, 1970), esp. pp. 197–208.

Until 1972 it was a picturesque sight to watch the great logs floating sedately down the northern rivers to the mills at their mouths. But roads and trucks now permit faster transportation and, more important, year-round delivery and year-round balanced work. Other floating materials are not so picturesque, and strenuous efforts are being made to reduce the pollutants issuing into the rivers and the Baltic from the pulp mills.

Second only to her forests, the mines of Sweden have been the basis of foreign earnings. The great "copper mountain" at Falun enabled Sweden to send her armies to the continent during the Thirty Years War (aided also by foreign subsidies). The iron mines in central Sweden have been consistent producers. The greatest recent production has come from the northern pits around Kiruna and Gällivare, whence the ore is shipped to world markets, to Belgium, Britain, and the United States, and especially the West German Ruhr. In 1972 exports of ores had risen to over 28,000,000 tons. Besides iron the Boliden Company and others mined significant amounts of silver, gold, nickel, zinc, arsenic, and pyrites and value of all ore exports (1972) was $292,000,000. Much of the arsenic is pure excess and must be buried in concrete blocks in the Gulf of Bothnia; some is used for plant sprays and for an impregnation material that prolongs the life of wood in railway ties, silos, and telephone poles. The scientific search is to find uses for all the by-products dug from the ground.

The rich return from northern mines could be realized only after the government, early in the twentieth century, built the railway to Kiruna, and when Norway built the connecting link down to the harbor of Narvik. By arrangements associated with railroad building the Swedish government became half owner in the mines, with the right of taking over from the private operators. This right was exercised in the 1950s, and the prime example of government-business cooperation ceased to exist. Mining in itself employs only a tiny fraction of the Swedish labor force. But the product amounts to 5 percent of world production of iron ore, and it enables Sweden to manufacture one percent of the world's steel. More vitally, it has provided both material and impetus for the mechanical and engineering industries.

Sweden is one of the world's largest consumers of energy (surpassed on a per capita basis only by the United States, Great Britain, and Canada) but produces less than one-third of her requirements. She has no coal; the weak "brown coal" of Skåne is no longer mined. The eager search for oil has so far failed to match Norway's success, though a strike in southern Gotland in 1974 may offer some hope. Sweden's total import of oil for heating and power cost her in 1970 nearly $600,000,000, and in succeeding years this cost rose startlingly.

Sweden's homemade energy came from her snowy mountains and the rivers that turned the electric generators. This power ran the railroads, lighted the cities, and heated the ovens of the steel mills. In wet seasons electricity is abundant and a surplus can be sent by high power lines to Norway, Denmark, and the continent. In dry seasons these same lines can reverse the power flow and bring it north from Denmark and Germany. Sweden's demand has increased so much that it must be supplemented by fuel-produced power. Only half of her water power resources are harnessed, but expense and ecological demands restrain further development. Some of nature's magnificence in the northern wilds must be preserved. Power stations underground already enhance both beauty and efficiency; they increase the natural fall by dropping the water further into the earth. The Water Act requires that for all purposes in construction around water "the benefit to society outweigh other considerations."

In any case the energy of the future will come from nuclear plants. The first such Swedish installation dates from 1963. In 1972 a purely commercial plant was inaugurated north of Oscarshamn on the east coast. This one, known as "Oscar I," uses uranium from the United States and will produce almost a half million kilowatts; by the 1980s it will be joined by brothers up to "Oscar VI," with a total capacity of over 5,000,000 kilowatts.

Plants on the west coast and elsewhere were calculated to make Sweden, for her population, the world's largest producer of nuclear generated power; it was meant to supply 20 percent of national energy requirements. But in the mid 70s people became sufficiently alarmed at the ecological dangers involved that the building program was at least temporarily slowed.

Industry as revolutionizer of life. Industry is the spectacular sector in Swedish economic development. In the mid-nineteenth cen-

tury Sweden was an underdeveloped country, the economy dominated by a primitive agriculture and almost no industry. Railways
came slowly. In the latter half of the nineteenth century foreign
investment built railroads and domestic capital began to support
an expanding industry. It could not, however, keep up with the
galloping birthrate, and Sweden of this period lost hundreds of
thousands of young workers in transatlantic migration. Early in
the twentieth century the pace of development began to quicken.
Forestry and mining produced savings and, because domestic industry could still not absorb all the earnings, Sweden exported
capital.

The accompanying chart showing the phenomenal increase in
value of Swedish manufactures from 1850 to 1971 indicates that
Sweden was more than keeping pace with general industrial development. About half of the 1967–1971 total came from the
metal and engineering industry, but other branches were strong
too: forest products, manufactures, and food products almost
tied for second place with somewhat over 15 percent each; then
came the chemical industry, textiles, mining, and other products.

The figures in the chart tell a story not only of extraordinary
productive ability but of significant structural shifts in the
economy—no longer merely digging ore wealth out of the ground
or cutting tree wealth out of the forest. Now the emphasis is on
sophisticated processing and a direct appeal to the world market.

Among the achievements of the engineering industry are two
makes of automobiles, the only ones manufactured in Scandinavia. One out of every four trucks and cars on the roads of
Sweden is manufactured in the country. Of the total production
about 70 percent is exported, which amounts to 8 percent of all
export value. The leading producer is Volvo, with 287,000 vehicles in 1971, and a worldwide but somewhat selective market: in
1970 its export went 31 percent to the United States, 21 percent to
Norway, Denmark, and the United Kingdom, 18 percent to EEC
countries, and smaller percentages to Brazil and certain countries
in Africa and Asia. Volvo may serve as an example of Sweden's
engineering success story and also of its problems.

Although Volvo's main plant was in Gothenburg, diffusion became policy. In the early 1970s, a new factory was being established in Kalmar (taking over the Tjorven plant abandoned by

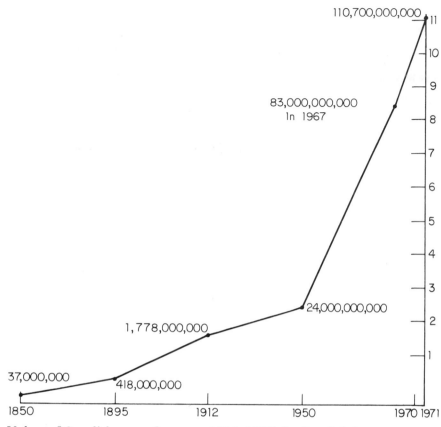

Value of Swedish manufactures, 1850–1967 (in Swedish kronor).

Source: Statistisk årsbok för Sverige, 1970, 1973.

the government), one in Skövde, and additional works scattered through the country. For several years some manufacturing and assembling had been done in Norway. Volvo also began in 1965 the making of cars in Ghent, using labor no longer needed in the textile industry and agriculture and gaining the advantage of a base inside the EEC. By 1972 the company was building 50,000 cars in Belgium. In northern France Volvo combined with Peugeot and Renault to manufacture a new and cleaner engine, planned to be put on the market in the late 1970s. The company also bought a German plant producing truck motors, planning to move it bodily to Sweden. And it had definite plans for a factory in Virginia.

Like many large manufacturing concerns Volvo began having trouble with labor because of the dull monotony of the assembly line. Absenteeism was high and hindered effectiveness, and the annual turnover was one-third of the workforce. Pehr Gyllenhammar, the head of the company, felt that the work must be humanized. After due experimentation a new pattern of work practices was introduced, and the factories in Kalmar and Skövde were planned to accommodate new methods. A worker, instead of standing and turning a single bolt on a car moving along the line, became part of a team of fifteen to twenty responsible for a major part of a car—axle, or brakes, or wheel. It was even arranged that different teams could work at different speeds if they wished, and individuals could work at different parts of the team job. Who would do what would be determined by the team itself, and by the foreman elected by the team. Still experimental, yes, but possibly at least a partial answer to the problem of letting a man feel he was creating something and participating with others in both work and decisions. Management pondered the possibility of having one man do the complete assembly of an automobile, but decided that this was economically not feasible. This personalized, small-unit system was of course in line with government policy and became part of a still wider drive for "humanization of the work place." To some extent it was only recognition of Swedish tradition. It had been pointed out to me as far back as 1967 in conversation with Curt Nicolin, head of the huge ASEA corporation, that in the decentralized iron and timber works the *brukspatron* (manager and often owner) enjoyed close relations with his workers and that Swedish industry retained the human approach.

On the level of general management two representatives of the workers were invited to sit on Volvo's board of directors. This is the kind of economic democracy in which the government is deeply interested and which it is gradually requiring of all major industrial establishments (those with over 100 employees). Götaverken, the largest shipbuilding firm, has a worker majority in decision-making committees concerned with working conditions and methods. Many companies are moving toward a monthly wage system to replace the older prevailing piecework basis of pay. Concern with health has brought rigid regulations on safety and hygiene and the employment of specialized industrial physicians (about 500 as of 1974). Similar trends are evident throughout Norden, but in Sweden discussion is particularly acute on the protection of the weak and the equalization of status; this is only natural because it has been in Sweden that the traditional distinctions have been sharpest between the "lower classes" and their "betters." Equality (jämlikhet) is thought of not only in terms of justice but in terms of its psychological importance for efficiency in production.

Much of the preceding discussion has used Volvo for illustrative purposes. But Volvo is not the only company, not even the only automobile manufacturer, that could serve as example of innovative practices as well as engineering and sales success. Saab is the second automobile company, and it "tries harder." Its Nordic character is emphasized by the fact that it has established a branch factory in Finland (which is 50 percent Swedish and 50 percent Finnish), and it does a large business in Finland as well as on the world market.

But the two auto manufacturers are only conspicuous examples of the twentieth-century achievements of Swedish industry. In shipbuilding the Swedes forged their way into second place (with Götaverken, Kockums, and Eriksberg), far indeed behind front-runner Japan but ahead of West Germany and Great Britain. L. M. Ericsson builds telephone equipment for world markets, and other companies are leaders in electrical equipment, household appliances, hygiene supplies, ball bearings, aircraft and munitions, matches, cellulose, and paper products. When *Fortune* magazine in August 1972 listed the 300 largest industrial concerns outside the United States it found that 15 of them were Swedish. The only Scandinavian firm besides these was Neste Oy of Finland. The accompanying table ranks these 15 in order according to sales.

Obviously these companies did not attain their stature from the Swedish market alone (with the exception of the Cooperative Federation and the State Company, which are special cases). They are concerns that originated sometimes with an invention—Alfa-Laval with the separator, Electrolux with the vacuum cleaner,

SKF with the ball bearing—and have grown through operations on the world scene. Stora Kopparberg, the world's oldest corporation, dates from the fourteenth century and has branched out far from the copper mountain that gave it birth. Like their northern neighbors the Swedes have also moved out far from home base in the application of their know-how. In Liberia, for instance, Swedish management has gone into partnership with American capi-

Swedish firms among the 300 largest industrials outside the United States.

Rank	Company	Sales (000s)	Products
61	(KF) Kooperative Förbund	$1,375,976	Food, paper, machinery
70	Volvo	1,196,237	Autos, trucks
88	(SKF) Svenska Kullager-fabrik	949,964	Bearings, tools
103	Saab-Scania	805,723	Autos, aircraft
108	ASEA	784,128	Electrical equipment
111	Statsföretag [State Company]	773,562	Mining, paper, tobacco
119	L M Ericsson	736,723	Telecommunications equipment
152	Gränges	596,218	Mining, steel, copper
189	Svenska Tändstick	483,704	Matches, building material
219	Electrolux	415,857	Household appliances
244	Stora Kopparberg	369,893	Steel, timber, paper
263	Atlas Copco	332,454	Compressed air equipment
264	Sandvik group	331,506	Special steels, carbide
272	Alfa-Laval	325,880	Machinery
299	Svensk Cellulosa	294,237	Cellulose, paper

Source: Fortune (August 1972), pp. 152–159. (Courtesy of *Fortune* magazine.)

tal and Liberian resources of ore and manpower for development of the large Lamco iron mine. In other cases Swedish companies have developed so strongly that they have drawn themselves into mergers with still larger international concerns, for example, the Findus food processing company with Nestlé of Switzerland, and Gevalia with General Foods. Swedish companies have a small homeland base but they manufacture ball bearings, telephone equipment, milk machines, and diverse other products in a large variety of countries scattered around the globe. SKF sells up to 93 percent of its production abroad. Since 1970 Swedish industry has put more than 20 percent of its investments into foreign operations. Seven Swedish firms have more than three-fifths of their labor force employed abroad. All told, Sweden has more multinational corporations, proportional to population, than any other country. The first of these major multinational operations, incidentally, were the plants started by Alfred Nobel after he invented dynamite.

Yet it has taken more than inventive genius and business acumen to achieve this unusual economic position. It is not automatically true that the maker of a better mouse trap will find customers crowding his doorstep. Free interchange of goods has long been plagued with quotas and tariffs and outright prohibitions, and such things can stymie the most clever inventors and the most vigorous business men. Sweden has been one of the leaders in the attempt to abolish nationalistic restraints on trade. She pushed particularly hard for the inauguration of EFTA, and this organization was created in Stockholm in 1959. Swedish leaders also worked eagerly for Nordek, a still-born try for closer economic cooperation among the five Nordic lands. However, when it came to the question of membership in EEC the government balked because of the political considerations involved.

Despite some failures and disappointments in the field of international trade Sweden has prospered amazingly. In the decade of the 1960s her exports to her free-trade EFTA partners quadrupled. Just as significant was the shift in the character of her total exports, which in the raw material category declined from 33 percent to 17, while they increased from 20 percent to 34 in the processed category (machines, paper, and so on). This was making the most of her productive capacity and technological skills, while at the same time making her trade more vulnerable in world competition. In 1970 the United States ranked third as supplier of Sweden's imports, with $600,000,000 worth, and bought from Sweden about two-thirds as much, $400,000,000. Of that amount $24,000,000 was represented by automobiles, a dramatic shift from the period prior to 1950 when the taxis of Stockholm were Dodges and 85 percent of the cars on Swedish highways were American; now Sweden was exporting to the United States twice as much in automobiles as she bought. Trade between Sweden and the communist countries of the east was about 5 percent of the total, and with the developing countries about 8 percent.

Achievements in industry and trade have of course left a profound mark on Swedish society. Some there are who reckon that Sweden has the highest material standard of living in the world; she is certainly close to the top. Since World War II the number of cars has increased from 50,000 to over 2,000,000, giving her a per capita car ratio second only to the United States, and the same comparison applies to telephones and television sets.

A "mixed economy." Sweden's extraordinary progress has been accomplished under a system of private enterprise, but private enterprise subject to challenge by the cooperative movement and to close control by an avowedly socialist government. Over 90 percent of business continues to be in the hands of individuals, but they have to operate within governmental guidelines. In this "mixed economy" the proportions in the mix are difficult to define. An account of some actual circumstances may clarify things better than theoretical analysis.

In its own name the state owns not only the railroads and the telecommunications systems, but the great iron mines (since 1957), the tobacco monopoly, the Uddevalla shipbuilding company, an oil company and two restaurant chains, the atomic power company—a total of 58 concerns in 30 of which the government holds the entire share capital. Plus four state monopolies for liquor and lotteries and seven financial agencies. Most of the state's industrial enterprises have recently (1970) been gathered together under the State Company (Statsföretag AB) which in turn is under the authority of the Minister of Industry. Some of these, like the iron mines and the tobacco monopoly, are big and profitable businesses. About 6 percent (200,000 persons) of the total labor force are employed in enterprises wholly or partly government owned. These produce (as of 1970) about 3.5 percent of the country's industrial production. Another 3.5 percent is made by the cooperative societies which are building much of the new housing and handle 18 percent of retail trade. But such statistics do not measure the influence or the participation of government in the economic life of the country; let us take some examples.

In 1968 a state defense workshop was faced with the need to lay off workers. The time seemed propitious to take over three struggling machine tool companies, consolidate and expand operations, and maintain employment. The state would thus set an example of social responsibility and good business practice. However, for various reasons the attempt turned sour, and in 1971, on sales of $14,000,000 the new company lost $7,000,000, and worse, it had to drop two-thirds of the employees. Another example from the period of aggressive socialist activity in the late 1960s is of the Tjorven factory established by the state in Kalmar. The idea was to go the Volkswagen a big step better and build a cheap plastic minicar for local use such as shopping and mail delivery. But people did not buy the little car. The workers in the factory were saved at last when Volvo took it over for its new plant. But there were also successes, and good profits in the mid-70s.

The glass and shoe industries are traditional and established. However, in the early 1970s they were losing money, factories were closing, workers were being "released." In a socialist state, or any state, such a situation becomes a national problem, a political problem (we might even be reminded of the Lockheed Corporation). In Sweden the Industry Department of the government responded to this crisis by creating a "guarantee company" that in the course of three years (1972–1975) was to have $20,000,000 at its disposal. It is a daughter company of the state's Investment Bank, and through loans can support restructuring of the affected companies. It is to encourage stronger firms, not necessarily engaged in the same branch of manufacturing, to take over other firms in trouble. The period of guarantee will extend ten to fifteen years.

The Salén shipping concern stretched its resources to order three turbine tankers from Kockums of Malmö. In order to support both Saléns and Kockums, the state put in 20 percent of the needed capital. The intricate interrelations of ownership and management become highly complex in such arrangements. For instance, the government has joined with the Swedish company, Uddeholm, and the American Combustion Engineering Co., to manufacture heavy components for the half-state-owned company Asea-Atom and other atomic and chemical concerns.

The government participates in management and financing because the Social Democrats, who have held power since 1932, believe in the principle of social control of the means of production, because they feel that it is the responsibility of government to provide full employment, and also because they possess the means. They prefer control to outright nationalization.

When the Swedes established their supplemental pension system they provided for the accumulation of a huge fund from which pensions would be paid and through which the state could guide investment. The United States followed a different method, which is largely a pay-as-you-go system backed by a comparatively small accumulation, with contributions made by workers and employers in a given year being paid to retirees of previous years. In Sweden the contributions are held for future use, and the fund is growing vast. In 1972 the General Pension Fund paid in pensions only a quarter of its income. The total accumulation as of August 31, 1973, was over $12,000,000,000 (62,333,000,000 S. kronor). Of this amount 9 percent was in government bonds, 47 percent in home mortgages, 10 percent in loans to communities, and 33 percent to industry and agriculture. The placement of loans from these immense reserves is a decisive factor in the life or death of many enterprises. The Investment Bank (founded 1967) had a capital of over $200,000,000, and other credit institutions at least 50 percent government-owned had almost $100,000,000 more. The accumulation in the National Pension Insurance Fund was estimated to rise to about $35 billion by 1980. This is the main fund in the public savings account that is already about one-half of all national savings; private savings have decreased in the last decade from three-fourths of the total to about one-half. The meaning of this development is that capital, the bloodstream of business, has come under the centralized control of government. It can be used to expand state enterprises or to encourage private industry or homebuilding or whatever the authorities prefer. Government funds were at first not permitted to buy land or shares of stock, but these restraints were being questioned. So far, the monies have been used primarily to support private enterprises that operate within governmentally approved guidelines.

The actual shift of emphasis in investment is partly the result of deliberate government policy, partly of general trends in society and the economy. But the shift is important to note. In the mid-nineteenth century housing took some 40 percent of Swedish investment, and agriculture took 25 percent. By the mid-twentieth century housing took only 20 percent, about the same as the shares allotted (each) to industry, transportation, and public services. Agriculture, lumped together with commerce and everything else, took only 20 percent.

Private interests themselves have attempted to enhance their strength by amalgamations. In 1971 two of Sweden's largest banks gained government approval to join forces—Skandinaviska Bank and Stockholms Enskilda Bank, to create Skandinaviska Enskilda Bank. On the heels of this merger came that of Göteborgs Bank and Smålands Bank. It was felt that only large aggregates of capital could be useful for Swedish business or for competition with the great American banks that were branching into Euope and elsewhere. Business concerns, following international patterns, had already fused many smaller companies into larger and, it was hoped, more effective units: Saab with Scania-Vabis, Facit with Electrolux, Pripps breweries with Abba-Fyrtornet. In 1972 fusions numbered 500, and for several years the annual average was above 200.

The scope of government-business interrelationships broadens out far beyond matters of finance and organization, and Sweden has faced this ensemble perhaps more frankly than many other governments. Even though they are antagonists on many issues business and government recognize that each has a role to play, and their mutual interests lead more to cooperation than contention.

In connection with labor the government has a keen interest in full employment. It is concerned also that industry have an adequate labor supply. Because of Sweden's burgeoning economy and shrinking birthrate a large immigration has been required in recent years, from 1930 to 1971. Yugoslavs, Italians, Germans, Danes, Poles have flooded into Sweden, and above all Finns. While scores of thousands become quickly naturalized others do not, and in 1972 more than 200,000 foreigners, half of them Finns, filled the ranks of factory workers, restaurant help, and the like. Through the 1970s the only additional labor supply in sight is married women. Business and government have had to cooper-

ate in control of the immigrant stream and in programs to facilitate assimilation. The demand for labor is of course one of the
primary factors in the expansion of democratic shop management, and in the participation of labor and government on boards
of directors.

Tax policy always hits tender nerves, even more so when an administration demands taxes not only for revenue but for the purpose of restructuring society. The Swedish social program is
treated elsewhere, and it must suffice here to mention two of the
tax items with direct impact on business. First was the introduction of a tax on advertising, in 1971, professedly to aid the press,
especially the weaker provincial press, by way of the political parties. The take began at about $7,000,000, but was to rise to
$10,000,000. An additional avowed purpose was to slow down the
expansion of advertising in newspapers and other media. Still
greater uproar resounded when the Minister of the Treasury
(Gunnar Sträng, a strong man in the government), proposed an
increase in the value-added tax (*Moms*) from 16 to 20 percent.
The bourgeois parties united in opposition and thought their victory was secure, for the communists were also opposed. The
clever administrative officials then switched to a raise in the
payroll tax from 2 to 4 percent, a move in which communists
could join with socialists. The liberal and conservative groups had
to swallow it. Someone commented that it was a case of "the Social
Democrats swiping the opposition's clothes while they were in
swimming."

Economic controls are difficult to manage—in Sweden as well as
elsewhere. In the summer of 1970 inflation seemed to be getting
feverish, and the government clamped down a strict wage-price
freeze. The economy cooled, and within a few months it was cold.
Businesses failed and unemployment rose. By the middle of 1971,
for the first time in forty years, emigration exceeded immigration.
Price restrictions were largely removed in the fall of 1971. Gradually good times returned but inflation increased. Ulf af Trolle,
"doctor of industry," declared that Sweden must either return to
the economic pattern of the 1950s, when the mix had more of the
private element, or move on to complete state takeover as in Russia; the Palme brand of state intervention in industry made devel-

opment impossible. The lines of conflict between business and government appeared to be hardening. But by 1973 business was once more booming and argument was somewhat muted.

Sweden's mixed economy has clearly produced both progress and tensions. And it is a situation constantly changing as it responds to political maneuvers and economic demands. Fundamental are the goals of full employment, equality within the labor force, participation of labor in management, and the phasing out of less productive industry and agriculture in favor of the more profitable. More dependent on Social Democratic political influence are such matters as use of the Investment Bank to enhance public control and state support of industry in sparsely settled areas. Up to this date the system can still be called socialization of incomes rather than socialization of production, and a concern with the public interest along with recognition of the advantages of private initiative. Yet the pressures of political necessity continue to drive the Social Democrats toward stronger ideological positions, and future change may be in the direction of greater state involvement. In any case the directing bureaucracy of government is powerful and unlikely to diminish.

Economic Planning in the North

Long before the "Five Year Plans" and the "Four Year Plans" of twentieth-century totalitarians the peoples of the North had tried various kinds of public planning: methods such as Copenhagen's zoning schemes of the twelfth century, Gustav Vasa's economic directives of the sixteenth century, the mercantilism that the North as well as all Europe practiced for a time, and the land reforms of the nineteenth century. But it is also clear that the upsurge of industry and the comprehensive state planning of the twentieth century introduced something new.

The recent economic achievements of the Nordic peoples did not happen by chance. Perhaps they merely awoke belatedly to the realization that they could live better. Maybe they were prodded into action by concern for the large number of youths who were fleeing to America for improvement of their lot. Or were they startled into self-examination by the industrial progress they saw in Germany and Great Britain and the United States? Whatever may have been the cause they shook themselves into action around the turn of the century, they invigorated each other, and they strode with increasing confidence on the road toward political democracy and economic well-being. The idea of planning for the future was implicit in the Swedish "Emigration Inquiry" in the years 1907–1913, and planning has grown steadily more purposeful and more precise. Two disastrous wars in Europe deepened the sense of community and demanded more careful calculation for the future. The Norwegian response to the need was particularly elaborate and all-embracing.

Problems and Programs: Norway

Norway was hard hit by World War II, and for rapid reconstruction a plan was essential—a survey of needs, a regulating of priorities, a clear indication of goals. The destruction of half the merchant fleet that earned foreign valuta, the devastation of north Norway, and the general disorientation of life required emergency measures on a national basis. Purchases abroad of replacement machinery and other goods not only involved the individual buyer but they created problems of currency exchange and affected national finance. Reconstruction was a concern of the whole community.

It so happened that in January 1940, even before the invasion of the country, Ragnar Frisch had written a memorandum on a "National Budget" and this term came to be accepted as the official name for the national plan. The ideas were an outgrowth of John Maynard Keynes' thoughts on estimates of supply and use of national resources. Wartime thinking both in Norway and within the exile government in London led to quick and close coordination, and the controls of the occupation period helped to lay a basis for peacetime procedures. The Joint Cooperative Program of the Political Parties agreed on in 1945 indicated unified purpose. The planning project got under way in the fall of 1945, and the National Budget for 1947 was a firm step in realization. This comprehensive document allocated income and expenditure not only for the government but for the nation as a whole. It was diagnosis and prognosis, but even more it was a program of action for the year ahead, a schedule of work for all Norway.

The 1947 budget was divided into a series of subbudgets. (1) *The manpower budget* estimated a one percent increase in the labor force, to be used primarily in forestry, manufacturing, shipping, and whaling; while agriculture, building and construction, and public administration were to use fewer workers. An increase in efficiency was counted upon. (2) *The commodity budget* was concerned especially with materials for building and construction—bricks, cement, and lumber. Production of these items was up from prewar, but was to be pushed further. Housing was emphasized, and materials were allocated to aid essential building and rationalization. (3) *The budget for trading goods and services with foreign countries* provided for an increase in 1947 of both imports and exports, with a still greater unfavorable gap between them than in 1946. But Norway was to import the means of new production and a minimum of consumer goods. Special efforts were to be made to increase exports for dollars, Swedish kronor, and other hard currencies. (4) *The foreign exchange budget* provided for "balance of payments classified by main currencies." The disposable foreign reserves of 1,500,000,000 kroner were to be used for goods, interest, and dividends totaling 950,000,000 kroner and for payments to the International Monetary Fund and installments on ships under construction. (5) *The production budget* carefully classified the total national product of 8,600,000,000 kroner, an increase of 9.6 percent over 1946 (quantity increase of 6 percent, and price increase of 3.6 percent). This was greater than prewar production, but because of the increase in population and the demands for restoration it would leave per capita consumption below prewar levels. (6) *The budget of consumption* estimated private consumption of 6,500,000,000 kroner and public consumption of 1,000,000,000 kroner—the latter down from 1946 by 100,000,000 kroner because of decreased expenditures for defense. The quality of consumer goods was reckoned better than prewar, but many items were not available, and individual consumption was to be not much above the 91 percent of prewar which was the figure of 1946. And the people got "movies in place of meat, radios in place of fuel, vacation trips instead of clothing." (7) *The investment budget* for both private and public capital formation was set at 2,000,000,000 kroner, 54 percent above 1946. Shipping and whaling equipment accounted for 550,000,000 kroner and the manufacturing and electrical industries for 410,000,000 kroner. Housing and inland transportation were also items of importance. (8) *The budget for the public sector* restated certain of the above items.

Admittedly trial and error entered into the execution of plans, but the people were ready to cooperate to achieve reconstruction. Controls were enforced largely by consent. All policies had to be subordinated to democratic values such as freedom of speech and occupational choice. Nevertheless the authorities established strict limits on imports and succeeded in reducing consumption of sugar, meat, margarine, and coffee to two-thirds of prewar levels, of eggs to one-fourth (as of 1948). Prices were controlled, and so was credit. Rents were fixed and, where housing was scarce, as in Oslo, homeowners were forced to take in roomers. Wage rates were geared to the Cost-of-Living Index, and labor lived up to its no-strike pledge. Controls on imports and private consumption lasted until 1952, licensing for building and materials until 1965.

Of the main objectives of the early postwar years three were achieved: full employment, high investment, and equalization of incomes. Two other goals met failure. Inflation was kept under control from 1946 to 1950, but then it rose rapidly. The long-term balance in external transactions could not be realized.

One of the chief planning administrators and perhaps the most effective apologist for the methods adopted was Petter Jakob Bjerve, a professor of economics. He emphasized that in the planning program there was no hidebound ideological line. Nationalization, for example, was but one means of working toward the major goal of social welfare. To attain this social welfare, by which he meant welfare for the individual in society, a program was necessary. Not merely a prognosis, which is what business and the bourgeois parties preferred. For Bjerve the national budget represented "a set of quantitative directives to subordinate government bodies, directives which are mandatory as long as the assumptions upon which they are based continue to be valid." [2] Although modifications were often necessary because of changed circumstances or new data the projections in the budget were nevertheless "a very important tool both for the design of economic policy and for execution of policy." "The national budgeting procedure brings into the open assumptions and projections that

2. For this and the following quotes in this paragraph see Petter Jakob Bjerve, *Planning in Norway, 1947–1956* (Amsterdam: North Holland, 1959), passim.

must be made by the policy makers—if they want to pursue a policy at all."

Despite occasional wishful thinking in the planning stages and faulty execution in the administering stages the budgets were valuable. They provided a firm basis for debate in the Storting on, for example, the choice between consumption and investment, and they often had a persuasive effect on municipal and private bodies by convincing them that certain items were in short supply. The state increased its own investment to one-fourth of the total budget. The government could also stimulate the rationalization of industry with better machinery and larger producing units. Publication of the budget sometimes tempted the administration to make things look rosy to the voters, but it had the salutary effect of forcing the government to play the game with more open cards. Government officials had to observe the figures in the budget, but on private companies and individuals the pressure was only of a moral nature.

As successive national budgets were prepared the planners perfected their econometric methods, still under the guidance of Frisch and Bjerve. The Ministry of Finance won increasing control of the process, and for the years 1962–1965 outlined for the first time a long-range quantitative plan. Plans were made on a rotating basis, each year looking forward to the next four years. The urgency of Norway's situation challenged the talents of her econometricians and unified the national will behind a far-reaching and effective planning structure, and then miraculously the situation changed and demanded a different kind of planning.

In the late 1960s the discovery of oil in the North Sea promised Norway, along with Britain and the Netherlands, a huge bonanza; it was like the winning of a lottery ticket, yet far more complicated. Income might be great, but it would come only in the future and only after stupendous outlays for development. Norway did not have the necessary capital and hence had to make arrangements with the international oil companies that had already taken the initiative. The problem complex involved not only planning for development of the oil resources and the distribution of future profits. It involved decision between two fundamental concepts: did this oil underlying the North Sea, in the Norwegian sector, belong to the private companies that explored it and wanted to exploit it, or did it belong to the Norwegian people?

The government took the view that it was a national resource and that the entire process of further exploration and exploitation must be carefully controlled by government action. Plans were outlined in detail in a book-size report issued by the government. A state company, Statoil, was founded to manage operations and to participate in all phases of drilling and handling the oil. Two other Norwegian companies, and only two (Norsk Hydro and Saga Petroleum), were to be allowed to take part. The foreign companies associated in discovery and operations were to pay the state royalties in percentage of oil extracted. Exploitation would proceed at a controlled pace in the fields south of the 62nd parallel; north of 62° even basic exploration would be kept restrained for a few years and would be guided by Statoil. Decisions in such matters were in the first instance economic and technical, but in the background loomed serious military-strategic considerations, and ecological—pipelines and platforms in the rough open sea were highly vulnerable. At least the principle of community ownership seemed to be clearly established.

A second question was related to the first but went beyond it. What should be done with the "windfall" profits accruing to the state? Obviously, if the oil wells and the gas belonged to the state the resulting moneys were also national. But how should these funds be invested?—in industrial development or in construction and programs for social welfare? Further exploration for oil would itself demand large expenditures, and of course it was to the advantage of the state to do some of this on its own account. A large share of the immediate income must be reinvested. Norwegian industry as a whole had long been starved for capital and could happily use a major portion of the funds now in prospect. The social sector could use it, too. Schools needed rebuilding and expansion, and so did hospitals, roads, and many good causes. Could a frugal people now enjoy affluence? Limitations on their dreams were not only financial. Finance Minister Per Kleppe pointed to one of them: "We have struck oil, but we don't have any more building workers or nurses." [3] Nevertheless, it appeared that building programs for social purposes would be highly favored, and that taxes would be reduced. The people of Norway were neither so optimistic nor so naive as to expect the utopian

---

3. In *Svenska Dagbladet*, October 1, 1974, p. 3.

circumstances of those Arab sheikdoms where no taxes were necessary, but they hoped for some relief, and began to get a little in 1974.

It had to be recognized that a sudden influx of capital could seriously derange the economic balance, upsetting wage and price scales, and threatening the simple life style that Norwegians had known for centuries. The government is trying to hold a firm rein, for Norway is too good to be spoiled. Thoughtful leaders realized that someday the oil would be exhausted, and that people must not become accustomed to patterns of living that they could not maintain. Future generations must be protected. The first locality to be affected by the money-shower was Stavanger on the southwest coast. Several hundred drillers and oil rig operators from Texas and Oklahoma were established there by 1974, and the total American population in the town was about 3500, and the American school had 400 pupils. The town was more or less prepared for its task and its prosperity by its long tradition as a fishing and shipbuilding center, but it had definitely become a boom town. Drilling and servicing of loading platforms and pipe lines would provide work and wealth for a long time to come. Foreign expertise would be required only until Norway could develop its own, and the foreign oil companies were rapidly being edged out of the decision-making process.

The foreign oil companies were naturally less concerned with Norwegian social considerations than they were with oil to sell and profits to be put in the bank. It was clear that there were conflicting interests and that the ramifications of the oil discovery spread widely to involve not only drillers and engineers but politicians, financiers, shippers, businessmen, environmentalists, social planners—just about everybody.

Among the difficult questions was, should Norway join the International Energy Agency, whose function was to arrange for the sharing of oil supplies in the event of a future oil crisis. In the fall of 1974 Norway rejected membership in the IEA, but this refusal to cooperate bothered people who realized that Norway is a part of the Western world and who worried, too, about being wealthier than their neighbors. They saw themselves in a strange new situation and were forced to ponder the problems of the rich man's burden. The difference between the Norwegian situation and the British was that, whereas Great Britain might get two or three times as much oil as Norway, the British would use it all domestically, but the Norwegians would export most of theirs.

Far-reaching decisions of many kinds would have to be made. In Storting and press and among the citizenry there grew a realization of the wide ramifications spreading from the oil drilling. The boundary with Russia in the Barents Sea became a matter of potential importance. Perhaps even more important was the fact that the largest Soviet fleet, including submarines, was based in Murmansk, and that its route to the North Atlantic lay around the North Cape and down through the Norwegian Sea. When exploration increases in the waters north of the sixty-second parallel the Russians may well be concerned about the possibility of NATO observations from the drilling platforms, and Norway may have reason to worry that the platforms are vulnerable to forces beyond weather. However, despite complications, the Norwegians could rejoice that they could plan for something positive and possibly amazingly profitable.

These two examples of Norwegian planning, the "National Budget" and the planning for the oil bonanza, are uique in some respects, but they are also illustrative of basic Scandinavian methods and habits of thinking. For social planning is not at all a new thing in Norden. It is therefore worth a backward glance to see some prototypes of earlier attitudes and procedures and then some other recent planning.

Although Americans have prided themselves on the freedom and the individual opportunity offered in their great open spaces, the United States itself offers some early examples of social planning, most notably perhaps the Northwest Ordinance of 1787 providing land for schools and prohibiting slavery in the vast Northwest. In European societies, owing to the paternalism of kings and the intimate living together of close-knit groups and the eternal demands of defense, planning was more natural and more common. The enclosure movement in England was planning by both landowners and government, and it set an example that inspired reorganization of rural life in both Denmark and Sweden.

Danish Land Reform

The reformation of Danish agriculture was a slow-moving rural revolution that increased productivity, changed farming from grain raising to animal husbandry, and shifted ownership from the large landholders to the men and women who worked the land. The full development went beyond what was first envisaged, but planning was both real and farsighted. As with most planning it was forced by circumstances. When the Danish peasant began in the 1780s to be released from feudalism he was encouraged by government under the stimulus from Reventlow to become an independent proprietor. But it took two nineteenth-century forces to boost him to his twentieth-century freedom. One was the liberal constitution of 1849, the other was the teaching of Bishop N. F. S. Grundtvig which created faith in economic and political progress. The movement from communal to individualist agriculture was slow but steady, aided by government and private societies and by the folk high schools. By the middle of the nineteenth century 58 percent of Danish farms had become freeholds.

In the latter half of the nineteenth century external factors accelerated the programs of the reformers. Cheap grain from virgin fields overseas destroyed Denmark's markets in Great Britain. Landowners and rural proletariat alike faced ruin. Many of the able-bodied moved to industrial centers or emigrated to America. Rural prosperity could be restored only by revamping the agricultural system. The new agricultural schools pointed the way, and the discouraged squires followed their lead. Intensive farming of individualized plots with raising of livestock instead of grain for export seemed to offer salvation. The holders of the large estates were willing to let their workers have five-acre plots of their own if they would also work part time in the larger fields and thus maintain something of the old economic structure.

Therefore the Rigsdag passed an act in 1899 offering state loans of 90 percent of the cost of such small holdings. Within twenty years the government put 58,000,000 kroner into this program, and thousands of new small holdings were established. In 1919 the program was broadened, and more money was provided. In the first years the peasants. had to buy land from the owners. The great estates were parceled out, but only partially. Increasingly it was realized that the old system of both agriculture and of landholding was obsolete and that Danish prosperity must depend upon individualized farming. This required small holdings not of five acres, but of fifteen to thirty-five acres, with each family earning its living entirely off its own land. The government, therefore, bought private lands for redivision and used the old glebe lands also. At the same time the government laid a heavy tax on the landed estates unless they would surrender one-third of their land, for compensation, to the state. Thus the private estates were diminished and small holdings further extended. Between 1920 and 1932 the government provided an additional 100,000,000 kroner in smallholder grants, and over 6,000 new holdings were established.

The state continued to give loans to qualified smallholders, and it also introduced a different system, based on Henry George's ideas: the holder paid no purchase price for his land but paid an annual ground rent of 4 percent of the value of the land as reappraised at periodic intervals. Rents at first fluctuated with farm commodity prices, but this worked out unfortunately, for it caused rents to rise during hard times when grain supply prices rose, increasing the costs of animal feeding. Hence the method of determining rent was changed to follow a sliding scale calculated each year by the Bureau of Agricultural Economics, and based on the earning capacity of small farms. Detailed regulations and controls were worked out in legislation of 1933, 1938, and 1943.

Altogether the state invested 300,000,000 kroner in the small holdings, and about 25,000 holdings were started. Many other smallholdings had been established earlier through the influence of the cooperative societies and the agricultural schools. The smallholders also organized societies which became strong political forces. In the 1960s and 1970s the push was toward consolidation and enlargement of the farming units, supported by legislation encouraging joint operation. The number of holdings was steadily decreasing (136,000 as of 1970) and the average size increasing; only one third of the holdings in the 1970s were of twenty-five acres or less.

The revolution demanded by social reformers for human reasons became merged with the agricultural-economic revolution demanded by world market changes. This coincidence made change more acceptable. State intervention was supported by group pressures and private leadership, and the state thus guided a socioeconomic change agreed upon by society. In the process the people were conditioned for wider governmental planning and control.

Early Swedish Planning

Sweden's agrarian reform differed in detail but was born of similar causes and had similar results. Twentieth-century developments take us into a new realm. The preliminary phases of twentieth-century overall planning in Sweden stemmed from World War I and the depression. At first they were financial in nature, for the government thought that through monetary measures it might avert disastrous shifts in the price level and the cost of living. The details of monetary controls need not detain us, but the method is significant.

The goals of monetary policy were outlined by the government, and the implementation was left to the directors of the Riksbank. They in turn consulted with such financial theorists as Knut Wicksell, David Davidson, and Gustav Cassel, for "the professional economist . . . commands an honored place in the scheme of things, in marked contrast to the scepticism or the polite indifference with which he is regarded in this country [England] and in the United States." [4] However, the theorists did not wholly agree, and the bankers would not follow any one consistent theory. When during World War I gold began to flow to Sweden from the belligerent countries, the bankers were worried about inflation; they could not accept Wicksell's idea that "economically we could do nothing better than exchange our barren reserve of 100 million kronor of metal for useful goods abroad." [5]

The Riksbank did forbid further importation of gold, yet because of the established monetary agreement it could not stop its influx from Norway and Denmark, and contradictorily lowered the discount rate. The measures taken slowed the progress of inflation, which never got out of hand as it did in Germany, but inflation came in a degree slightly greater than in the United States and Great Britain.

When the world depression enfolded Sweden in 1930 monetary policy concentrated on the maintenance of internal purchasing power. The real purpose was to "stabilize the cost of living" and to avoid labor unrest by maintaining jobs and prices. Sweden was fortunate to have a reserve to throw into public works and relief

4. Brinley Thomas, *Monetary Policies and Crises* (London: Routledge, 1936), p. xx.
5. Ibid., p. 4.

(accumulated from the alcohol monopoly). The government borrowed heavily, and demand for iron ore and timber happily remained relatively strong. Export prices rose in 1931–1933, while import prices were held low.

Finland profited, too, by the continued demand for her timber products, but her internal purchasing power suffered severely. Norway was at the mercy of autarchic policies elsewhere which deprived her ships of cargo and curtailed her markets for fish. But in Sweden, by 1933, "the monetary policy had brought the economic decline to a standstill, and in the favourable situation which thus arose the recovery in export trade started a general business revival." [6] By the combination of guidance and good luck Sweden weathered the storm remarkably well. Belief in planned controls was strengthened. In succeeding years exports were encouraged by keeping the krona below its normal free market value.

Such experiences and attitudes form the background for the more sweeping plans of the 1940s. The early short-term calculations were adjustments to circumstances. With the advent of World War II the Swedes decided to do more than adapt themselves to conditions. As Gunnar Myrdal stated the new concept, it was to try in the existing situation to direct developments in the desired direction.[7]

One of the first steps in the new activist policy was the appreciation of the value of the krona in July 1946. The scheme contemplated in 1937 was now carried out, but in 1946 it was directed at the dollar instead of at the pound sterling. The Swedes reasoned that the krona was undervalued and that inflation was coming in the United States. By increasing the value of the krona they hoped to minimize the reaction of that inflation on the Swedish economy. They expected demand for Swedish pulp and other products to remain strong regardless of this price increase, a price increase which would affect goods sold to other countries also, including the USSR under the trade agreement then being negotiated. They expected to be able to buy goods abroad more advan-

6. Arthur Montgomery, *How Sweden Overcame the Depression, 1930–1933* (Stockholm: Bonniers, 1938), p. 66.

7. See Myrdal, *Beyond the Welfare State: Economic Planning and Its International Implications* (New Haven: Yale University Press, 1960).

tageously. One result, Myrdal wrote a few months later, was that "price control had a less restrictive effect on imports than would otherwise have been the case." [8] But Sweden imported so much that she soon spent her dollar reserves and had to restrict imports drastically in 1948 and 1949. And she priced many of her own goods out of the American market.

For planning in its broader aspects, however, the story must go back to the war period.

Wartime Planning

In the early months and years of World War II the Scandinavian countries could follow only the catch-as-catch-can policy. They stockpiled foreign goods as much as possible and rationed scarce items of importance. Finland's war and postwar plans were channeled by immediate needs and by the imposed program of reparations, which necessitated industrial reorganiztion. The Finns had to plan for the resettlement of their dispossessed people from the ceded areas in the east and north. From 1940 to 1945, planning in Denmark and Norway was controlled by the Nazis, yet some worthwhile and permanent projects of roadbuilding, and construction of railways, airfields, and factories were undertaken. Devastated homes and industries provided the great common problem, and plans to meet it were formulated both at home and by the Norwegian government in exile in London.

In January 1943 the Danish minister of finance appointed a commission to study the danger of inflation and allied problems. The membership included representatives of government and banking and professors from Århus and Copenhagen. In March the commission recommended price ceilings and a price-wage policy. In 1945 it produced a two-volume report and recommended wide governmental intervention in economic activity: government orders to stimulate export and investment industry, including purchase of durable consumption goods such as furniture; government subsidy of repair to buildings and of shipbuilding; possible reduction of the interest rate on housing loans. Public works were to be a second alternative. Imports should be restricted on account of the shortage of foreign exchange. Possi-

8. *Svenska Handelsbanken Index*, supplement (December 1946), p. 10.

ble unemployment should be distributed by staggering workers' time off. Unemployment benefits should be increased to encourage buying and thus to offset a decline in production. Taxes should be reduced on short notice before a depression could get out of control and should be raised on short notice to control a boom. Much of this program was made law. In fact, partial steps of a similar nature had been tried in the depression of the 1930s through subsidies and discount cards for children of low-income families. Denmark was geared for her stringent postwar controls.

The Swedes had the best opportunity to show the natural Scandinavian method of operation: they established a planning commission in February 1944. Chairman of the commission was Gunnar Myrdal, minister of commerce, a trained social scientist and professor. The twenty-one members of the commission represented the main political parties, industry, trade unions, the employers' association, chambers of commerce, the cooperatives, agriculture, and women's organizations. The commission had no authority to act but was charged to formulate principles.

This Swedish commission had almost completed its work by September 1945. It took for its starting assumption that exports and investment were "the active force behind changes in the business cycle." The commission expressed aversion to manipulation of exchange rates, subsidies of exports, or similar measures. But it recognized a need for state encouragement to industry to produce and store goods for future export. It foresaw some of the difficulties which would follow when Swedish exports would be demanded by countries with "weak" currencies, whereas Sweden would wish to buy from countries with "hard" currencies. A period of governmental control was therefore essential, but control should be applied only as necessary. Investment should be evened out between depression and boom; special tax policies could encourage this, and an Investment Planning Commission was established. Industrial construction and public building were to be aided by an "investment reserve," with new projects available to be put in motion at the start of a depression. Housing construction was to be stabilized at a high level. Consumption was to be promoted in depression periods by increases of relief allotments and by subsidies to families with several children, to encourage them to purchase durable consumers' goods. The importance of free competition was emphasized, and price control was to be held in the background, but lowering of the price level and stabilization of incomes were to be sought. The labor exchanges were to be improved, and industry further rationalized.

The Commission's program represented what government, labor, and management could agree on; it might be labeled "reluctant semisocialism." Much more definite was the postwar program of Swedish labor, but it too stayed within the broad path of the "middle way." More recent and still more specific was the "long term investigation for the 1970s," [9] which was worked out in the Ministry of Finance. This was a statistical survey of the trends of the 1950s and 1960s and the probable trends of the 1970s in population, demand and supply of manpower and womanpower, investment, resource availability, prices, and many other factors affecting economic developments. Alongside this government investigation came a report by the Business Research Institute based on a questionnaire sent to businesses and industries and also utilizing the government findings. Planning had become the business of every leadership branch. But the most sweeping prognosis of all was to come from the Social Democratic government itself, with the imprimatur of the Prime Minister.

The Ultima Thule of Social Planning:
Sweden's Regional Plan for the 1970s

"It is the betterment of conditions for the individual that stands in the center of our regional policy. . . . All people wherever they live in our land shall have a part in the material, social, and cultural welfare." [10] So Eric Holmquist, Minister of the Interior, announced the newest of Sweden's regional plans in the fall of 1972. Its implications were far-reaching, and it was the most ambitious of a long succession of such plans. It was physical planning on the national level based on the concept that technical and economic development should be subordinated to man's needs and desires. Local considerations must yield to the regional and interregional to produce "integrated social planning." Prime Minister Olof Palme pointed out how the well-directed resources of the nation's economy were continually increasing the security and freedom of

9. *Svensk ekonomi, 1971–1975, med utblick mot 1990*, SOU, 1970: no. 71.
10. Quoted in *Svenska Dagbladet*, November 2, 1972.

the individual, and that the public sector was continually expanding, especially in northern Sweden. For instance, in 1970 the State Company (*Statsföretag*) employed 13,000, and the placement of the nation's investment funds supported an additional 4000 jobs in private industry. Palme mentioned the progress made in controlling water and air pollution. All in all, he was convinced that Sweden was on the right track and that now was the time to go further.

Participation of citizens in decision-making must come earlier and more effectively. New productive work opportunities must be provided. The three most important items were work, service, and milieu. People in the sparsely settled communities as well as in the cities must have access to good daily services within reasonable distance, by which he meant trouble-free access to doctors, hospitals, schools, roads, theaters, and varied recreational facilities, as well as grocery stores and shops. Growth in urban areas must be curtailed. Expansion of the public sector can influence the location of industries and the labor structure, and all future construction must be guided into the areas where, for the good of all, it ought to be located. The community as a whole must have increased responsibility for the administration of land and water resources. Inequalities between the regions must be evened out.

To implement this idealistic program the government laid before the Riksdag a series of specific proposals including: decentralization of governmental agencies (already begun by moving a number of bureaus from Stockholm to scattered inland cities, to the distress of many employees and their families); support in sparsely settled areas for employment, education, and supply; subsidies for noneconomic bus lines and other services in the outlying communities, even for bringing people to the shops; redistribution of taxes to less favored communities; increased support for entrepreneurial associations and a system for improved exchange of information between business and people; conservation of the coast and of interior wooded areas suited for recreation and general public use, with a significant reservation that angered some landowners: it could not be considered just that an owner of land should expect compensation if in the public interest he was forbidden to use his property as he might wish; northern rivers so far undisturbed by power development should be left untouched.

In short, here was the outline for a new utopia. But the dreamers who envisioned and promulgated it were not ivory-tower philosophers, they were bureaucrats in government offices. The program dealt with the economy, but it was people-oriented, not business-oriented. It did not deny to private concerns the right to exist but it asserted unequivocally that the ruling principle must be the welfare of society as a whole. This was its very essence. At the same time its proponents denied that they were thinking of "society" in an abstract or impersonal sense. They insisted, rather, that the purpose of the proposals was to enlarge opportunities for the individual and to make his life better. They would do so through governmental action aimed at equalizing opportunities for all.

A Summary Comment on Economic Patterns in the North

1. Up almost to the mid-point of the twentieth century, Scandinavian industry was based on the raw materials supplied by her own farms and fisheries, forests, and mines; this is less true with each passing year. Iceland and Norway produce no bauxite, but they import and process it with the use of their power resources and send aluminum to world markets; Finland imports much of the materials for her manufacture of electrical equipment and icebreakers; Sweden imports more steel (though of lower quality) than she exports. As manufacturing becomes more sophisticated, the tendency increases to buy specialized parts (as for automobiles) from distant producers and incorporate them into domestic products. Thus the interchange of goods has increased markedly.

2. Limited variety of resources remains a basic characteristic of the economies of the North. One vital resource they all share is easy access to the sea and therefore to supplies and markets.

3. The importance of technological research is keenly realized and is applied throughout industry, perhaps most spectacularly in connection with the development of weapons systems, notably the "Viggen" airplane. The Scandinavians keep carefully abreast of discoveries and techniques abroad through reading and also travel and working in other countries.

4. Nordic economies are rapidly becoming internationalized,

and the area of choice left to national institutions is therefore more and more restricted. Illustrations of the trend are the growth of large multinational companies (especially in Sweden), cooperation of governments and private firms with foreign corporations (as in the Norwegian oil fields), establishment of plants abroad, and expansion of connections with the Common Market.

5. 'Government participation in economic enterprise has increased to large proportions in each of the countries. This takes the form of guidance and control and sometimes of mixed ownership through investment of public savings. Direct government ownership and operation is so far minimal, but decisions on economic choices are made by the government. The system has been called "socialism without nationalization." By whatever name, it is a significant expansion of the public sector of the economy and a relative diminution of the private sector.

6. In each country the relative position of agriculture has weakened in both economic and prestige terms, as technological and industrial progress has been emphasized. The degree of change has been roughly similar to that in other developed countries of Europe.

7. The forced pace and the monotony of labor on the assembly line is beginning to be recognized as dehumanizing and counterproductive; innovative steps are being taken (by Volvo, for example) to make such work seem more creative.

8. Increasingly, the Scandinavians who had applied intelligence and skills to their own technical and material betterment are exporting not only products but know how to aid the development of other countries. Danes build cement plants in far countries, Finns build water towers in Arabia, Norwegian and Swedish engineers are everywhere.

9. The socializing tendency has caught the attention of the prophets of doom who, looking at Sweden in particular, have repeatedly predicted the breakdown of the economy: heavy progressive taxation would destroy incentive, rising wages would require higher prices and discourage markets, welfare policy would ruin morale and morals, central control of the economy would dampen responsiveness to consumer demands, public management would destroy efficiency, equality would weaken the role of leadership, and so on. When year after year results

negated prophecies, the prophets merely projected their warnings into the future. Do the 1970s indicate fulfillment of the forebodings? In Denmark, Burmeister and Wain is in deep trouble. In Finland factories can not employ the increasing population. In Sweden wildcat strikes broke out and a general strike was threatened in June 1971; unemployment rose temporarily to 3.5 percent (bad in Sweden although considered quite acceptable in the United States), and immigration dropped. Are the difficulties basic or superficial? The enigmatic future will someday give its answer.

10. Despite the difficulties and the doubts indicated above, despite the disadvantages of climate and distance from market centers, the peoples of Scandinavia still maintain strong positions in shipping and shipbuilding, in automobile manufacture, aluminum, wood processing, fisheries, and other branches.

11. The advantages of economic cooperation in EFTA proved far-reaching, yet not sufficient to persuade everyone to accept the tighter bonds of EEC. Always there were doubts and objections. Mercantile interests favored cooperation, but these nationalistic Nordics feared being dominated by others politically or economically. Norwegians voted decisively to stay out of EEC. Denmark voted to join. Sweden, Finland, Norway, and Iceland too, made commercial agreements with EEC, preserving some freedom of action.

12. Social characteristics and fundamental attitudes of the people are significant elements of the functioning economy. Racial homogeneity, the traditions of the Lutheran religion, an inbred pragmatic philosophy, the small-state psychology that enhances a sense of individual importance, a habit of work, freedom from corruption in government—all are valuable foundation stones.

13. Both peoples and governments are firmly committed to the idea of careful planning for the future. Assuredly, all modern governments attempt to foresee developments and to influence the economy in favorable directions. But there are few if any of the "free" countries of the West that plan ahead with such mathematical precision as does Norway in her National Budget, or with such frank statement of social idealism as Sweden in her "Regional Plan for the 1970s."

5 *The Search for Security*

The fundamental thrusts of Scandinavian purpose are three: building strong economies, providing equality of distribution of the good things of life, and establishing national security. Security of the state has been sought through a combination of neutrality, international cooperation, and varied emphases on defense.

Neutrality: Tradition, Policy, and Practice
(to 1814)

The Scandinavians learned generations back that war "does not regard the neutral powers," that a state which would keep out of war must take care of herself. From the sixteenth to the eighteenth century, as the concept of neutrality evolved, the problem was mainly to gain rights for peoples not participating in war. In the nineteenth and twentieth centuries warring states insisted that states claiming neutral privileges must also obey certain rules. In other words, neutrality is a two-way street. In the evolution of rights and obligations of neutrality the Scandinavian states have played a prominent part.

Neutrals were not always pious proponents of international law and not necessarily pacifist. They were pursuing their special interests through neutrality while others were striving for their own interests through war. Through the eighteenth century the Scandinavian states were still unconvinced of their peaceful destiny; they were alternately belligerents and neutrals, and their policies alternated accordingly. Opportunism remained a characteristic of neutrality even after peace became a permanent goal. Neutrality was expediency, not principle.

The catch-as-catch-can aspect of neutrality was clearly stated by Christian Günther, Sweden's foreign minister in 1943:

A policy which does not take account of the actual situation of the moment, but stands on a preconceived doctrine without asking where it leads *then*—such is no policy at all, but pure bravado at a time when the whole world is rocking. Sweden's neutrality policy has been formed by world events in these fateful years, there is no reason to hide the fact under the bed and it needs no excuses.[1]

Günther's statement explains why Sweden's policy shifted like a weather vane during World War II and was a better indication than the stock market of how the fortunes of war were treating the warring powers. This policy was the product of experience deep rooted in the past.

The rivalries of power and trade in the Baltic in the seventeenth and eighteenth centuries are enlightening but too complex for these pages. Denmark and Sweden, Holland, Lübeck, France, Prussia, Poland, England—all were involved in attempts to interdict each other's commerce and during wars to try to preserve their own. Trade was important, especially that in naval stores. The northern states sought to frame regulations on siege and contraband and to set rules which would safeguard them when at war yet permit trade. Dutch depredations against Baltic commerce at last led to joint Danish-Swedish convoys and confiscation of Dutch ships in Denmark. Success in this venture led to the "armed neutrality" of 1691 and 1693, which insisted on freedom of navigation, joint convoys, and joint action if warfare resulted. For three years the English lords of the sea responded by treating the Scandinavians with leniency.

In between the campaigns for neutrality came, of course, those bloodier campaigns for national security: Gustav II Adolf fighting

---

1. *Svensk neutralitetspolitik under stormaktskriget* [Swedish neutrality policy during the Great Powers' War] (pamphlet); speech at Eskilstuna, May 7, 1943, p. 17.

across the Baltic and both Danes and Swedes invading Germany; Charles X marching through Poland and Denmark and winning the southern provinces of Sweden; Charles XII unsuccessfully sparring the Russian threat by leading his armies to the Ukraine. But very little security was attained.

When Denmark and Sweden were at war with each other, they issued decrees that sounded just like those decrees of the western powers which they denounced in periods of their own neutrality. They also cooperated occasionally, as during the Seven Years' War after France had induced them to rebuild an armed neutrality. Sweden tried to insist that "free ships make free goods," but the Danes insisted rather on freedom to act "as existing contingencies and the national interests should require."

During the wars of the mid-eighteenth century both Sweden and Denmark-Norway tested the policy of opening their ports to captors of both sides: "neutrality consisted in impartiality alone." They found that this worked out to help the French, for the French used Norwegian ports as bases for attacking British commerce and bringing in British prizes. But the British could not capture French ships in those waters for the simple reason that French commerce did not use those routes. The British argued that impartiality should mean total exclusion of all ships, but they were not consistent, for they were doing from Mediterranean ports exactly what they objected to the French doing from Norwegian ports.

Britain was the most important customer for northern goods, and her prosperity was therefore vital even to those who defied her overweening naval power. They could not live happily with her, but their trade could not live at all without her. Hence the small countries of the North, like the big countries of the East and the West, made strong statements of policy, but were ready quickly to reverse themselves.

The Armed Neutrality of 1780 followed the pattern. It was born out of a temporary community of interests between Denmark, Sweden, and Russia, with some stimulation from France; it was in force briefly; it disintegrated, and soon every one of its members was applying principles contrary to those of the treaty. The neutral league was built on a plan outlined by Count A. P. Bernstorff, the Danish foreign minister, in 1778, and restated by the Empress Catherine of Russia. Denmark and Sweden agreed in 1779 to convoy their merchantmen, Russia was ready to act in the waters north of Norway, and in 1780 they all got together. The principles of the Armed Neutrality can be summed up as:

1. Neutral vessels may navigate freely port to port and on coasts of the powers at war.
2. Property of belligerents on neutral vessels is to be free, except contraband.
3. Contraband is that which is so listed in treaties of Sweden and Russia with Great Britain.
4. Blockade is to be recognized only if it is effective.

In October 1780 the United States Congress passed a resolution agreeing to these principles, and in December Francis Dana was authorized to sign treaties on such bases. Dana then discovered to his embarrassment that the alliance was for neutrals only. The first American treaty with Sweden, April 3, 1783, did incorporate the principle of "free ships, free goods," and thus opened the path of official Scandinavian American relations. The Swedes foresaw great opportunities resulting from the American Revolution, as indicated in the comment of a Swedish statesman: "What future may this greatest field of Swedish commerce expect if the English colonies win their independence and they, in peace and with liberty's stimulus, carry all such undertakings to that height to which their country with so much advantages seems to entice them?" [2]

Early in the period of the French Revolution Sweden and Denmark-Norway combined again to protect their neutral commerce. The Swedes approached the United States about acceding to the agreement, but the Danes thought America would be more of a liability than an asset. American statesmen were working at cross purposes: Alexander Hamilton informed the British that the United States would not join the Scandinavian alliance in any case, while Thomas Jefferson was doing everything possible to frighten the sea lords. Russia now stood with Britain instead of with Scandinavia, and the Empress Catherine threatened to station her

---

2. *Dagboksanteckningar förda vid Gustaf IIIs Hof af Friherre Gustaf Johan Ehrensvärd . . .* [Diary notes from Gustaf III's court by Baron G. J. Ehrensvärd], 2 vols. (Stockholm, 1878), II, 115.

fleet in the Baltic to prevent Scandinavian ships from sailing for France. The Armed Neutrality could get no subsidies and soon died. As Gouverneur Morris said, it was "a demonstration of a force and a temper which do not exist."

No issues were settled, either then or when Czar Paul persuaded the Scandinavians into a new armed neutrality. This one collapsed with the British attack of 1801 on Copenhagen and led only to some British compromises.

In the years which followed, Denmark-Norway became of less political and economic importance while Sweden's commerce fattened rapidly, especially in the period 1808–1813. Imports of cotton, wine, sugar, and tobacco increased astronomically; total goods in bond in Sweden grew from 511,000 riksdalers in 1807 to 10,200,000 riksdalers in 1813. Much of this goods found its way to Europe, through holes in the back fence of Napoleon's Continental System. This was the major reason for that extraordinary massing of 1200 merchant ships in the harbor of Gothenburg in 1812. But Sweden's neutrality and her illicit commerce both ended in 1813, as she fought her "war to end all wars," won Norway, and gave up her continental holdings.

Two centuries of neutral striving proved that effective neutrality must be armed neutrality. They proved also that the neutral purpose was to promote commerce while others fought. The purpose was wholly reasonable, but it is useful to remember that it did not involve pacifism nor any other "higher morality."

A Century of Success, 1814–1914

With 1814 began a new phase in Scandinavian neutrality. Up to that time the Scandinavian governments had attempted to make the most out of their occasional nonbelligerent status, but a change to war status was easy if advantages appeared, such as subsidies from France or Britain or a chance to win territory. Abstention from diplomatic bargaining and the international tug-of-war was not considered. But when in 1810 Bernadotte became Crown Prince Carl Johan of Sweden he conceived of a new system: Finland, taken by the Russians in 1809, would be forgotten; the German territory of Pomerania would be renounced; Norway would be added to the Swedish kingdom in what looked to a French general like a natural geographical unit; and Sweden-Norway would withdraw forever from the quarrels of Europe. Denmark, beaten and deprived of her co-kingdom of Norway, was at the nadir of her fortunes and could think only of nursing her wounds and preserving what was left. Norway wanted only peace and as much of independence as she could get. The whole of Scandinavia was neutrality-minded, though the people did not indulge in much theorizing about it. The nineteenth and twentieth centuries spelled out the methods and developed the principles. Not only commerce but national existence was now at stake.

Toward the end of the Napoleonic Wars the great powers decided that the smaller states should no longer participate as equals in international affairs; the four (later five) great states would alone maintain the concert of Europe. Scandinavian leaders observed affairs with interest and were occasionally tempted to adventure. But they held their peace. Sweden's position had deteriorated with Russian acquisition of Finland and her fortification of the Åland Islands.

In the Crimean War Denmark and Sweden-Norway declared neutrality in similar but independent announcements. Then Sweden in 1855 signed the November Treaty with Britain and France, pledging herself not to cede to Russia even so much as fishing or pasture rights in the Lapp lands of the Far North. The neutrality bases of 1834–1856 emphasized the right to trade with both Britain and Russia and the right to receive in port the naval vessels of both, a right which meant much more to Britain than it did to Russia. The English took advantage of it to use the harbor of Fårösund on Gotland for two years during the war.

In general the descendants of the Vikings restrained themselves, outsiders let them alone, and luck was with them. At the close of the Crimean War Sweden got a guarantee of nonfortification of the Åland Islands, but she had antagonized Russia anew. At the same time there was rousing talk of a real Scandinavian union. King Oscar I of Sweden-Norway, at a student festival, proclaimed that not only was war impossible between the Scandinavian states, but that "our swords stand ready for our mutual defense." But King Frederick of Denmark rejected either an alliance or the proffered guarantee of Slesvig.

Militarily the great threat and perhaps the great opportunity of the nineteenth century came in 1864 when German aggression gobbled up Slesvig and Holstein, the two duchies which had been under the Danish crown. The Danes fought valiantly but against hopeless odds. The glib promises of Swedish aid by Karl XV, new king of Sweden-Norway, yielded nothing, and neither France nor Britain raised a finger. Henrik Ibsen attacked passionately what he saw as the craven selfishness of the men in power. The Danes died alone; pan-Scandinavianism died with them. Bismarck was on the march. The Swedes and the Norwegians and the Danes knew that the odds were against them; with a mixture of satisfaction and resignation they turned their energies into building up their internal economy and culture.

In the century and a quarter between 1814 and 1940 the only actual outbreaks of war in Scandinavia were in 1848–49 and in 1864, both in Denmark. But there were other threats, and there was constant attention to the problems of defense and of neutrality, particularly in Sweden. The Swedish minister Manderström was mirror and mouthpiece of the perennial principles of neutrality: "In political things it is not permissible to entertain sympathies and antipathies, at least not when one has no possibility to make his attitudes valid." [3] When the Franco-Prussian war was threatening, Manderström told the French Minister that his hearty sympathies were with the French, but asked "What can we give them?" The Frenchman thereupon read Manderström a political sermon:

No European state [he said] can reasonably leave it to others to play the game of European politics without itself taking part and being prepared to take part. Sweden has no army and no fleet. Neutrality can be a great advantage for the moment, but is it so in the long run for a state like Sweden which lies isolated between two unscrupulous neighbors? [4]

Manderström merely listened with resignation.

Sweden's notes to Prussia urging a plebiscite in Slesvig were brushed aside because Prussia saw in Sweden neither the force nor the will to act. A frank renunciation of influence abroad was written into the Swedish King's speech from the throne in January, 1867:

3. Hans Lennart Lundh, "Svensk neutralitetspolitik åren 1865–1866" [Swedish neutrality policy, 1865–1866], in *Studier tillägnade Curt Weibull* (Göteborg, 1946), p. 261.
4. Ibid., p. 284.

Without any desire to participate in the solution of the problems which disturb or threaten to disturb other parts of Europe, I have well-founded hope that the united kingdoms, surrounded on all sides by natural frontiers, shall continuingly be able to enjoy the blessings of peace.[5]

Could isolationist neutrality be more bluntly or more complacently stated?

In later years the Rigsdag in Denmark passed various resolutions in favor of neutrality on a permanent legalized basis, but the government did nothing to implement the resolutions. Norway, after 1907, strove to obtain an international guarantee of her integrity and her neutrality. She obtained a guarantee only of integrity.

Perhaps the efforts toward neutrality might have been more vigorous if Nordic statesmen had then known the contents of a letter written by the British statesman Sir Charles Hardinge to Sir Arthur Nicolson, then ambassador in St. Petersburg:

As for the Baltic and North Sea agreements they will hold good for us so long as they are not violated by others. If in time of war the Straits [Skagerrak, Kattegat and Öresund] remain open that is all we want. If Germany tries to close them we shall regard ourselves as absolutely free to do what we like and even to ignore the integrity of Norway should we require a naval base on the Norwegian coast. For these reasons the agreements are hardly worth the paper they will be written on as we know that Germany has made preparations to invade Denmark in case of war with us.[6]

Of all the talk and all the hope the most practical neutrality act came after the separation of Norway from Sweden in 1905. Tempers had been strained by long tension, and the wounded sensibility of the Swedes was as inflammable as the nationalistic pride of the Norwegians. Yet the Swedes swallowed hard and then formulated some sensible demands; the Norwegians had the good sense and courage to accept them. The result was that Norway went in peace out of the union with Sweden; the boundary in the long mountains between them was neutralized; all forts on the border were demolished, and perpetual friendship was pledged.

5. Ibid., p. 287.
6. Letter of February 5, 1908, *British Documents on the Origins of the War, 1898–1914* (London: HM Stationery Office, 1926–), VIII, 165–166.

The Swedish-Norwegian frontier, the boundaries of Switzerland, and the frontiers between the United States and Canada (since 1817) stand as examples to the world of effective neutralization.

The Testing of Neutrality, 1914–1918

The "guns of August" brought shock and fear to Scandinavia. People became imbued with a sense of weakness in their innocence, of uncertainty from day to day, and of disillusionment in the good faith and intelligence of men.

Declarations of neutrality were issued independently by the three governments, Norway, Sweden, and Denmark. (Finland was still a Russian archduchy, and Iceland was subordinate to Denmark.) By the twelfth of November, 1914, the first joint note of protest was sent to the warring powers by the three Scandinavian states, and a practice was instituted which continued to annoy the belligerents throughout the war. The United States was also sending its notes, and several times the various governments of the North suggested cooperation in this work with the United States. But the United States never accepted the proposals. King Gustav V of Sweden took the initiative in calling a meeting of the sovereigns of the three Nordic countries in Malmö (December 1914), his first meeting with King Haakon of Norway since the bitter incidents of 1905. The foreign ministers met several times during the war and established firmer and firmer bonds.

The Declaration of Paris of 1856 concerning blockade and other aspects of international law during war, the Declaration of London of 1909, and the whole accumulation of custom on neutrality was assumed to be fundamental and dependable. In the first few weeks of war both Britain and Germany acted in accordance with these principles, and for practical purposes it was only these two states with whom Scandinavia was concerned until the United States entered the war in 1917. The Scandinavians maintained, as did the Americans (1914–1917), that neutrals had a right to trade whatever they would, except contraband, with whomever they would—a principle that the British could not tolerate.

The old maritime laws of war were torn to shreds. "Conditional contraband" lists were extended time after time. In October Germany began to seize neutral ships in the Baltic and to take them to German ports for search. Denmark needed fodder and coal; Norway normally obtained all her coal from England; Sweden imported one-third of her cereals: all Scandinavia was dependent on foreign trade. Ships with food and necessary raw materials were delayed in English ports, blown up by mines, torpedoed by German submarines; factories had to be closed because raw materials could not cross the oceans. Fishermen sold their catch at fantastic prices, sometimes thirty times the prewar price, without even taking the cargo into port. Wages rose too, but there was little to buy. Housing construction ceased. "Coffee" was stewed from roots. Scandinavia was at peace, but her life was debased by war.

Shipping had a double importance for the Scandinavian countries: the carrying trade as a business, and the import-export of goods. Norway's huge fleet was the chief means of earning foreign exchange for the country as a whole. The war on the seas destroyed over 1,000,000 tons of Norway's shipping—half her fleet and 2000 sailors lost; the Swedes and the Danes lost over 200,000 tons each and hundreds of men. Oceans had ceased to be paths of commerce; they were preempted as the playing fields of belligerent powers. Both coal and food became short. Swedish supplies of wheat and rye were 55 per cent lower in 1917–18 than in 1913. Diplomatic protests sometimes gained petty concessions, but in the main the warring powers were ready to attack whatever came in their way. Convoys were tried, but did not succeed very well, and there developed no armed neutrality league on the old pattern. In the latter part of the war Britain furnished armed escort for commerce of interest to her, for she grew worried that neutral shipping might be driven from the seas. She tried to force ships to stay in service by making them promise to return with cargoes to English ports, and she would release from port one neutral ship only when a compatriot ship arrived.

Most interesting of the devices for neutral living in that chaotic world were the arrangements negotiated by the Northern countries for "compensation trade." Agreements were made for carefully balancing trade each way in return for concessions. In Sweden this was arranged partly through "Transito," a private joint stock company, supposedly Swedish, but actually controlled through the British Legation in Stockholm; Transito effected a partial reconciliation between the interests of Sweden and the Allies, permitting imports to Sweden, but forcing Swedish merchants to agree not to reexport to Britain's enemies. Sweden allowed the export of dairy products, meat, and horses to Germany, in return for which Germany agreed to send to Sweden coal, potash, fertilizers, salt, drugs, and some iron and steel (processed from Swedish ore). The need for a strict balance resulted in some drastic changes. For example, in peacetime Sweden had bought about 90 percent of her coal from Britain, but during the war about 47 percent (down to 27 percent in 1917), while 53 percent was obtained from Germany. By 1917 Sweden had to permit 90,000 tons of timber to go to Britain in order to obtain safe passage for nineteen shiploads of grain from Halifax. Sweden also had to limit her iron ore export to Germany to 3,500,000 tons and to charter 400,000 tons of her shipping to the Allies.

Such agreements with Britain placed a neutral state's entire shipping in the "enemy" category in German eyes (after April 1918); but Germany was willing to make exceptions and to issue letters of safe-conduct to neutral vessels which pledged that they were supplying only their own people. Norwegian fishermen had to obtain their coal, salt, and hemp from Britain, and the British objected to supplying this equipment in order for the Norwegians to catch and sell fish to the Germans. In January 1916 the British government set aside £10,000,000 for "blockade buying" of the fish-catch; in July they arranged to take 85 percent of the catch, at a fixed price in a rising market. On Norwegian insistence they permitted 15 percent to be freely exported to Germany.

This agreement for a meager 15 percent incensed the Germans and led to a period of submarine retaliation against the Norwegians. At this stage Britain and France permitted Norway to make some additional concessions to Germany; they did not want to have Norway forced into war even on their side, for the extension of their defense zone would have been a heavy burden. By June of 1917 Britain chartered most of the remaining Norwegian merchant fleet, sent it to distant and safer waters, and with her own armed vessels took over commercial operations in the North Sea. In May 1918 the Norwegians signed an agreement with the United States further limiting their shipments to Germany, guaranteeing certain products to the Allies, and getting permission for food and raw material imports.

Denmark agreed to the British demand not to reexport contraband to Germany but insisted that she could sell noncontraband. In general Denmark was, however, the best example of the mutual tolerance showed by the belligerents, and for a simple reason. She sold food to Germany, but in order to produce food she had to import animal fodder from Britain; to get this fodder she must obviously also sell food to Britain. The Germans, in order to get some food from Denmark, tacitly allowed this trade, and in one case captured and then deliberately released two ships bound with food for Britain.

The Danes knew that they must play a careful game. They fixed prices and established export quotas on the basis of prewar trade. Thus 75 percent of the pork exports went to Britain, most of the rest to Germany. In 1915 butter was treated in the same way, and in 1916 eggs, too. In 1917 butter and pork were put on a 50-50 basis, because Denmark had to obtain additional supplies from Germany—Britain had cut down drastically on her exports to Denmark, and the United States had begun to clamp down on fodder. In September Denmark too was forced to put half her fleet at the service of the Allies. In essence Britain and Germany, at war with one another, determined rations of coal and grain and coffee and raw materials for the "independent" neutrals of the North.

Did the neutrality of 1914–1918 profit the Scandinavian lands? It is a question which cannot be answered. Granted the original fact of war it is obvious that the Scandinavian countries were fortunate not to be drawn in. They avoided destruction and bloodshed and a part of the social disruption that comes with war. But it would be untenable to suggest that these peoples earned a positive benefit because of war around them. Prices rose to levels three to five times as high as those of 1913, and a few individuals reaped rich rewards. Governments were enabled to pay off up to two-thirds of their foreign debts, and their citizens became owners of many foreign-built enterprises. But markets were disrupted, wartime trade was often artificial and temporary, destruction of shipping was tremendous, wage rates and currencies were thrown out of balance, and the Scandinavian monetary union was destroyed.

War also stimulated political change. Sweden furnishes an excellent example. The serious disruption of her trade and internal economy led to a Conservative loss in the elections of September 1917. Compounding the economic-political problem came the Anglo-American exposure of the fact that Sweden's neutrality had been far too benevolent toward Germany. The Foreign Office had permitted coded German cables to be sent over its lines from America to Berlin, and one of these from Count Luxburg, German minister in Buenos Aires, carried the notorious recommendation that two Argentine vessels should be *"spurlos versenkt"* (sunk without trace). Publication of the cable created a furore, discredited the Swedish government and her neutrality, and unlocked the door for long desired political reform. There followed not only a change of government but also the establishment of ministerial responsibility.

Only two territorial changes affected the North directly: the Danish acquisition of North Slesvig and the independence of Finland. In 1864 Prussia had promised a plebiscite in North Slesvig but had never held it. German defeat brought it at last after World War I. The voting showed a considerable penetration of German people and influence since the 1860s but brought to Denmark by clear popular choice 184,000 people and 984 square miles of territory in the fertile Jutland peninsula. Here was a satisfying example of historical rectification.

Another factor which can be recorded on the positive side was the wartime impetus to Scandinavian cooperation. From July 29, 1914, on to the end of the war this cooperation grew and spread, diminishing old antagonisms and building new foundations for useful working together.

In trade the first effect of the war was to diminish intra-Scandinavian business, because of the concessions demanded from the individual countries by the belligerents. In March 1917 a Scandinavian trade representatives' meeting in Stockholm reversed this trend and private and official committees cooperated to expand this internal commerce: butter, pork, cheese, and eggs from Denmark to Sweden; salt herring from Norway to Sweden; iron and steel, lumber, paper from Sweden to her neighbors. Here was laid the basis for still further expansion.

Governmental activity was greatly stimulated by the needs of war. In many cases private associations of businessmen and shippers in the three Scandinavian countries dealt as groups with

foreign governments, indicating the preservation of "free enterprise" even in a wartime emergency. Yet by the end of the war
the governments had assumed vastly increased powers. A government commission in Denmark allocated export quotas and levied
an embargo against certain exports; government fixed prices on
food and underwrote shipping insurance. In Norway the government was authorized to forbid the laying-up of privately owned
ships, local councils were empowered to fix maximum prices, agriculture was made compulsory, and various commissions and ministries were established: Fish Department, Fat Board, Food Ministry, and Ministry of Industrial Supplies. In Sweden the same sort
of things happened. Centralization and the direction of economic
activities by the state became a wartime habit and was never entirely discarded.

In short, despite neutrality, the Scandinavian lands experienced many of the same forces as did the nations at war.

An Era of Widened Cooperation, 1918–1939

Scandinavia relaxed in November 1918 and settled down to
work on a philosophy of "*as if* we shall be left in peace." Serious
soul-searching preceded the decisions to join the League of Nations. Independent neutrality had been strengthened by regional
cooperation from 1914 to 1918 and had kept the North out of
battle. Why should these peoples, who had no aggressive ambitions, get involved in the sanctions system of the League? The
Covenant appeared to outlaw neutrality, and when a Dane asked
about it Lord Robert Cecil replied that a member of the League
had three obligations: (1) to stop commercial relations with a state
breaking the peace; (2) to authorize passage of League forces
across its territory; (3) to participate in military and naval action.

The Danes and the Swiss agreed that a neutral could break
commercial relations but that it could not take the other steps.
The League insisted that all must be prepared to defend the right
and quell the wrong. The Scandinavians remained skeptical, and
they debated anxiously the whole problem of their international
position. The Norwegian Labor Party voted *no* because of its distrust of great power idealism. In the end the Scandinavians all
joined the League, but they considered that they were abandon-

ing neutrality in doing so. Once in, they acted energetically and intelligently.

One of the little known but significant chapters of League success was the Åland Islands agreement. The islands between Sweden and Finland had been settled by Swedes and had remained Swedish in culture and speech. In 1809 Russia had included them in her annexation of Finland. When Finland gained her independence at the end of World War I the Ålands thus legally became a part of Finland. The Swedes hoped, however, that the principle of self-determination might be applied there as in Slesvig and other areas which were changing hands. Ninety-five percent of the people of Åland voted for reunion with Sweden. The League Council heard the question debated, and its *rapporteurs* then took the legalistic position that Finnish sovereignty was incontestable. The decision involved a closely related people eager to join Sweden, and it also involved a vital security problem for Sweden, for the islands are a perfect base for attack against Stockholm by sea or air. Nevertheless Sweden accepted the situation with good grace, and by doing so did her part toward strengthening international law and the authority of the League in its infant years.

These small states were often useful in avoiding open clashes in the League between the great powers. At one time the British opposed a French proposal in the Council but dared not say so because of public opinion on the issue. The British delegation wired home for instructions, and received the cryptic reply: "Britain expects every Swede to do his duty." The Swede blocked the proposal and Britain was saved from taking a public stand.

The jealousies of the great powers, the absence of the United States, and the shortsightedness of weak statesmen, however, soon made the League a feeble instrument. No one could find a formula for disarmament; Britain and Germany went off by themselves in a naval agreement of 1935; and the League could only issue a report on the Japanese invasion of Manchuria. The Scandinavians became irritated at the failure to apply effective sanctions in the Ethiopian affair. In July 1936 they joined with the Netherlands, Switzerland, and Spain in a note claiming the right to determine for themselves when and how to apply sanctions, a right which the great powers were in practice exercising.

Self-interest as well as idealism led the Scandinavians toward international collaboration. Yet the collaboration must include the great powers as well as the small, to be useful or acceptable. As a Frenchman said at the time, European statesmen could depend on the North if the continental states did not cause the northerners to despair of the power and the principles of their southern neighbors. But despair was growing, and with it a renewed tendency to look inward.

"Our frontier is within our boundaries, not at the borderlines," a Swedish scholar-statesman wrote for an American audience. He went farther and claimed, most modestly, that the Scandinavian nations were simply uninteresting in the realm of foreign relations. This smug boast reminds one of Benjamin Franklin's comment that there could not be a really modest man, for if there were such a one he would be proud of his modesty.

In 1938 and 1939 the Scandinavians felt anxious but also superior and self-satisfied, and it was in this frame of mind that they proceeded in 1938, in the months between January and July, to withdraw completely from the sanctions system. Chamberlain admitted that the League could not offer collective security, and that Britain should not lead the small states to think they were protected. The result was a formal joint declaration in July 1938 by the seven states of the Oslo Group: "The system of sanctions under the present conditions and by the practice of recent years, has acquired a non-obligatory character." The Scandinavian states, disappointed in the League, were going to go their own way, but characteristically they thought they should tell the world so in legal fashion.

In 1938, with the powers flexing their steel muscles, and with a German geographer studying the Åland Islands, Finland and Sweden grew nervous. They proposed joint fortification of these islands, demilitarized since 1856. Although the ten signatories of the Åland Agreement were in sympathy, Russia objected and the plan fell through.

The temperature of diplomacy continued to rise; the Nazis "Anschlussed" Austria and absorbed Czechoslovakia. It began to look as if Munich might not bring "peace in our time." President Roosevelt in the spring of 1939 asked if Germany's other neighbors were safe, and Hitler replied with a direct question to each:

Did it feel threatened? Each quivered and replied "Of course not." When Hitler offered to each a nonaggression pact Denmark felt it impossible to refuse. Finland had a pact of friendship since 1932 with Russia and begged off. Sweden discussed the question with Germany and avoided entanglement. Norway said no as politely as she could.

None of the Scandinavian states in 1939 had any military commitments nor any military security. The League was powerless, neutrality had been compromised, and armaments were not impressive. Finland had a vigorous military tradition and a sense of danger; she had her forests and she had her Mannerheim Line of fortifications and an intense nationalistic spirit, but less than four million people. Sweden had excellent munitions factories. Norway had the natural fortifications of her fjords. Denmark had nothing; Prime Minister Stauning had said that Denmark should put all her funds into social welfare and hope for peace. Iceland was all but forgotten.

Was there a common line of action among these states allied by geography and culture? In 1927 they had signed a series of mutual arbitration pacts among themselves. In 1930 Denmark, Norway, and Sweden had joined with Belgium, the Netherlands, and Luxemburg in the Oslo Group. In 1932 Finland was added to the society. These small and democratic states of western Europe attempted to combat depression and increase their mutual trade by a mild form of tariff cooperation. But the British saw visions of a powerful bloc which might destroy Britain's trade advantages, and claimed the agreement was contrary to the "most-favored-nation" clauses in treaties. The Oslo Group was frightened and weakened before it accomplished anything significant, although it held meetings of the Group as late as 1938.

Closer cooperation was attained by Denmark, Finland, Norway, and Sweden, whose foreign ministers met repeatedly in the years of the League and the "long Armistice." By cooperation they kept one member regularly on the Council of the League. At one of the foreign ministers' conclaves in April 1938 it was unanimously agreed that the Scandinavian states should stand outside all power combinations, refuse to be drawn into war, and aid each other economically. The Finnish foreign minister, Eljas Erkko, expressed the sentiments of all when he said that no one could convince the Nordics that in the name of peace they could be drawn into the schemes of the great powers to any advantage to the world or themselves.

All five Northern states signed (May 1938) a set of neutrality rules, bringing up to date the regulations agreed upon in 1912. The one new item was a prohibition of military plane flights over the air territory of the northern countries. There were no regulations on transport or export of war material. This pact, like most of the other agreements, indicated independence in passive neutrality rather than any common positive action.

Estonia, Latvia, and Lithuania had sought a general Baltic military pact, but their neighbors held aloof. Finland was eager for an agreement with Sweden, but the nearest to realization reached in this combination was the abortive plan for joint fortification of the Åland Islands. Discussions among the foreign ministers doubtless touched on the possibilities of Scandinavian action in common, but the inequalities in armament, the differences in geographical position, and the failure to envision future dangers were factors too strong to overcome.

The history of neutrality in the North is the story of the more or less innocent bystanders attempting to protect their own interests. They tried by neutrality to avoid the horrors of war and to make what profits they could out of the needs of the belligerents. Consistency in neutrality policy they never attained. The very concept is negative and the practice must be opportunistic. The neutrals refuse to take part, the participants shape events.

World War II: Scandinavia Rent Asunder

Neutrality had worked fairly well from 1814 on into the twentieth century. Its success convinced the Scandinavians that with self-restraint, careful attention to one's own business, and a gentle firmness about justice peace could be maintained. If a state threatened no one why need it worry that another would threaten it? Or had the North simply been playing in luck? Munich, the fall pogroms of 1938, and the taking-over of Czechoslovakia raised doubts. Was the rest of the world headed for war again? However, the May 1939 meeting of the Scandinavian foreign ministers in Stockholm only reiterated the old determination to remain neutral and to have nothing to do with power groups.

Finland the First Victim

The Finns had few illusions about their fellowmen, and their only illusion about themselves was that 4,000,000 Finns could dare stand up against 180,000,000 Russians. When Germany concluded an agreement with the Soviet state in August 1939 and the panzers and the planes swept over Poland in September, the Finns knew that danger was imminent; they and all the Northerners quickly declared neutrality.

Estonia, Latvia, and Lithuania were powerless to resist, and by the summer of 1939 they were absorbed as republics of the USSR. On October 5, 1939, while discussions were proceeding with the neighboring states, the Russians approached the Finns, suggesting negotiations which would yield military and naval bases to the Soviet Union in return for cession to Finland of forest land in Karelia. A few Finns thought the country should make the best out of obvious necessity. Foreign Minister Eljas Erkko, however, pointed to the fate of Estonia and her sister states and said that it was suicide to begin making concessions. The Finnish people were in overwhelming agreement.

On October 12 a combined Danish-Norwegian-Swedish statement in Moscow affirmed that "a blow against Finland is a blow against the North." On October 18 the president of Finland, the kings of Denmark, Norway, and Sweden and their ministers met in Stockholm, and popular reaction showed strong inter-Nordic feeling. Yet no government was ready to ally itself with Finland. Humanitarian aid and supplies were promised, but no military support. The Finns nevertheless stood upon their rights. On November 30 the Russian bear lumbered into action, and the Finnish tiger counterattacked in full fury.

The story of the Scandinavian neutrals in World War II went like the children's game of "The Ten Little Indians." Down went one, and then there were nine . . . until all were gone. The game of "The Little Neutrals" began with five and ended with one. Finland was first.

Denmark and Norway declared their neutrality in the Russo-Finnish conflict; Sweden, with closer ties of geography and sentiment and a vitally direct strategic concern, carefully did not declare neutrality and pointed this out in a note to Russia. The

Swedish, Danish, and Norwegian foreign ministers met in Oslo on December 7 and strongly supported Finland's appeal to the League of Nations. The League took its boldest step and its last and excluded the Soviet Union from membership. But this did not stop the Red armies. When the Assembly suggested the application of sanctions, it was Sweden's Östen Undén who spoke for the three northern countries, expressing the shock and the sympathy of the peoples, but refusing to take a stand on the proposal. Sweden was both profoundly worried and supremely cautious.

"Finland's affair is ours" became the slogan of the day in Sweden, and among the masses of the people there was a surge of anti-Russian feeling. Over $100,000,000 in gifts and loans from government and people were sent to Finland, 84,000 rifles and 50,000,000 rounds of ammunition, 300 cannon and 300,000 cannon-shells (all the heavy artillery came from Sweden), 25 airplanes, and quantities of clothing and other goods. Over 8,000 Swedish volunteers were enrolled.

The Swedish government stood firm in its well-studied position. When the Russians protested Swedish partisanship the government replied without mincing words: There is strong pro-Finnish sentiment in Sweden and a free press; volunteers are recruited privately, in accordance with international custom, commerce is continuing freely; and the Swedish government sees no reason for complaint; Sweden, like the Soviet Union, wishes to avoid all complications. The government was just as firm with its own people. The king declared it was with sorrow in his heart that he judged that Sweden must not go militarily with Finland. In such a case, he said, Sweden would almost certainly find herself involved in the general war, and then could do still less for Finland's sake.

Finland fought like a nation of heroes. The concrete pillboxes of the Mannerheim Line held at bay the southern attack from Leningrad; the "Molotov breadbasket" bombs did not frighten Helsinki; and the Finnish armies made steady progress on the central front. The organized women's corps, the Lottas, helped at the front and behind the lines. The nation was united as in the days of storied Ensign Stål against the threat from the East. Many Finns were communists, and people faced a decision; which were they *first*, Finns or communists? The answer was the answer of Finnish patriots. Otto Kuusinen, a Finnish communist emigré, was set up as president of a communist republic. His followers were a pitiful handful. If the Russians really expected Finland to crack from within they got the surprise of their lives.

Through weeks of bitter cold, filled with stories that remind an American of the tales of Valley Forge, the Finns more than held their own. Russian losses were tremendous. When the men in Moscow decided they could no longer leave the fighting to the troops of their northern army, they sent to Finland their best in men and planes and guns. They rocked the Mannerheim forts on their foundations, they drove with overpowering mass and limitless reserves against the thin Finnish lines. The Finns had neither men nor women left to stem the tide. Four million was not enough against 180,000,000.

Finland's resistance aroused worldwide sympathy, but effective aid was difficult to send. The nazis and the communists were hand in glove; Germany controlled the southern Baltic and Russia reached north to the Polar Sea. The only route by which troops and supplies could reach Finland was across Norway and Sweden. Britain and France were eager to send such forces, but Norway and Sweden refused passage. They feared the aid would be insufficient, and they knew that if they granted such a privilege they would find their lands a theater of war. Britain and France hesitated to demand free transit of troops unless Finland herself would issue a clear and public request for it. By March of 1940 Finnish defenses were breaking before the newly massed strength of Russia and unless aid could come quickly and in great force the agony would only be prolonged. Finnish military and statesmen could see no hope, and on March 12 Finland signed a treaty with Russia. Norway and Sweden did not have to make the difficult decision with which France and Britain would have confronted them. But Finland, for the moment, was lost.

For Scandinavia as a whole the tragedy of World War II was in her wealth of iron ore and in her geographic position, the same geographic position which had given her security once, but whose significance had changed with the changing technology of war. Germany needed the iron ore of Sweden which came out through Narvik and down the protected Norwegian coast. Britain needed to stop that traffic. Germany needed northern bases from which her submarines might attack British shipping. Britain needed to prevent Germany from getting them. And any of the Scandinavian countries could provide useful air bases for a flank attack on either Germany or Britain—good for each to have, and good for each to prevent the other from having. Scandinavia was in the maelstrom of the new geopolitik.

Norway Fights

The Norwegians knew the facts as well as anyone, but they deluded themselves in their own moral innocence. "It can't happen here." The army was a token force. The navy, with 2100 miles of coast to defend, consisted of fifty-seven obsolete craft and a few antiquated coastal fortifications. The Labor party (social democratic) had long preached pacifism, and it had been the governing party since 1935. Prime Minister Nygaardsvold and a few others saw the danger. But the military were hesitant in drawing up plans and requests. Behind the somnolent military was a somnolent Storting and a somnolent people.

Norway was nonetheless in the arena of conflict. In the fall of 1939 Norwegian shipowners contracted to put 2,000,000 tons of shipping at the service of the British. During the winter fifty-four Norwegian ships were sunk and 377 sailors killed. Most ominous for the country's future were the geographic factors that enticed the Germans to run ore ships and captured vessels down the channel inside the island shield. One was the American *City of Flint*. More notorious was the German transport *Altmark* with its 299 British prisoners, which the British came in and captured (February 16, 1940). The British would not tolerate the ore traffic and other German violations of Norwegian neutrality and therefore decided it was necessary that they themselves violate that neutrality by mining the offending route. Foreign Minister Halvdan Koht was drawing up a protest against this British action when the Germans made their strike during the night of April 8–9, 1940.

German landings, carefully prepared, came almost simultaneously at Kristiansand, Stavanger, Bergen, Trondheim, and far north in Narvik. Airfields were overwhelmed. Norwegian defenses inflicted surprising damage—the fortress of Oskarsborg sank the huge cruiser *Blücher* and another ship coming up Oslofjord; an old mine layer with the proud name *Olav Tryggvason* sank a transport and a destroyer. But the nazi might was overpowering. By early afternoon of April 9 German army personnel were in the streets of Oslo and airborne troops had dropped into Oslo's airport, Fornebu.

At 4 o'clock that morning the German minister, himself taken by surprise, had handed Foreign Minister Koht a nineteen-page ultimatum. The Germans demanded surrender, control of transportation and communication, cooperation of Norwegian troops, and a diplomatic break with the allied powers. Without a dissenting voice the government rejected the ultimatum. King and government took a special train at 9:30 A.M. for Hamar, and there the Storting gathered that same afternoon. The sacrificial resistance of Oskarsborg and the ships in Oslo Fjord had given the government time to think and act. The German plan to capture the king and all his men had failed.

The people of Oslo were stunned. Gradually a deep and abiding anger hardened in their minds. Young men from the captured towns put on knapsacks and escaped over the hiking trails to the mountains, still deep in snow. They formed themselves into companies and battalions and were at least partially welded into a fighting force by General Otto Ruge.

Was there treachery? Some, as at Narvik, where Colonel Konrad Sundlo, friend of Quisling, gave over the city to the invaders. Knut Hamsun, one of the great novelists, spoke for the nazis throughout the war. There was Major Vidkun Quisling himself, former assistant to Nansen in Russia, once minister of war in Norway, but since 1933 out of office. In 1940 he was a political leader without a single party representative in the Storting. His *Nasjonal Samling* was a party strictly on the nazi model, and it did not appeal to the democratic Norwegians. Quisling was a sincere but disgruntled man. He had converted himself to the principles of Mussolini and Hitler. He too was surprised at the timing of the invasion, but he stood ready, as he claimed, to save Norway from a bloodbath. When the king refused to appoint him prime minister he declared himself the head of state. Hitler, when his ultimatum was rejected, backed Quisling. But the people refused to accept him, the overwhelming majority identifying themselves with the king and the government fleeing through the woods.

The German forces drove the king and his party from Hamar

to Elverum; on to Nybergsund where they tried by bombing and machine gunning to destroy king, crown prince, and ministers; to Molde which was burned and from which the government sailed with a British ship to Tromsö, hoping to hold the northern section of the country. Around Narvik fighting was intense, heroic Norwegians aided by British sea and air squadrons, French Alpine chasseurs and Polish mountain troops. But soon after they recaptured Narvik (May 28) and seemed to be in control of northern Norway, the disasters in France and the Low Countries demanded every man that Britain and France could muster. Norway had to be abandoned.

Fortunately plans had already been made. The ministry was broadened by the addition of other party representatives, and the conservative C. J. Hambro became a leading figure. The government was voted full powers to act as was necessary for the good of the country and to transfer its seat out of the country in case of emergency. Everything was legal. The Supreme Court had been given no orders on that hectic morning of April 9, and under the wise guidance of Paal Berg, chief justice, it stayed in Oslo and became a potent factor on the home front.

On June 7 the king and his entourage sailed for London, and on June 9 announced that organized opposition had ceased but that the fight would be continued from abroad. Though small and unprepared, Norway had held out longer than any of the continental states against blitzkrieg, sixty-three days (Poland had lasted twenty-nine days, France thirty-nine, Belgium nineteen, Holland four).

The Norwegian Nation Underground

The Norwegian government in London proceeded throughout the war to govern Norwegian seamen and fleet, to radio news and directions and inspiration to the population at home, and to plan for the day of return. The gold reserve was saved and the Bank of Norway did business in London. The free fleet of over 4,000,000 tons carried 40 percent of the oil cargoes of the allies to theaters of action around the planet. Half of that fleet and 3000 sailors were lost, but it had been more useful than an army. Not a single ship free on April 9 turned back to the German quays. The shipping companies pooled their activities in an organization called

Nortraship, with headquarters in New York. Their fees and taxes paid the expenses of the entire government and left a surplus for use in the liberation. Insurance provided much of the means for rebuilding.

Some air force personnel escaped to England and after a few months went on to Canada. There, to Camp Little Norway, flocked scores of eager boys from Norway. They escaped in small boats to the shores of Scotland or through the woods to Sweden, then across Russia or out by plane to England. They returned to pilot bombers over Germany. By the spring of 1944 a Norwegian unit of the RAF had established the highest record for effectiveness and safety. The British government cooperated wholeheartedly with this active government-in-exile and helped it to build a new navy. Britain allowed Norwegian courts to function and gave them the use of British jails. The Norwegian king and ministers were honored guests.

Meantime even the Norwegians realized that some form of government must be set up at home. Their aim was to make that government merely an administrative structure which would not give moral or practical advantages to the invaders. The proper formulas were difficult to find. In the early days of the conquest, even while the king was still in the country, the Supreme Court had taken responsibility for appointing an Administrative Council (April 15). Quisling's "prime-ministership" had been abolished that day by the Germans. It had backfired against the nazis because of the popular reaction against Quisling. On April 24 Josef Terboven became Reichskommissar, and Norway was governed as a conquered province. Nevertheless the Norwegian people were honored Nordics, and the Germans wanted desperately to align them with nazism. When the Storting refused to grant legal powers to the nazis, Terboven proclaimed that political parties were dissolved and that the royal family was "no longer of significance." In the Act of State of February 1, 1942, Quisling was again brought forward and made minister-president to form a national government. But this move too failed to win friends.

The Norwegians were slowly discovering, as did the Danes later, the political potential in voluntary social organizations. On August 24, 1940, the leaders of the political parties, and of the large organizations of employers, laborers, and producers, agreed to sink all party and occupational differences and to work together for the interests of Norway. In October the small church organizations joined with the state church in the Christian Council for Joint Deliberation, nucleus of an increasingly effective protest group. In November the sportsmen refused to be organized under nazi leadership and during that winter only 4 out of 3000 athletic teams participated in contests. About 90 percent of the schoolteachers refused to be nazi-organized. Only two out of ninety professors at the university were nazi. Some farm leaders joined the nazi organization, but neither farmers nor fishers would be nazi-organized.

The church at last came out, in February 1941, with a pastoral letter which in ringing tones denounced the lawlessness and brutality of the Hird, the Norwegian counterpart of the nazi brownshirts, and attacked the nazi invasion of Christian rights. A year later, after Quisling had become minister-president, the nazi government became more repressive. When people were stopped from entering Trondheim cathedral for service the bishops of Norway resigned, and on Easter Sunday practically all the clergy did so. But they kept on with their work, if not arrested, and were supported by the people. In February 1942, 12,000 of 14,000 teachers refused to obey orders to nazify the children; 1,300 were arrested, and more than half of those were sent to work with Russian prisoners in labor camps at Kirkenes.

Violence had been tried before without success. In September 1941 a strike of workers gave the nazis the opportunity to arrest and execute two popular labor leaders, though both had opposed the strike. Through 1942 the noose was pulled tighter. In September Quisling attempted to establish his long-cherished corporative state, but the answer of the people was mass resignation from the nazified trade unions, and the Germans forced Quisling to give up the scheme. The next step was a roundup of the Jews; of the 1500 in Norway about 800 were captured and sent to camps in Germany. Thirteen returned. In November 1943 the Germans took action against the recalcitrant students of the university. Some 650 students were transported to Germany to have "right ideas" forced into their heads. An international roar of protest went up from many lands, including Finland and Sweden, and the king of Sweden sent Hitler a strong personal note.

The Germans were driven to desperation by the unexpected strength of opposition. Even Quisling's handful of young men gradually diminished. Month after month more became "rowers," men who rowed away from the sinking ship. Probably never more than 2 percent of the population had associated themselves actively with the quislings, but some 20,000 of these were dealt with severely after the war.

The regular press was taken over by the authorities and published the German handouts. One of the attempts to win friends and influence people was to publish each day the picture of a quisling with a statement, "Why I am a member of *Nasjonal Samling*." People ceased to read this nazified news or go to the nazi movies. Underground newspapers appeared, ultimately about 230 with a combined circulation of 250,000–300,000, spreading the news by courier and by chain-letter methods. Radios were confiscated in September 1941, but boys and technicians constructed new sets, sending as well as receiving. The contact with England was never lost. Repression bred resistance and forged stronger the nationalistic communal bond. Every office and factory had at least one active worker. Word of decisions and activities could be passed on quickly through trade organizations, church societies, and schools. Food was collected for the needy, passports forged, bridges blown up. When the nazis wanted forced labor from the classes of boys born in 1921, 1922, and 1923, the population objected and cooperated in evasion. Birth certificates were lost or changed, offices with records were burned, and the nazis got only 300 of the 80,000 eligible.

Through it all the Norwegians, "the world's most serious people," kept a soul-saving sense of humor. They loved to pass on little jokes like the one about the twelve-year-old boy and the Viking ships. It was September 1940 when German planes were failing in their attempt to bomb England into submission. Across from Oslo some German soldiers were looking at the Viking ships in the Bygdø Museum. As they exclaimed "*Wunderbar, wunderschön,*" the boy came up and said, "You like our old ships, do you?" The Germans outdid themselves in admiration. The boy cocked his head on one side and remarked, "Yes, those are the boats our ancestors used when they went over and conquered England every year."

Often the Germans caught a saboteur or a suspect, and they filled Norwegian concentration camps like the notorious Grini and sent hundreds to Germany. When they caught up with Lauritz Sand, leader of the Norwegian counterespionage, they tortured him for weeks, and broke twenty bones. But Mr. Sand gave no information. The Norwegians are a stubborn people.

High in the fjelds at Rjukan was the "heavy water" plant, and the Germans needed the heavy water for their work in atomic fission. A band of young Norwegians was carefully trained and equipped in England. They succeeded in blowing up the plant and then hid out in the fjelds to the end of the war. Again and again saboteurs destroyed trains or tracks, and they kept the British fully informed about German building and movement in Norway.

The Home Front had no courts, no army, no stately buildings. It had power because of the national will. Its leaders rose through natural selection, no formal election. Not only Chief Justice Paal Berg but the postwar prime minister, Einar Gerhardsen, was an active leader, as was many another official. Confinement in a concentration camp became an honor, an important item in a man's record in *Who's Who*.

The most tragic chapter was written in the snows of the north. Soviet forces came in from Petsamo and took Kirkenes on October 25, 1944, and a Norwegian force soon joined them. Together they drove the Germans back slowly. But as the Germans left they carried out a thorough scorched-earth policy, slaughtering livestock, destroying bridges, burning buildings, and leaving the people to freeze to death in the Arctic winter. That bitter memory has not been effaced.

Threats of a similar devastation of all Norway were not carried through. On the eve of the nazi collapse in Germany a secret army of 40,000 men had been built by the Norwegians and at the end the German forces surrendered to this authority. May 5, 1945, was a great day and greater still was June 7. Exactly five years from the day the king and the government departed from Tromsö, Haakon VII and the government of Norway steamed up Oslo Fjord. Norway was once more free.

The people had earned the tribute penned by the poet Arnulf Överland, that although they "owned no ready sword" they fought like heroes against tanks, machines, and planes, they fought until they fell, for a broken will would leave only a "life without meaning."

Denmark Bows to Fate

Denmark remembered her disillusionment of 1864 and understood her weakness. Thorvald Stauning, the social democratic prime minister, declared in 1937 that Denmark would not be the watchdog of Scandinavia. With mighty Germany at her doorstep what was the use of fighting? When Germany requested a ten-year nonaggression pact in 1939 Denmark signed; it lasted ten months. Danes detested nazism and feared German power, yet they could put no faith in their own strength or their geography or their neighbors. They lived virtually without an army and without a foreign policy, hoping that luck would be with them.

Warnings had been coming for weeks prior to the invasion of April 9, 1940, and columns of troops were reported near the border on April 8. The German minister dissuaded the Danish foreign minister from requesting mobilization; it would be a disastrous affront to a friendly neighbor. At four o'clock the next morning he was presenting the German ultimatum and the attack had already begun. Denmark had 14,000 troops under arms that day. Border guards fought bravely but briefly against an armored division and 80,000 men. German soldiers crawled out of "coal boats" that had been lying in Copenhagen harbor; bombers flew over the city. The Germans came to "protect Denmark from the British," but threatened if opposed to level Copenhagen like Warsaw. Resistance was suicide, and at 6:30 A.M. the king ordered that it cease.

The Germans did at first act with forbearance. They wanted Denmark to be a "model protectorate." The Danes could eat well if the Germans could have the surplus, and Danes probably ate better than any other Europeans throughout the war. Stauning and a few others urged the Danes to adapt themselves. An emergency government of the four major parties was established. As foreign minister Erik Scavenius, a repeat from World War I, came in to guide adjustments. He was neither pro- nor anti-nazi; he was a realist. After the war he wrote a well-reasoned defense of the politics of the possible (*Forhandlings Politik*), as good a defense as can be made of the need to live to fight another day. Owing to his skillful handling and to restraint by the Germans major conflict was avoided for many months. It was a test of how things might be done differently than in Norway. But tension was strong from the beginning.

Out-and-out nazi sympathizers of course existed—racialists, ambitious opportunists, adventurers, German-born. Some were of the German minority in North Slesvig. But all together a dozen personal cliques could never amass as much as 3 percent of the popular vote.

King Christian X had ordered resistance to cease, but he was no compromiser. He personified the pride and the shame of Denmark, and was beloved by his people as the incarnation of their feelings. One story was that when the Germans demanded that the Danish flag be taken down from a building the king refused. The Germans said, "We will then remove it ourselves." The King: "If you do I shall send a soldier to put it up again." The German: "If you send a soldier we will shoot him." Christian X replied calmly, "I will be the soldier." The flag continued to fly. And the king continued his daily horseback ride in the streets of Copenhagen until injured by a fall in 1942.

J. Christmas Møller was one of the dynamic conservative leaders who joined the coalition government but soon withdrew to tour the country and inspire opposition. He and Frode Jacobsen organized "The Ring" of young people to spread information and prepare for the time when action would be feasible. In the spring of 1942 Møller escaped to England and there became the central figure in the Free Denmark movement abroad.

In Washington Denmark was fortunate in having one of her ablest diplomats, Henrik de Kauffmann. He it was who on April 9, 1941, signed with Secretary Hull the agreement which placed Greenland under the wartime protection of the United States. He was immediately dismissed under German pressure, but he calmly continued to represent Danish interests and had to wait only until May 1945 to see this agreement and his whole policy ratified by the Danish Rigsdag. Others of the Danish foreign representatives gradually followed Kauffmann's example. It was the old and permanent Denmark which was represented in the free countries of the world.

The Danes were not as amazed at the German attack as were the Norwegians, hence not as bitter in their disillusionment. For them the disillusionment had come in 1864 and the wound in the heart was partially calloused. The first months of occupation were not too difficult. Danish contempt and hatred of the Germans was shown by the cold-shoulder policy: Danes simply did not see the Germans on the streets, ignored them. The Germans acted correctly and tried to smile. They would force these stubborn Nordic brethren to be friends. Some of the Germans, boys who had been given happy vacations in previous days of Danish hospitality and adopted into Danish families, felt disillusioned when they found that their nazi leaders had lied to them and that they had invaded the country of people whom they loved. Others played happily the role of "protector."

German requisitions on Denmark amounted to little in 1940 and prices were good. Some 340,000 pigs were sent to Germany, 15 percent of the whole stock. As the war continued, the German need of supplies from Denmark increased. But fertilizers could not be obtained nor sufficient fodder, hence the land was despoiled and livestock was slaughtered too fast. Industries, especially shipyards, were put to work on German orders. The Germans promised to send coal and other materials in exchange, but at the end of the war German deliveries were far behind and the cost was left to Denmark.

The Danish people had thought it necessary to yield, but they were chagrined as they saw their Norwegian cousins fighting and their British customers and friends enduring the devastation of bombs. Abroad a Danish Council was set up in London in September 1940 to coordinate the work of 3000 Danish sailors serving the Allies; 40 percent of the merchant fleet escaped German control. Christmas Møller roused hope at home. An underground press managed to give to the people forbidden news from beyond the curtain of censorship. As fast as one paper was suppressed others jumped into print or mimeograph. Party differences had been subordinated to the national interest and a Committee of Nine organized to represent the diverse elements in an extralegal body.

In January 1941 the Germans asked the king to appoint a government of other parties omitting the social democrats. This he refused to do, for the exclusion of the largest party would violate the constitution. Then in June came Hitler's attack on Russia and the demand for a supporting Danish "free corps." Recruitment attracted a fraction of youth into the Schalburg Corps. This special guard incorporated criminal elements and became a curse on the domestic front.

The entrance of the United States into the war, despite the early disasters in the Pacific, gave new hope to the Danish opposition. The death of Stauning on May 3, 1942, did not change the official government attitude. When Wilhelm Buhl, minister of finance, became premier he expressed appreciation of German behavior and urged cooperation. Yet dissatisfaction increased and sabotage gained momentum. The Russians continued to "reject the inevitable," the British counterattacked at El Alamein, the Americans and the British landed in North Africa. At the end of October 1942 Scavenius was called to Berlin and told to set up a government friendly to the Germans. For this he could not gain cooperation of the parties and ended by picking a government of his own, with himself as both premier and foreign minister.

Authority was in the hands of Werner Best, Hitler's diplomatic representative, and General von Hanneken, military commander. Yet neither the conciliation policy of Best nor the brutality policy of von Hanneken converted the Danes. An election for the Folketing in the spring of 1943 was exploited by the Danes to show themselves and the world where they stood. Ninety percent voted, and 95 percent of these voted for democracy. An out-and-out resistance party, Dansk Samling, won three seats. Definitely nazi tickets won only 2 percent of the votes. The Danes lifted their heads with new faith in each other.

During the summer of 1943 the nervous nazis tried to guard against the rising tempo of sabotage, and the more they did so the more obstinate became the Danes. Explosions and strikes broke out everywhere. At Odense shipyards workers struck against the German guards on a ship under construction and the owners sided with the workers and paid their wages during the strike. Reprisals merely incensed the population the more. At last, both hope and patience gone, the Germans discarded the idea of the "model protectorate" and took over with a proclamation of martial law, Sunday morning, August 29, 1943. Hundreds of underground workers and suspects were arrested, many of them prominent business and professional men and women. The navy went down with éclat. Orders were issued to escape with the ships to Sweden if possible, otherwise to scuttle. A few escaped, a few fell into German hands, most were scuttled.

Scavenius could not get together a new government, and the king refused to appoint a ministry that lacked the approval of the Rigsdag. From August 29 the country was governed by the German military and Danish officials merely maintained the administration. Martial law continued to October 6.

What had gone wrong? Why had the model protectorate refused to cooperate with the German protector? It must be the Jews! said the Germans. In Denmark there were but 6–7,000 Jews and there had never been a "problem." But now the Germans were applying the heel and in the night of October 1–2 the entire Jewish population was to be rounded up. Word leaked out in advance, and by bicycle and car, by boat and raft and swimming, some 6,000 of the intended victims were spirited to Swedish boats and over to the Swedish shore. The nazis bagged only 600, most of whom died in Buchenwald. The king protested in vain, and the people intensified their efforts to destroy German production and transportation. The nazis in turn increased violence and allowed the Schalburg Corps to run wild. Kaj Munk, minister and poet of international note, was assassinated, as were many others.

By June of 1944 the Germans were attempting to control sabotage with a curfew from 8 P.M. to 5 A.M. One afternoon thousands of workers at the Burmeister and Wain shipyards just went home, writing an official explanation that they were not on strike but that if they could not work in their gardens in the evenings they would do so by day. The Allied landing in Normandy had raised fresh hope. The Germans shut off Copenhagen's supply of gas and electricity and cut off food supplies.

When the "strike" began the Freedom Council took over. This Freedom Council grew out of the success of democratic cooperation in the elections of 1943 and was already a strong centralizing power in the August days. Basically it rested upon one-man representation from each of the four big resistance organizations: The Ring, the youth organization already mentioned; *Frit Danmark* (Free Denmark), a newspaper organization widespread through towns and parties in the whole country; Denmark's Communist party; and the Christian political and activist *Dansk Samling* (Danish Union). After the government was shelved on August 29, 1943, the Council grew into a voluntary, extralegal government of the Danish people.

Hence it was that the Freedom Council took up the spontaneous movement of June 1944 and laid down demands to the Germans: curfew must be abolished, the Schalburg Corps suppressed, public services restored, and no reprisals. After five days of chaos the nazis had to yield to the unanswerable unanimity of the nation. From this time on the position of the nazis weakened steadily in France, in Russia, at home in Germany, and in Denmark. Sabotage increased and the number of underground newspapers rose like an inflationary curve. The Danish police were set aside by the nazis in September and 1900 of them were transported to concentration camps. The Danes kept order by self-restraint.

Sabotage was planned to delay production and to stop transport, yet to do little permanent damage. Key pieces of machinery broke or disappeared to halt the work of a whole factory; a section of railroad was removed, or a single car of soldiers dynamited. One detachment passing from Norway to the western front was delayed a week in transit through Jutland. Forty or more single acts of railway sabotage might occur in one night. The Danes counted up 2156 acts of sabotage against railways and 2548 major acts against factories. No conceivable force could keep track of it. Regular connections were maintained with England and with Sweden, and parachutists landed nightly with orders and equipment. Denmark had become a peaceful battlefield.

The Danes were late in awakening. Their pacifist policies of the 1930s and earlier had deprived them of the means of self-defense. Only gradually did the people as a whole come to understand that other countries were suffering for a common cause, including theirs, and that they had a duty to do at least something for themselves. Their cold stares at the Germans and their sabotage of trains built no major road blocks against the nazi war machine, but by the later part of the war there was nothing more they could do. At the end they did what they could. When the Germans collapsed in May of 1945, and the British troops entered

Denmark, the Danes felt that they too had played a part in the liberation.

Iceland Occupied

When Denmark fell under the shadow of the nazi bombers on April 9, 1940, her distant possessions were left to themselves. The Faroe Islands were taken under British protection and provisioning.

Since 1918 Iceland had been autonomous, united with Denmark through the king and the foreign ministry. On April 10, 1940, the Althing met and gave over the royal power to the government of Iceland. Sveinn Björnsson was made regent, and Iceland was prepared to go alone. But the country had no army and no navy, and lay in an exposed and strategically important position. As the Germans extended control over western Norway the British worried increasingly that they might establish another flanking position against Britain in Iceland. For once the British acted first. On May 10, 1940, a British naval force landed troops and took over the protection of the country, promising to respect Icelandic independence and to see it restored at the conclusion of hostilities.

Iceland was as much in the American sphere as in the European, and when Russia was plunged into war in June 1941 the north Atlantic island took on new significance as a station on the supply route from North America to Murmansk and Archangel. Hence, on July 8, 1941, by previous arrangement with the British and the government of Iceland, American forces landed to take over defense responsibilities.

No more than Denmark did Iceland wish to be occupied, but the people realized that they faced only two alternatives. They did not want or invite either the British or the Americans, yet they felt that if they had to be occupied by Germans or by Anglo-Saxons they had been granted the lesser of the two evils. Forty-five thousand foreign soldiers in a country of 125,000 people created inevitable social problems and some unfortunate incidents occurred. They were, however, individual incidents and there was neither general opposition nor sabotage but, rather, friendly cooperation and a number of marriages. The occupation was as friendly as an occupation could be.

The Keflavik airfield was made into a base for transatlantic planes and the harbor of Reykjavik became a lively center of trade. Iceland's fish were paid for by the Americans and sent to Britain on lend-lease, and supplies which had come from Denmark and England now came from the United States. Prices rose and Iceland prospered. There were incidents of submarine activity offshore, the sinking of a few Icelandic ships, an occasional nazi plane—but Iceland essentially felt the war indirectly rather than directly, and through an artificial prosperity and inflation rather than through destruction.

Sweden Steering between the Rocks

"Each of our countries in full agreement with the others should follow the tried policy of impartial neutrality to which all the Northern States have declared their allegiance . . . the peoples of the North are imbued with a common desire to live in peace with all others. They are also inspired by a common determination to live as free nations." These are the words of King Gustav V, on October 19, 1939.

Sweden, last of the Northern neutrals, had the will, the skill, and the luck to stay neutral. How could it be done, and what did it mean?

In Finland's Winter War of 1939–40 the Swedes did not pretend to be neutral but did what they could for their neighbor short of fighting. When that war was over Finland asked Sweden and Norway for a defensive alliance and both expressed willingness. Then came a Russian warning and the German invasions in the North. The agreement did not materialize.

The ninth of April 1940 posed bitter problems for Sweden. She was neighbor and kin to Denmark and Norway as well as to Finland. But she had emptied her armories for Finland, and there was little left. The situation was complicated by Denmark's immediate acceptance of the German occupation, and more importantly by the fact that the kind of aid given Finland, if extended now to Norway, would certainly lead to immediate war. The German minister assured the Swedish government on the fateful morning that Sweden would not be attacked if . . .

Swedish policy was to be legally strict in interpretations of the Hague regulations on neutrality and then, admittedly outside the law, to adjust to circumstances as seemed possible or necessary. Transportation of war material, for example, could be either granted or refused, and it was refused. Transit of troops and equipment was prohibited by the Hague convention and the rule was not brought in question for some time. When the Germans tried to smuggle munitions through Sweden the customs authorities detained the cars and returned them to Germany, although many such cars undoubtedly slipped through. Sweden had already established a policy of refusing export licenses for arms and munitions to warring powers.

Strict neutrality required that Germany and Norway be treated exactly alike, at least publicly. When Sweden refused to permit transportation of war materials for Norway's benefit the Norwegians protested. The Norwegians were also often bitter over the detention of Norwegian refugees who escaped to Sweden hoping to arm themselves and return to fight (on this and other matters policy changed with the course of the war). In both cases Sweden was attempting to apply the rules, rules which for Norway's own sake it was important to maintain. The Swedish government was friendly to the Norwegian cause, and the Swedish people were overwhelmingly sympathetic. Nevertheless, in the balancing act incidents resulted which left lasting scars. For instance, German ships with military supplies for the Norwegian front were often allowed to pass through Swedish territorial waters; all that was required was that they fly the flag of distress. This was arranged by agreement with Swedish naval officers friendly to Germany—and had not the great Admiral Nelson set a precedent for putting the telescope to a blind eye? The fact was that enforcement of regulations had to be left to human beings, and men's sympathies were sometimes stronger than their duty to obey the rules. Much more often it was the sympathies of border guards who permitted Norwegian refugees to cross into Sweden, or of local police who gave asylum to American pilots in distress and occasionally helped to spirit them out of the country again.

The Norwegian government knew that it was far better for Norway that Sweden remain neutral. In a postwar Norwegian publication is a memoir from Foreign Minister Halvdan Koht complaining that Sweden did not observe toward Norway the same kind of neutrality that she had toward Finland, but insisting that in no case should Sweden be driven into war. If Britain required, for example, Sweden's stoppage of ore traffic to Germany it might drive Sweden in on Germany's side. That would be tragic. If on the other hand Sweden should enter the war on the side of the allies they would all have Russia to fear. Norway had had a warning that the USSR would not tolerate the influence of a great power, especially Great Britain, in northern Norway; for the same reasons the Russians would react against British influence in Sweden and British sea power in the Baltic. The result of Sweden's "aid" might well be a Russian attack on both Sweden and Norway.[7]

The Swedish people on their side wanted to maintain peace but they also wanted to help the Norwegians as they had helped the Finns. The pro-Germanism which had existed during World War I had been weakened by the excesses and the antidemocratic propaganda of nazism. It was almost snuffed out by the attacks on Denmark and Norway. Wide differences of opinion and a profound confusion were reflected in a blend of patriotic bravado and a sense of futility. "It is a little land" was a common confession of weakness and disappointment. Many felt that they had let their neighbors down. Yet as a young Norwegian put it, "Sweden's only crime is that she was not invaded." Per Albin Hansson, respected prime minister, expressed the general opinion in a speech of April 12:

> Our emotions are shaken by what has happened to our Scandinavian brother peoples . . . I am convinced that the Swedish people are ready to endure heavy sacrifices for their peace and self-determination . . . to preserve that which is dearest to all of them, freedom and independence.

A significant lack in the speech was that there was no reference to any sense of obligation to other peoples.

The "special regard for Sweden" entertained supposedly by the big nazi Hermann Göring was used by the Swedes whenever possible. Göring's first wife had been Swedish and he had spent some pleasant visits there. To him, therefore, a private Swede hopefully

7. Memoir to British and French governments, May 19, 1940, *Norges forhold til Sverige under krigen, 1940–1945* [Norway's relations with Sweden during the war, 1940–1945], I (Oslo: Gyldendal, 1947), 21–23, 235–236.

proposed in mid-April the withdrawal of both German and Norwegian troops from the Narvik area and occupation there on a
trusteeship basis by Swedish troops. Germany was interested. The
idea was passed on to Norway's foreign minister Koht, who was at
first cool, later became favorable. The plan was approved by London on June 1. Koht and Günther signed an agreement on it at
Luleå, Sweden, on June 3, and this was presented to Germany. It
was too late. On June 7 both the allies and the Norwegian government fled the country. A potentially unique chapter of war history
was not written.

On the withdrawal of the Norwegian government to London
the Swedes were confronted with a situation without exact parallel. The Germans immediately claimed that since Norwegian opposition had ceased the Swedes could have no objection to German transit through Sweden to Norway for the German forces of
occupation. The Norwegians, however, were continuing to fight,
and their allies, the British, were vitally concerned about German
strengthening of Norwegian coastal bases. The Swedes thought
hard and squirmed. They had permitted one German train, supposedly carrying only Red Cross personnel and material, to pass
through Sweden to Narvik in late April. Other demands they had
rejected. At first determined to deny the new German request,
they delayed a response.

But the situation rapidly grew worse for the allies. It was the
month of Dunkirk, and until Winston Churchill infused new vital
ity into the British government it looked as if there might not
always be an England. The Swedes were therefore told officially
in London that Britain might have to make peace on whatever
terms she could get, that her policy would be guided by common
sense, not bravado. The Germans kept pressing for concessions,
especially rail passage through Sweden for German soldiers on
leave and the right to transport materials; refusal would be
regarded by the Fuehrer as an unfriendly act. The Swedish government, frightened by the British warning as well as by German
threats, accepted the first step in appeasement. On June 19 the
German government was informed that Sweden agreed. Transit
began over Swedish roads of general goods (not war materials)
and "leave soldiers" without arms. To the protesting Norwegians
Sweden said specifically that "all neutrality policy had its limits in

the possibilities open to the neutral state." Pragmatism, nothing doctrinaire.

When the Germans attacked Russia in June 1941 there came new demands on Sweden, and the Germans were allowed to send one entire division (the Engelbrecht Division) across Sweden to Finland. This concession aroused heated controversy within the government and was granted not only because of the danger from Germany but because King Gustav thought it essential and because a refusal would have thrown domestic politics into chaos. It was counted as aid to the Finns and was frankly admitted to be a departure from neutrality but a "one-time" departure, not to be repeated.

What the Swedes did for the Norwegians during the early months did not seem much to their hard-pressed neighbors, but they did permit export to Norway of maps, helmets, clothing, and hospital supplies. In the years of occupation and hardship which followed, Sweden sent prefabricated houses for the shelter of the homeless and quantities of food to maintain the "Oslo breakfast" for the school children of Norwegian cities. They kept cottages near border escape routes from Norway equipped with food and fuel. They took in hundreds of youths who fled from fear or who used Sweden as a way-station to get to England or Camp Little Norway in Canada, there to gird themselves for effective fighting. Others continued their education in Uppsala or Stockholm or trained in Sweden as "police" to take over in northern Norway when opportunity permitted.

For the Danes also, particularly for the Jews whom they helped to escape from Denmark just prior to the roundup of October 1943, the Swedes opened homes and opportunity to work. Altogether more than 15,000 Danes were sheltered in Sweden when the war ended. Some 35,000 refugees from the Baltic states were given shelter; 70,000 Finnish children were given shelter and schooling through Swedish foster homes.

It was the Swedish Count Folke Bernadotte who in the spring of 1945 arranged for the release from German prison camps of the Danish police and many of the Norwegian political prisoners (19,000 people in all). Shiploads of food were taken as gifts from the Swedish people to Greece, and the Swedish Red Cross was helpful in distressed areas throughout Europe. It was a Swedish captain and crew who turned back in all but suicidal conditions to rescue the men of the sunken *Jarvis Bay* in the north Atlantic. Talk of obligation to others was at a minimum, but there were daily acts of helpfulness and sacrifice.

Both warring groups recognized the locked-in situation of Sweden and her dependence on imports. Britain tolerated the continuance of iron ore export to Germany and the manufacture for the nazis of ball bearings and other vital goods. The Swedes did not sell arms and ammunition. Safe-conduct agreements with Germany allowed five ships per month to enter and leave Gothenburg for the West, but even this traffic was subject to the whims of the nazis, who repeatedly stopped it for weeks or months at a time. Eleven ships and 100 lives were lost in this *allowed* commerce.

Despite such strangling pressure Sweden maintained the trade agreement made with England in December 1939 and steadily decreased shipments of iron ore to the German area from a 1939 figure of 11,300,000 tons to a well-controlled 8,200,000 tons in 1942. By 1942 total exports were down to 47 percent of normal, imports to 45 percent. Food was rationed, *akvavit* had to be made from wood instead of from potatoes, and cars were driven by wood gas instead of gasoline.

Sweden was willing to adjust to circumstances, but she had no intention to submit to whatever might happen. Government and people made it clear as the northern air that they would battle any invader. Neutrality had always been an armed neutrality, and there remained a pride in the exploits of Charles XII. Sweden was much stronger in a military way than any other of the northern lands. She restocked the supplies sent to Finland, and increased production from the great Bofors munitions plant. Her iron ore and her heavy industry strengthened her position, though she lacked coal.

Sweden's defense budget was $50,000,000 in 1938–39, $400,000,000 in 1939–40, and $600,000,000 in each of the next two years. She could quickly mobilize 600,000 men and 110,000 Lottas (WACS) in case of danger. On several occasions that force was fully mustered, and it may have been that trigger-readiness which made a bold man in Berlin fear that the conquest of Sweden, though possible, would be too costly. The Swedes were reputed to have the best antiaircraft guns in the world and they used them; during 1940 they shot down thirty German planes which had flown over Swedish territory. In the summer of 1942 repeated U-boat attacks in the Baltic were found to be Russian, but no country would admit responsibility. The Swedes did their best at self-defense. At the end of 1942 Sweden had twenty-three destroyers with six more building; twenty-seven submarines with one building; one mine-carrying cruiser almost ready; eight old coast defense vessels, and twenty-odd torpedo boats.

A pamphlet of *Directions for Citizens of the Kingdom in Event of War* was issued, the essence of which was: "Resistance shall be made in all situations. Any announcement that resistance should be abandoned is false." This was distributed in June 1943; by that time Sweden felt surer of herself and of others, and her neutrality had changed tone. It was obviously a weather vane kind of policy. It gave Sweden a reputation in the West even worse than she deserved, for her concessions to Germany were always known, those to the allies had often to be secret.

Sweden's merchant fleet agreement with England of December 1939 gave to Britain the use of 600,000 tons of Swedish shipping (for commodity use only) until it was sunk. Two-thirds was gone by 1943. Courier planes flew regularly above the clouds from Stockholm to England, and they carried businessmen of the West, Norwegian escapees, and "others."

From the Swedish west coast swift 100-foot motor ships carried much-needed ball bearings to Britain, in greatest secrecy. SKF smuggled to Britain and Russia $20,000,000 worth of bearings and machinery, about half as much as was sold openly to Germany. But by the spring of 1944 both Britain and the United States were pressing Sweden for the cancellation of her agreements to sell ball bearings to Germany. The Swedish product was only 3 percent of Germany's needs, but that 3 percent was of high quality and important. The Swedes kept on selling until October 15, 1944, when they ceased completely. To the United States as early as 1940 were smuggled the designs for the Bofors anti-aircraft gun, which was modified somewhat and manufactured by the thousands in the United States.

The Swedish press did not have to go underground, and the old law on the freedom of the press was its protection. Occasional issues were confiscated after publication because the government feared particular articles might provoke retaliatory measures from the nazis. The Germans were often exasperated by the vitriol of the Swedish press and returned it with interest, calling the Swedes "swine in dinner-jackets." Such papers as Torgny Segerstedt's crusading *Handels- och Sjöfartstidning* kept up a steady attack on the Germans and kept reminding the Swedish government that an Allied victory was vital for the continuance of Swedish democracy. There were, on the other hand, several papers owned outright by Germany, as was true also in Demnark, and a news service under nazi control. Stockholm was a buzzing information center where newspapermen and spies from east and south and west grabbed for morsels of fact or opinion for their papers or their governments.

The elections of September 1944 gave significant indication of Swedish feeling, and undoubtedly stiffened the back of the government. The outcome of the war was by then fairly clear. The socialists elected half of the second chamber, 115 out of 230, but lost 19 seats. The communists raised their Riksdag seats from 3 to 15. The coalition government continued and Per Albin Hansson was still prime minister; neutrality was obviously approved. Yet the strong communist trend indicated, at that moment, an increasing urge for action, for in the fall of 1944 Russia represented the most vigorous anti-nazism.

As the conflict advanced to its final stages Swedish neutrality all but ceased to be neutrality. In August 1943 the goods traffic between Germany and Norway was limited more strictly and was stopped in April 1944 after Sweden found large numbers of military maps of Sweden in some German shipments. German couriers were given circumscribed routes. After September 1944, only hospital cars were allowed to move through Sweden from north Finland to Germany. All Swedish waters were next closed to German warships, and the ore traffic was brought to a halt by the stoppage of insurance and credit.

The credit operations of wartime trade had been drawn so as to provide Sweden with imports from Germany large enough to balance her exports over each six-month period. Sweden was not going to be caught with a defeated debtor unable to pay. In the autumn of 1944 she sacrificed both trade and import possibilities when she ceased all credit and prohibited foreign trading to her

Baltic ports. She also announced that she would not harbor war criminals. It was all clear indication that she had little to fear from Germany and that the war would soon be over. It was also a boost to the allies in speeding that end.

How neutral was Sweden? If by neutrality one means impartiality, there was none. Sweden did first what she had to do in order to placate Germany; later she did all she dared to help the allies. Neutrality was the policy of the possible, "cold-bloodedly selfish." No one claimed it was heroic. It was Sweden's way of struggling for survival, just as war was the way of other countries of struggling for survival. In judging the justice of the policy one must remember that it was impossible for Sweden to get foreign aid, coal, or foodstuffs, except from Germany or with German consent. Peacetime trade was as much with Britain as with Germany, but this was war, and peacetime trade was curtailed by geographic circumstance. To paraphrase a Swedish statesman with geographical insight, Sweden lay where she lay.

There was in Sweden admiration for German cultural achievements and among conservatives a sympathy for German "order." But feeling had changed since World War I. It was social democrats, not conservatives, who now held political power in Sweden, and liberal thought was stronger. Very few Swedes favored the nazi ideology, and the nazi party in Sweden could not elect a single member of the Riksdag. What many foreigners interpreted as pro-Germanism was more two other things: (1) the supercaution of a small nation before the over-might of a ruthless power; (2) anti-Russianism, which was age-old in Sweden, and which saw in Germany the only real protection against the threat from the east.

Toward Great Britain the Swedes felt both admiration and love, more in commercial Gothenburg and Malmö than in governmental Stockholm, but deeply everywhere. Political sympathy with Britain was a fact of as great significance as the respect felt for German science. A second factor is that Sweden had also to fear Britain. Both Britain and France in the winter of 1940 wanted to involve Sweden in the war and to use her territory as a base against Germany. Churchill describes some of the schemes in his memoirs. Hence Sweden had to guard against Britain as well as against Germany.

Who was responsible for the Swedish neutrality policy? Probably two men bore the brunt of leadership: King Gustav and Prime Minister Per Albin Hansson. Gustav V had been at the helm in World War I and had then been pro-German. He had, however, used his influence to keep Sweden out of war and to unite the Scandinavian countries in a common neutrality policy. He was shrewd, experienced, and widely acquainted. Like the kings of Denmark and Norway (altogether that was a remarkable trio in strength of character, as well as in height and age!) he was beloved and respected by the people, and his firm stand for neutrality was influential. "Per Albin," the prime minister, was a man of the people, one with them and yet their leader, liked and respected by the king. He stood wholly for the interests of the Swedish people, thoroughly neutral, isolationist. These top figures could of course have been overruled. They dominated policy because they represented the will of the overwhelming majority of the Swedish people. In foreign policy that will was embodied in neutrality, a concept that became a fetish.

Finland Involved Again

The Finns had no historic basis for thinking that the treaty of March 1940 would establish eternal peace between them and the Russians. In the Winter War they had fought alone and lost. Next time they must have allies.

The preliminaries of new conflict began almost as soon as the Winter War was over. First, the strategic situation was altered by the nazi invasion of Denmark and Norway and by the advance in the West. For Finland herself the new issue was the nickel of Petsamo, in which the Russians had not previously seemed interested. But the Germans were, and when they got into the northern tip of Norway, leaning over toward Petsamo and the Russian border, the Russians became concerned about both ore and strategic geography. The concession for mining the ore was held by British and Canadian interests, and Britain was willing to adjust to Russian demands for nickel, at least for the duration of the war, but Britain was unwilling to let Germany have any. The Russians, still in alliance with the Germans, were agreeable to allowing the Germans up to 60 percent of the ore for a year or two. But Finland owned the mine and insisted on control; the Russians demanded that the manager of the mine be a Soviet citizen. When, after months of increasing tension, Finnish Ambassador Paasikivi continued to reject the Soviet proposal, Vyshinsky told him in no uncertain terms that Russia was "a great power, and its demands were therefore 'categorical and definitive' "; Finnish rejection was "rank effrontery."

Paasikivi was frightened, but the government in Helsinki had reason to hope that in the event of renewed war the Germans would come to their aid. Not only did the Germans want the nickel of Petsamo but also the Arctic highway from Kirkenes in northern Norway down to the headwaters of the Baltic Sea. Most important, Hitler had decided on a war against Russia (Operation Barbarossa), and by early December 1940 he had determined to include Finland "as a participant." In September the Germans had made arrangements with the Finns to allow German troops to travel north through Finland to Norway, and discussions had been held on German supply of arms to Finland. As for the Russians, we now know that they were considering action to force Finland into the Soviet Union, as they forced Estonia, Latvia, and Lithuania in the summer of 1940.

The nazis told the Finns nothing of their plans and made no commitments. At the same time, Finns who sat in the foreign office and could read the directional signals knew by the spring of 1941 that a German attack on Russia was at least a possibility. They knew that Finland would be a good base for a flanking movement and that it would be easy for the Germans to redirect to the east troops "in transit" through Finland. Actually, German plans had been carefully prepared, and many Finns welcomed the situation. On June 15 a northern sector of Finland was assigned to German command. The Finns could hardly have been surprised when the Russians bombed Helsinki. On June 25 they recognized a state of war, and the Swedes gave permission for passage from Norway of one German division to aid on the Finnish front. Finns were not allied with Germany, but, as Hitler announced, they were fighting "side by side."

The first days of the war, even the first months, went well for the Finns. By July 10 Marshal Mannerheim could sign a jubilant "order of the day" calling for the liberation of Karelia. By September 14 the old frontier of Finland on the Karelian isthmus had been rewon and by the end of 1941 practically all the territory lost in 1940 had been reconquered. Germany had succeeded in drawing Finland into war and in getting Russia to strike the first blow. They could not, however, persuade the Finns to join fully in their war. They asked Finland to aid in an attack on Leningrad but the Finns refused. Some 1400 Finnish volunteers had gone south to train with the nazi SS, and the government asked that they be sent back. The Germans, however, held them to their term of enlistment and they fought as the only group of Finns in the Ukraine. Finland maintained that she was not a partner of the nazis and insisted that she was fighting a separate war against an old enemy.

The "separate war" idea was reasonable enough from the Finnish angle of vision. It was somewhat similar to the American position in the War of 1812 when the United States fought against Britain but did not consider herself an ally of Napoleon. Germany was now fighting with Finland, and Finland's Russian enemy was now the ally of Britain and soon would be an ally of the United States. Finland remained the same, while Germany, Britain, and the United States all changed their stance toward Russia!

Russia could not accept the separate war idea, and she pressed England to declare war on Finland. The Germans from the other side pressed Finland to break relations with England. This the foreign minister, Rolf Witting, awkwardly and foolishly did, and then an official and most friendly party was given to the departing British diplomats. In the fall of 1941 Churchill tried to find a way to assuage the Russian urgency and to freeze the situation on the Finnish border. Russia, Britain, and the United States were deeply concerned lest the Finns and Germans advance eastward and break the last slender rail connection carrying supplies south from Murmansk.

The British demands led to cautious Finnish assurances, so vague as to leave the British unsatisfied. A declaration of war was issued from London on December 6 to take effect at noon on December 7. That same day Pearl Harbor blew the United States wholly into the war.

The United States had maintained her friendly relations with Finland despite the growing antagonism with Germany, but as early as August of 1941 Secretary Cordell Hull warned Finland of the possible consequences of collaboration with the nazis. Increasing pressure led to the closing of Finnish consulates in the United States in August 1942. At the end of the year the Finnish Information Service in the United States was throttled and the legation staff was restricted in travel. The Finns took no new aggressive steps, but still there was no definite assurance that they would not. The Americans were annoyed and worried, and their Russian allies wanted action.

In 1943 the long-continuing war became increasingly burdensome for Finland, and the prospects for the future did not improve. Internal differences of opinion came to the surface. There were appeals for peace and counterappeals. A fresh warning from Secretary Hull brought a recommendation by the leading social democratic paper that a peace approach should be made to the Soviet Union. But when the Finns informed the Germans of their desire to get out of war, the nazis blocked shipments of food to Finland and cut in half the promised oil and gasoline; they demanded a political pact to bind the Finns more closely. Parliament refused to sanction such a pact. Eventually von Ribbentrop accepted assurances and dropped the retaliations. The same thing was repeated in the autumn of 1943. It showed the spirit of the Finns, but it showed also the German stranglehold on the Finnish economy.

As trade with her Scandinavian neighbors declined and as trade beyond the Baltic area was choked off, Finland could get only from Germany the necessary quantities of potatoes, grain, textiles, fertilizers, oils, machinery, and munitions of war. In the prewar years her imports from Germany were about 20 percent of the total; in the years 1941–1944 this import jumped to 75 percent. Her normal exports to Germany were about 15 percent and these jumped to 65 percent.

From February to April 1944 actual peace discussions got under way. To Juho Paasikivi, Finnish diplomatic troubleshooter, Mme Kollontay, Russian minister in Stockholm, gave an outline of Russian terms:

1. Finland must sever relations with Germany and intern the German forces in Finland; Russia would be willing to help.
2. The 1940 treaty must be reinstated and Finnish troops withdrawn to the 1940 border.

3. Russian prisoners must be returned immediately.
4. Questions for discussion: demobilization, reparations, Petsamo.

Western leaders advised acceptance, but Finns considered the terms impossible. A Finnish economist reckoned that the projected reparations figure of $600,000,000 would amount to 45 percent of the nation's productive capacity for a five-year period—"The Finns would have to learn to live without eating." By June of 1944 the Allied landings in France and a new Russian offensive in the North created a bleak outlook for Finland. On the 20th the key border fortress of Viipuri fell, and on the 22nd the Finns made a new peace proposal. However, on that same day von Ribbentrop flew in from Berlin and promised both food and strong military aid if Finland would stay with Germany to the end. In an unusual Machiavellian move President Risto Ryti, in a letter to Hitler, personally and alone took responsibility for not making a separate peace.

But the situation continued to worsen. The United States broke diplomatic relations on June 30. As the German armies were pushed back in the west Germany not only could not send Finland the needed support but withdrew her air force and some infantry regiments. The Finns had at last to abandon their "private war," yielding not so much to their own defeat as to a world situation. President Ryti resigned on August 1 so that his personal pledge to Hitler could be canceled. Marshal Mannerheim became president, and the Germans were informed of Finland's desperation. The Russian conditions were more stringent than before, but on September 2 the parliament voted 108–45 to accept them. The Finns were to cease firing on September 4, the Russians only on September 5; and the Finns must demand that the Germans evacuate Finland by September 15, 1944.

The treaty left a hardy people room to exist and no more. The eastern boundaries of 1940 were restored, which once more sheared off 10 percent of the arable land and once more threw nearly 450,000 people back into a smaller and a war-worn country. The Petsamo area in the far north was ceded to Russia, excluding Finland from access to the Arctic and taking from her the rich nickel mines of the north. Hangö was renounced by the Russians in return for a fifty-year lease on the Porkkala peninsula (renounced in 1955), which gave the Russians a strangling strategic position around the corner from Helsinki and permitted them to control a section of railroad from Helsinki to Turku (Åbo). Finland was obligated to try in court and to punish the "war responsibles," and to disband all "fascist-minded" organizations. The reparations figure was set at half the amount mentioned in the spring, but $300,000,000 in American dollar values of 1938 was a stupendous sum for Finland. Could the country survive?

The Germans amazed the Finns by the atrocities and devastation they left in their wake as they were slowly pushed out. On to April 1945 there was bloody fighting and the towns and farmsteads of the northern third of Finland were laid waste. For years the lone chimneys of burned homes still marked the north country.

The Finns had tried to treat their German partners fairly. They both had a common cause. But the motivation of the people had not been pro-German or pro-nazi, although there were those in government and army who were quite ready to use Germany to strengthen Finland's position against Russia. The end result was defeat by the Russians and hatred and disillusionment toward the Germans.

Finland had not been careful enough in her neutrality and had allowed Germany to compromise her. Once involved in war she was dependent on Germany not only for guns but for food. She clung to the notion that a single nation could wage a separate war while the world chose sides; she was just as mistaken as were those nations who thought they could have separate peace. She fought skillfully and with a bravery which made the shields ring in Valhalla. Politically she played her cards so badly that the Russians feared her, the German "brothers-in-arms" distrusted her, and her sincere friends in Britain and America could not know what to count on. It was both a miracle and a tribute to her stubborn strength that she survived as a nation.

Scandinavia and the Costs of War

The costs of war can never be stated precisely. Only some of the lesser but tangible items can be measured. The sensitivity of the Scandinavian countries to European and world conditions was evidenced as early as October 1939; Finland's income was reduced 20 percent, food rationing was begun in Norway, gasoline rationing in Denmark, and export of eggs from Sweden prohibited. Sweden's minister of finance, Ernst Wigforss, warned the workers of what happens when their products cannot be sold; the old standard of living could not be maintained. The cost of living index, which had held fairly even from 1937 to 1939, began to rise rapidly.

The financial situation in the occupied countries is illustrated by Norway. There the note circulation on April 9, 1940, was under 600,000,000 kroner. But the Germans opened a Wehrmacht credit in the bank in Oslo, and by 1945 the note circulation was over 3,000,000,000 kroner. In 1940 there were 113,000,000 kroner deposits on current account; on May 7, 1945, the amount was 5,900,000,000 kroner. It made little difference that the exile government in London had paid its way; this inflation remained as a ball and chain on the country. Denmark faced a similar problem, for she had sent Germany her foodstuffs, and Germany never caught up in payments either in coal or in money; at the close of the war the debt stood at 7,640,000,000 kroner (about $1,500,000,000).

Shipping losses were stupendous. Of Norway's 4,850,000 tons, a fleet of 4,000,000 tons was abroad on April 9, though some of it was caught in the ports of Denmark, or Germany, and later in Vichy France. Of that 4,000,000 tons, much of it in modern tankers, just half survived the war. Insurance made good the losses but could rebuild only a few ships. Hence earning capacity was lost for years to come. Over 3000 sailors had perished. The whaling fleet, small and specialized, was particularly hard hit, losing nine out of thirteen of its "floating factories."

Denmark had a merchant fleet of 1,176,000 tons in 1939, but only 921,000 tons in 1945. Finland had 645,000 tons in 1939 and was down to 330,000 tons in 1946. This loss was due to the sinking of 113,000 tons, reparations payments to Russia of 82,500 tons, and confiscations by Germany, Britain, and the United States of about 120,000 tons. Sweden had 1,582,000 tons in 1939; even in her neutrality she lost about 250,000 tons, but since she was able to build anew she ended the war with about 1,600,000 tons. Iceland had only 31,000 tons in 1939, but she felt keenly the loss of some of her fishing boats and one of her two large passenger vessels.

Loss of life was especially large in Finland and Norway. The Finnish toll in two wars was 78,000, 2 percent of the population. Finnish losses, furthermore, included 17,800 square miles of territory, reparations of $300,000,000 in goods (in terms of 1938 dollars), and the destruction of some 1600 houses in the Russian wars, and of 25,000 in the devastation by the Germans as they retreated in the north. There was additional destruction in the area ceded to Russia. The damages inflicted by the Germans were reckoned at $120,000,000.

In Norway the destruction led to staggering reparations claims against Germany. Damage to industry and commerce was estimated at $100,000,000, that to ocean shipping at $395,000,000, railway and other transport at $215,000,000, man-years lost to the national economy or used in the war against Germany at $761,000,000, additional costs of German occupation at $2,738,000,000, and other items which all added up to $5,217,000,000.

Such figures are impressive, but Mars presented a bill which was larger still, incomprehensible in worldly statistics, including items like disillusionment and mistrust between neighbors. War had changed Scandinavia.

The Aftermath of War

The trauma of war left a bitter residue. Hard feelings toward Sweden, which had been more fortunate than the rest of Norden, persisted for years after. The Finns faced stupendous problems of reconciliation and adjustment. The Danes and the Norwegians both had to deal with minorities who had collaborated with the Germans. Feeling in Norway was particularly harsh toward those who had failed to resist and toward those few who, like the famous writer Knut Hamsun, attempted to justify the nazi ideology and action. The death penalty was reinstituted to take care of those considered to be out-and-out traitors like Vidkun Quisling. There were fewer executions in Norway than in France, for example, but the number of imprisonments for collaborationism rose to 20,000, highest in Europe on a per capita basis. Not only courts but citizens and neighbors had to decide how to treat the

"German girls" who had consorted with the invaders, and their children, what attitude to take toward fellow-citizens who had honestly sympathized with the nazi ideology, those who merely lacked strength to resist, and those who opportunistically accepted advantages from the occupation authorities.

The occupation of Denmark and Norway had intensified the sentiment of nationalism in the overwhelming majority of people. It had forged tighter the bonds of community as people suffered together hardship and humiliation and as they worked together in clandestine operations. No man stood alone any more. "What occupation accomplished was to abolish the concept of the unlimited privacy of the decent man. Under inhuman pressures the communal bond was pushed until it became extraordinarily tangible, and an anatomy of the social bond itself . . . became easier both for the novelist and the psychologist." [8]

However powerful had been the bond of common suffering, it was discovered once the war was over that the bond of victory was psychologically less demanding, less binding. Recrimination and retaliation often gained the upper hand. And soon debunking writers began to denigrate the patriotic fervor of war and to question the solidarity of men under stress. Some tried to restore Quisling to respectability. Others, easily enough, proved untrue those little stories of heroism and challenge that had bolstered courage in dark days. Surely it must be remembered that in no society are 100 percent of the citizens patriots, and that still fewer are heroes. And part of the heritage of war were the atrocities and injustices committed in the name of justice after the war was over. The human and social costs of war are diverse as they are incalculable.

More measurable and more reparable were the physical damages wrought by the great conflict. Except for Finland and northern Norway destruction in Scandinavia was not comparable with that in Great Britain or on the Continent. Yet the impact of war was shattering physically as well as emotionally.

In Oslo after the war houses could not be painted nor rugs replaced; new housing could not be built and rooms in private homes were rationed like food—all available materials were sent

8. John Hoberman, "The Psychology of the Collaborator in the Norwegian Novel" (manuscript), p. 9. Cited by permission of the author.

to northern Norway which had been burned and laid waste by the retreating Germans. The regional problem was made a national responsibility. Sense of community and of need brought a no-strike pledge from Norwegian labor, and work stoppages were rare throughout Scandinavia.

Finland had not only the task of rebuilding the devastated north but of finding homes and farms for the 450,000 Finns from Karelia who had to be resettled for the second time. Forest lands were cleared for some, others had to be squeezed into subdivided farms in areas already settled. One of the sadder things was the obligation to return to Russia refugees in Estonia and Inger-manland.

Denmark found herself flooded with 210,000 East Germans, fleeing from the Cossacks. The Danes took the hardheaded atti-tude that these people would not make good Danish citizens, hence kept them in concentration camps until diplomatic pres-sure could get them wedged into one zone or another of Ger-many—they were mostly women, children, and old men and the Russians would not take them. For some of them the Danish stay had been almost four years. Another 300,000 German refugees had packed into South Slesvig, an area which many Danes wanted to annex after a plebiscite, as they had done with North Slesvig in 1920, but Danish agitation on this issue faded away after 1947.

Into Sweden, during and immediately after the war, came some 35,000 Balts, mostly Estonians. One group that reached Swedish shores in uniform were returned on Russian insistence, in accor-dance with strict legal propriety—a yielding by the Swedish gov-ernment that roused bitter protests. Others feared the long arm of the Soviets and pushed on as rapidly as possible to Canada, the United States, and wherever they could get farthest away. The largest number were absorbed into the burgeoning Swedish econ-omy but less readily into Swedish society. They kept their own schools and newspapers and continued for years to hope for re-turn to Estonia.

The aftermath period in a larger sense involved reorientation in internal politics, in diplomatic relationships, restructuring of the economy, and a general readjustment to changed conditions in the world.

The luxuries of partisan political strife had been laid aside during the war, and coalition governments had acted in the spirit of national unity. Freedom brought return to party programs, reinforced by deepened convictions. In the special case of Finland a coalition government continued until the summer of 1948, and in her case alone was there any real bitterness in the resumption of one-party responsibility. In each case the social democrats were the strongest single group (technically not quite so in Finland), and they took over the administration. This parallelism in the five countries facilitated inter-Scandinavian cooperation, especially in the field of social legislation.

It was exactly in social legislation that these countries headed into contradictions and troubles. The governments assumed new responsibilities for guiding the economy, but it was a puzzling and uncertain time for all economies. The governing parties had promised everyone a long and happy life of security, and they swelled the budgets for social affairs. They legislated two and three-week paid vacations for workers, yet they had to insist on extraordinary production and to persuade people to wait for some of the promised beneficence. Where the leash was not held tightly, inflation, as in Finland and Iceland particularly, robbed the people of the advances which looked good on paper. Finland had not enough goods, and by 1948 prices soared to eight times the prewar levels. Only the automatic increase of wages prevented chaos.

In Denmark and Norway, and even in Finland, people were understanding and optimistic. In Sweden, where war had not disrupted life as much, people were surprised and disgruntled to find that peace brought little relief. Sweden was ready for business in a big way, but her war-built dollar reserve was exhausted in two years, too much of it going for purchase of plastics and nylons and other consumer goods instead of for basic production goods such as machinery. In 1946 torrential rains drowned important crops; 1947 followed with killing drought. Government planning for abundance degenerated into controls for existence. People complained of "red-tape Sweden," and Stockholm in 1948 was placarded with signs "Save for worse times ahead."

Such was the northern milieu in which communists tried to spread suspicion and dissension. They had behind them in 1945 the prestige of the Russian resistance to the Germans, and in

Norway the Russian prisoners doing labor for the nazis left a good impression. In Denmark the communists enjoyed prestige for their effective work in the underground. In all these countries they won election support, 1944–1946, of from 8 to 15 percent of the voters. In Finland they combined with left-wing socialists and won still greater support and a strong ministerial position. In Iceland they had two members of the cabinet.

Then the communists began to overplay their hands, both internally and internationally. In Denmark, where the food rations were twice the European average, they induced a group of workers to demonstrate against a shortage of potatoes. In Iceland they rioted, and the communist members of the government withdrew in protest against the continuance of United States use of Keflavik airport. By the end of 1947 their votes and their influence were declining significantly. The decline became a toboggan slide with the Soviet coup in Czechoslovaki and the Russian demands for a mutual assistance pact with Finland.

The social democratic parties of Denmark, Norway, and Sweden staged a joint campaign against communists in April, trying to wash themselves clean of the taint of fellow-traveling. The Finnish elections of July 1948 cut the communist-popular democrat strength by 25 percent, and when they wanted still to hold important places in the coalition government the other parties revolted and allowed the social democrats alone to form a cabinet, though they had only 54 members out of 200 in the diet. In the Swedish Riksdag the communists lost seven of their fifteen seats and in the Norwegian Storting all eleven. Pressures continued, but the heyday of communism in Scandinavia had passed by 1949.

The USSR made a strong bid for trade with the Nordic countries, and at a crucial time when Germany was still down and out and when Europeans distrusted American economic stability. The largest of the Russian trade agreements was with Sweden, calling for a Swedish credit of a billion kronor (almost $200,000,000). The amount seemed ominous and brought an official protest from the United States. But fears were highly exaggerated. The total trade contemplated was only 15 percent of Sweden's export, and only a third of this was actually contracted. None of the five states swung into the Soviet economic orbit.

The Russian demands on Finland were severe—both the

$300,000,000 of reparations and the requirement that payment be in goods which Finland did not normally produce. But the Finns set to work and built the plants for ships, electrical equipment, and machinery, resulting in a permanent restructuring of their economy. And after four years, half of the remaining payments were forgiven.

Politically the USSR pressed even harder on Finland in demands for a mutual assistance pact. There must be no more threat on the northern border either from Finland herself or from possible allies such as a resurgent Germany. The Finns for four years were stubbornly dilatory in responding, but in the spring of 1948 they had to yield. By taking advantage of the simultaneous uproar over Russian action in Czechoslovakia they at least got a wording for the pact that was as mild as any such agreement could be. It did little but state in a legal document the condition of affairs which geography and power made inevitable. All the states along Russia's border to the south had acquiesced. How could Finland refuse to say that she had no aggressive designs on her big neighbor? Finland promised to defend her territory against "Germany or another state allied with her," to enter into discussions with Russia in case of war or threat of war, and to accept Russian aid. Finland insisted upon accepting no responsibility for action outside her own territory. Promises of noninterference in internal affairs were mutual; the term was for ten years; the date was April 6, 1948.

It was in July, after this treaty had been ratified, that the elections clipped the wings of communist power in the parliament. In the summer of 1949 the communists started a series of strikes in key industries like lumber and metals, evidently intending to cripple the entire economy and overthrow the government. But non-communist workers refused to quit work, the illegal strikes were condemned by the federation of labor, and the offending unions were expelled. Able leadership and the solidarity of the majority preserved the government and the national independence.

Soviet compulsion on the other northern countries was comparatively gentle. There were fulminations in press and radio, becoming occasionally virulent against the states that joined NATO. Rumors of possible military moves never materialized. Suggestions to Norway for cooperation in the defense of Spitzbergen were politely rejected; later harmless agreements were consummated.

Fundamental to the search for security was the reestablishment of sound economies. This was a problem that included all of Scandinavia but that spread worldwide in intricately interrelated patterns. To consider for the moment only Europe and especially northern Europe, the long concentration on war had disoriented industry and commerce to a tragic degree. The great German productive machine was nonfunctioning, and all Europe was out of money. Dollars and a few other hard currencies were in demand, and all too many countries had only soft currencies.

Without dollars Finland could not build the factories to pay her reparations, Denmark could not buy the fertilizer to make her fields yield crops, Sweden could not buy the machinery to make her industry function. The trouble was not laziness, as some Americans thought, nor socialistic programs: it was an international disease of war-devastated economies and artificial barriers to the interchange of goods. The same disease was affecting England, France, the Netherlands, and other countries.

To aid Europe as a whole to reconstruct its economy, to stimulate a new flow of trade, to make the Western democracies function in order to save them from communist revolution, the United States first granted loans and then inaugurated the Marshall Plan, or ERP (European Recovery Program). It is to the everlasting credit of the United States that her political leaders and the people as a whole saw the need in time and acted promptly and generously. The result was not only the much-touted *Wirtschafts-Wunder* in Germany but rapid resuscitation of all Europe. The Scandinavian countries each received some form of help. To war-devastated countries like Denmark and Norway generous aid was given as grants, with loans in addition; to more fortunate countries like Sweden the aid was in the form of loan only.

The first ECA (Economic Cooperation Administration) loan went to Iceland in July 1948, a $2,300,000 credit for a ship to "increase the production and processing of fish oils and their related products and their exportation." Denmark estimated that each dollar of the support given her was multiplied four times in Danish production; Norway on the basis of this aid and her own efforts raised her industrial production index in 1948 to 140 as compared with 100 in 1939. By the end of 1948 progress was evident throughout the North. Sweden during the course of 1949 achieved the trade balance set as a goal for 1952. Finland alone, because of Russian objections, was not within the ERP, but a series of special loans to Finland by the United States helped toward the accomplishment of the same object.

To the American citizen and taxpayer this five billion dollar per year program was intended to aid people in distress, to give business assistance to important working partners, and to help build a political bulwark against Russian aggression. The Scandinavians could appreciate the last two motivations but found it difficult to believe in Uncle Sam's altruism. They saw other aspects of American policy which seemed like stupid contrariness. For example, the United States was giving aid to Denmark to rebuild her export industry and agriculture, but the American forces in nearby Germany bought their meat from the United States. The United States was helping Norway to reconstruct her merchant fleet but curtailed the earnings of that fleet by requiring that at least 50 percent of ERP goods be shipped in American bottoms. Despite these and other disturbing problems the Scandinavians cooperated wholeheartedly in the total program.

Trade difficulties and the dearth of dollars slowed progress and forced unnatural controls. Danes could not replace their broken cups and saucers, they could not buy new silver made in their own workshops without bringing in for trade an equal amount of old silver. But foreigners with dollars could buy handsome porcelain and silver. In most of these countries permits had to be obtained to export anything (even a toy wooden pig), and only the man with dollars could expect to get many permits. He was often so frustrated by red tape and high prices that he did not buy. Foreign exchange was under strict control: In 1947 Sweden allowed the government to demand from Swedish citizens, in return for Swedish kronor, their holdings abroad in hard currency countries. Such measures were stringent but successful. In September 1949 the devaluation of the pound sterling had its immediate counterpart in Denmark, Norway, Sweden, and Iceland. The Scandinavians considered that the move had been forced by the United States, and they felt some resentment. They had no choice but to go along because of their own dollar shortages and their trade with Britain.

By the end of 1948 Norway's desolated Finnmark was two-thirds restored and her fleet was almost back to prewar capacity. Narvik was being rebuilt in concrete on a larger scale and new piers installed for the ore traffic. Denmark was reclaiming her heath and Finland her forests. Iceland was improving her means of processing fish. Sweden was electrifying more railroads, building new power plants. All the countries were planning thoughtfully and striving energetically, expanding educational facilities and extending social legislation as fast as finances permitted.

Reorientation in Foreign Relations

To war's aftermath of reconstruction problems must be added major rethinking and readjustment of relations with other states within and without Scandinavia. War had changed both Scandinavia and the world.

Norway, acting through her government in London, participated in framing the charter of the United Nations and was an active member from the beginning. Trygve Lie became its first secretary general and, as he said, his election had a geographic cause and was not a personal tribute. It was a signal recognition of the importance of small nations and their statesmen in the new world order. In none of the northern countries was there this time any question about participation, as there had been with the League of Nations. All had learned that international organization was the only hope for them and the world. The only issue was how to make cooperation effective.

Each of the other Nordic states was in a different category. Denmark during the war had no legal government abroad and could not take part in the San Francisco Conference. But upon liberation in May 1945 Denmark at once joined the UN. Iceland and Sweden were admitted in the fall of 1946, along with the first group of nonwarring states. Finland's status was puzzling. She wanted to join, every one professed to want her in, but she was caught in the rivalry of East and West. When the United Nations refused to admit certain of the Russian satellite states, the USSR retaliated by delaying the inclusion of Finland, but she was admitted in 1955.

In the council chambers of the United Nations, in its secretariat, and in its affiliated organizations, the Scandinavians served with intelligence and success. Here was a forum and a working institution in which the Scandinavian will to peace and the Scandinavian genius for cooperative action could express themselves. Again and again one or another of the Nordic countries was called on to furnish peacekeeping forces in trouble spots like Cyprus and Jordan or to lend a statesman such as Gunnar Jarring to mediate in the Arab-Israeli conflict. The most active phase of the United Nations' life came during the period when Dag Hammarskiöld served as Secretary-General, and he was killed in the heart of Africa while on a mission for the United Nations.

When the Council of Europe was set in motion in 1949 the Scandinavians joined that, too, ready to use it to the limit of its possibilities—which have been narrow.

However, participation in general international organizations fell far short of solving all problems. In the tense power rivalries of the Cold War period and after, the Scandinavian states were called upon to choose sides.

World War II had left Norway disenchanted with her isolated position. When in 1949 the choice had to be made between a Nordic pact and association with Britain, the United States, and their allies Norway went with the North Atlantic group. Perhaps one reason was the report that Russia was about to ask the Scandinavian states to sign nonaggression treaties like the ones demanded from Finland and Czechoslovakia. The United States looked with skepticism on a neutral North, fearing that, although it would be stronger than the five countries separately, it would be still not strong enough, only a "widening of the soft spot." Norway's harbors and long coast line remained of strategic importance.

Denmark was less sure of her position than Norway, but once Norway's attitude was clear Denmark likewise joined NATO. Without allies Denmark is helpless. Danish sovereignty over Greenland is also important because of the island's meteorological significance and its relation to the Great Circle air routes. Iceland was left with little choice, though with occasional restiveness. Since 1949 Norway, Denmark, and Iceland have all been members of the western defense alliance, and in 1972 Norway hosted extensive NATO maneuvers on her west coast. Denmark and Iceland became increasingly "reluctant dragons." Both were in sore financial straits and hated to pour money into defense systems that could not in any case be adequate in an emergency. The left wing parties pressed this point at every opportunity.

Finland had as little choice as Iceland. She did not have to become a full ally of the USSR, but she did have to accept a mutual assistance pact designed to protect the Soviets from a repetition of German or other use of Finland as a base of operations. Her unique status of independence on a leash is popularly known as "Finlandization."

The country in the middle is Sweden, and it is her position that has been most discussed both within the nation and in the rival camps outside. The Swedes have reached an almost unanimous consensus, and their position, based on years of newspaper comment, government statements, and conversations with hundreds of Swedes from "John Q. Carlsson" to high officials, may be paraphrased as follows:

"We are with the West, and Britain and the United States ought to understand that. We will attack no one, and if we are attacked we will fight as long as we can. We went so far as to offer to include Denmark and Norway in our sphere of defense and to regard an attack on either of them as an attack on ourselves. This was the same kind of proposal the United States made to various states in the North Atlantic Pact. We thus magnanimously agreed to abandon our more than century-old neutrality, keystone of our foreign policy. We who possess the only real military and naval strength in the North were ready to pledge common action. But the offer was spurned, chiefly because of American pressure. Now we are forced to retire into neutral isolation, for otherwise we irritate our great eastern neighbor and possibly force her to take more positive action in Finland—which would be disastrous for our good Finnish friends, and bring Russian guns to the Åland Islands, the Gulf of Bothnia, and to our northern border in easy reach of the iron mines of Kiruna and Gällivare.

"Even if we should be so bold as to align with the West, what good could it do either the West or ourselves? The United States could not get aid to us in time to count, and, from what we gather, the strategy of the

West is to retire to the Atlantic shores of Europe in case of Russian attack, or at least to the Rhine and the North Sea. In any case we would be left to our fate.

"And neutrality is not impossible. Yes, the odds are against it, but it has worked since 1814, through World War I and World War II, and it just might work again. We can be no worse off for trying it.

"Do you speak of a moral responsibility to band together with others of like belief? How can an American raise such a question on Sweden's conduct? Was not the United States more neutral and isolationist than Sweden until she suddenly became a dominant world power? Nations must look out for themselves. The great states do, and so must the small."

Such an argument has logic, plausibility. It represents deep conviction. But it is also essentially negative and not fully satisfying. Out of a psychological need for something more positive has developed in recent years the attitude of "active neutrality." This has led to strong official pronouncements against Russian actions in Hungary and Czechoslovakia and also to stinging attacks on the United States over the war in Vietnam. Prime Minister Olof Palme defends these attacks by saying, "For us neutrality does not imply, can not imply isolation, silence. We maintain neutrality vis à vis the military blocs, but we can never be indifferent to the problems of the world we live in." [9] Washington could not agree that the rights of self-expression justified the Prime Minister in comparing the bombing of Vietnam to fascist and communist activities (Katyn, Guernica . . .). Palme has been denounced for an arrogant and "holier-than-thou" stance. His heated remarks and the overreaction to them by American officials produced an anomalous situation: Diplomatic relations between Sweden and the United States were chilled to the freezing point at a moment when relations between the United States and China and Russia were warming up—an illustration of how twisted can become the bonds between friends. But this was a problem that would pass. More fundamental problems remained, concerned with the mutual interest of Scandinavia and the United States.

Problem number one is: Can any state, either big or little, defend itself alone in this new world of great agglomerations of

9. From an interview in *Le Monde*, quoted in "Aktuella frågor" [Current questions], *Sydsvenska Dagbladet*, February 3, 1973.

power? In the last major war only Sweden avoided involvement, and she had occasionally to knuckle under to pressure.

Problem number two is: Can neutrality function during a war between power blocs? All the northern states except Sweden have decided that it is an obsolete hope.

Problem number three is concerned with geography: Can war swing off in another direction and leave an area such as Scandinavia untouched? Escape seems hardly conceivable for a region that lies directly under the air routes connecting the probable chief antagonists, an area, furthermore, that straddles the sea routes and that has within itself great productive potential—for food, iron ore, wood, and industry.

Problem number four grows from the first three: Could the West, in a confrontation that we pray will never come, count on the goodwill or aid of Scandinavia without specific agreements beforehand? In the last war did any country come to the aid of another if it had no commitment to do so? Friendship guarantees neither the willingness nor the ability to cooperate at a critical moment.

Problem number five reverses the question in number four: Can Scandinavia, without specific understandings, count on the assistance of the United States? American interest and American sentiment is strongly pro-Scandinavia. But without coordinated plans assistance is bound to be as futile as the British aid to Poland in 1939 or the British and French aid to Norway in 1940, not to mention Finland. American aid, in case of that crisis that everyone is trying to avoid, can hardly reach beyond her NATO obligations.

A generation after the end of World War II Sweden cut her military budget from 5 percent of her GNP to 3.5 percent and her leaders talked of a plan of "territorial defense"—that is, internal withdrawal. Conscription continued, but its effectiveness was questioned. Tales were told of conscripts getting their handaxes caught in their bicycle chains. Denmark in 1973 trimmed her allocations for defense to 2 percent of GNP. Her approval of NATO continued because it was for her a cheap protective blanket and it gave her a participating voice. But her military structure was weak and deteriorating. Mogens Glistrup, the tax and general political rebel, suggested that Denmark should establish as her defense department a telephone answering service what would say, in Russian, "We surrender." Finland would hardly need this; certainly she could not repeat the magnificent performances of 1939 and 1941. Finland's military establishment is severely limited by the treaty with the USSR. Her army cannot be more than 34,400 men, the navy 4,500, and the air force 3,000; ships are limited to 10,000 tons, planes to a total of 60. Submarines are forbidden and so are factories that might produce military equipment. Even the permitted limits are not fulfilled. Avoidance of war is absolute policy, for freedom of action does not exist. To emphasize Finland's peculiar status of ambiguity and suspense, she is a member of the Nordic Council and has a trade agreement with the EEC, and at the same time is associated with the Eastern bloc's Comecon (the eastern counterpart of EEC). Iceland's naval forces are only enough to annoy British fishermen and their convoys. Political opposition to the continuance of the American presence at the Keflavik air base is sure to continue despite the new agreement with the United States in 1974. Norway is the most firmly committed of all the Nordic lands to the Western defense system, and she has reason to look askance at the buildup of Soviet strength in the Kola peninsula in the past decade; Norway is occasionally critical of American policy and the weakening of NATO.

Clearly these countries of the North are not prepared to defend themselves either individually or in concert in case of outside attack. Most of them are no more prepared psychologically than materially. Both Sweden and Norway would probably resist, but their own power would not determine the ultimate outcome. Their independent resistance could last only a few days or weeks. They live on hope—which is perhaps all any nation can do!

Scandinavia and EEC

The difficult decisions for the Nordic countries, and the most practical achievements, have come in connection with those international agencies that combine economic and political problems. Most notable are the debates concerning EFTA and EEC.

The Scandinavian states, despite their many-sided cooperation, have never been able to construct an economic union for themselves. American prodding and pump-priming after World War

II produced the beginnings of general European collaboration
(ERP, OECD, and so forth), then the Coal and Steel Community
(1951). French statesmen, especially Robert Schuman and Jean
Monnet, built on this multiform system and added a political
dream in founding the European Economic Community (EEC or
the Common Market, 1955). But EEC united only six continental
states in a customs union with a common tariff frontier and with
the deferred hope of closer political cooperation; the Treaty of
Rome left the door open for later adhesion by other states. At first
Great Britain was omitted because of certain internal policies as
well as her complex relationships with the then far-flung Com-
monwealth. When she applied for membership in the early 1960s,
de Gaulle used his veto and EEC closed in on itself.

In the meantime the countries not invited to the party decided
to have their own. The initiative was taken in meetings in Stockholm in 1959, and by 1960 the "Outer Seven" began to function as
the European Free Trade Association (EFTA). It was a strange
grouping of Portugal, Switzerland, Austria, Great Britain, and the
three Nordic countries Denmark, Norway, and Sweden. Only
later (1961) did Finland join as an associate member, and Iceland
entered (1970) just before the benediction. In this society there
were no overtones of political purpose; the agreements were
purely economic. Furthermore, it was recognized that some, perhaps the group as a whole, might later affiliate with EEC. The
geographical diversity of EFTA obviously made impossible a common customs frontier; the goal was simply free trade among
themselves.

Thus the Scandinavian states were brought into economic association with each other by way of association with scattered states
outside their area. The results amazed them. Among themselves
they could and did develop a common customs frontier, and
foreign citizens could move within Scandinavia without passport
examination. In the first ten years of its existence, EFTA's total
import increased 108 percent and export 111 percent; within its
own tariff-free exchange the increase was 186 percent; for the
neighborhood group of Denmark, Finland, Norway, and Sweden,
the increase in trade with one another was 284 percent. These
spectacular results proved the value of free trade, but the external
tariff walls of EEC loomed as threats to further expansion. When

it appeared that Great Britain would abandon this effective but loose association in order to join EEC, it was essential for all EFTA participants to rethink their position. Hopes that this Outer Seven might treat with EEC as a group, or that at least the Nordic states might negotiate together, were dashed by EEC insistence on dealing with each individually and also by the fact that each had separate problems along with some that were general. The Kennedy-Round type of united approach was no longer feasible.

Among the common problems was the fear that "joining with Europe" would pull down the high standard of living attained by the Scandinavians: fear that they would be overrun by immigrants from the south, fear that their farms and recreation areas would be taken over by foreigners, fear that their prized social welfare systems would be overtaxed, fear of a cold and distant bureaucracy that spoke a different language—a pervasive suspicion, natural to the citizen of a small state, that his life style and his independence would be somehow submerged. This uneasy feeling was strongest in Norway, whose farmers didn't want to "take orders from Brussels"; Norwegians remembered four centuries of union with Denmark when they had to play second fiddle, nearly one century of union with Sweden when they continued to play second fiddle; the trauma of the nazi invasion; they wanted no more of it.

Decision was easiest for Denmark, closest to the EEC neighbors, geographically and psychologically long a part of Europe. Commercial interests vital for the whole country made it almost necessary that if Britain should join, Denmark must follow. Denmark had few political qualms, being already a member of NATO and not being obsessed with the ideals of neutrality. Nevertheless strong opposition developed, especially within the leftist elements among the social democrats and among all the communists; for the extreme leftists the strengthening of Western Europe could only delay the success of world revolution. Other parties split on the issue, and the outcome of the plebiscite in the fall of 1972 was in doubt, especially after Norway voted negatively. However, the people voted their pocketbooks and Denmark became the only Nordic country to become a full member of the European Community; the vote meant that some complex constitutional issues did not have to be resolved.

Finland had no trouble in saying no to membership. She was only an associate member in EFTA and had stabbed the now defunct Nordek (see below) in the back. But the Finns proceeded to negotiate a trade agreement with EEC and initialed it in the fall of 1972. This nonpolitical association with Europe ought to create no complications. But ratification was up to the government in Helsinki, and antennae keyed to Moscow as well as to domestic politics caused some long soul-searching. It was felt that only President Kekkonen's continuance in office could reassure the USSR and squelch controversy at home. Hence Kekkonen was voted an extraordinary additional four-year term. Even then he hesitated a while longer before he approved the agreement, wanting to be sure that Moscow would not object.

In Norway the question of entrance into the Community was decided by plebiscite, and the issue proved to be the most divisive problem since the war. It was a strangely violent political campaign in 1971–1972. People with "Ja" bumper stickers found themselves attacked and their tires slashed—this and other militancies were most un-Norwegian and indicated a wholly unnatural bitterness. Back in the early period of calm discussion in 1971 the leader of the Labor party, Trygve Bratteli, had emphasized the necessity of Norwegian membership in west European society and the importance of helping to promote democracy in Europe. On the economic issues the negative argument seemed to be *not* that Norway would win advantage by staying out but only that the disadvantages would not be great.

In a fascinating television marathon in mid-June 1971 these and other issues were debated, along with comments by Hilmar Baunsgard of Denmark, Olof Palme of Sweden, and Antti Karjalainen of Finland. The most effective Norwegian participants were the opponents of membership, and they played strongly on the themes of democracy and nationalism—Norway had always cooperated and could do so as effectively from without as within. As the debate continued through the following year, it became clear that party leadership, except for the communists and the Center party, favored adherence. But the Labor party was sorely divided. The farmers' cooperatives helped finance public opposition. Old religious antagonisms were revived—Lutheranism of the North versus Catholicism in southern Europe. The youth opposition was rooted, probably, in antagonism toward the materialism inherent in the pro-EEC argument. Both farmers and fishermen were opposed on economic as well as nationalist grounds. Already too many big foreign trawlers had encroached upon what the Norwegians insisted were their own fishing territories, and they were talking about extension of the national boundaries to fifty miles out, as the Icelanders were doing. EEC could not bring itself to making satisfying compromises.

The ultimate result was that the plebiscite of September 1972 registered 54 percent No to 46 percent Yes. Bratteli had thrown all his weight into the campaign by making the issue a question of confidence, though the plebiscite was technically only advisory. Hence the government had to resign; the former bourgeois coalition would not take over, and the premiership went eventually to the leader of the Christian Democratic party, leading a coalition of only 40 out of 155 members. Gradually people came to have morning-after doubts about their decision—had they committed economic suicide? They went hat in hand to Brussels asking for a trade agreement on the best terms they could get, and they got a surprisingly favorable deal.

Sweden's road to decision was long and wavering—like the "narrow, crooked, bumpy," roads of her central forests. Sweden's sacred neutrality was the deepest rut in the road.

Industrialists and business men considered membership essential for Sweden's economic well-being. The leadership of organized labor was favorable, but not the rank and file. Conservative and liberal leadership and some social democrats were in favor. The importance of trade for a country that exports 25 to 30 percent of her GNP underscored the desirability of obtaining a free market area as large as possible. EFTA had been good, EEC would be better.

However, the opposition proved stronger than all these elements. The reasons were partly the same as in Norway—nationalism, suspicion of "Catholic Europe," fear for the welfare system (with probably no grounds at all). Bertil Olsson blamed the situation on external forces: the line between "East and West" which drove a wedge right down the middle of Scandinavia. More than in Denmark and perhaps even more than in Norway there was a vague distrust of Europe, for Sweden has always been somewhat apart. There is also a fundamental egoism in the Swedish position—a desire to get, with little thought of the give and take of mutual relationships. Several Swedes have told me that Sweden was really more important for EEC than EEC was for Sweden, and the government seemed to think it possible that EEC would create an all-embracing free trade area including Sweden, while the rest of the members assumed more complete responsibilities of organization membership. In short Sweden took a rather high tone in early stages of the long negotiations.

But it was political issues, not economic, that determined the outcome. The possibility of Nordek as a group affiliating with EEC was quickly quashed in March 1970. Within a month after the Nordek agreement had been initialed, Olof Palme made a continental tour in which he evidently discussed this possibility with leaders of Common Market countries, and it may well have been the publicity about this trip that caused Finland to shy away from Nordek. This was a double setback, for Sweden now stood alone both in Scandinavia and in negotiations with EEC. For some months the Swedish government based its approach on an "open application," continuing to hope that some sort of membership arrangement could be reached allowing exceptions for Sweden's neutrality reservations. Then came the Davignon memorandum recommending meetings of EEC ministers twice each year to plan common foreign policy, and the Werner report concerning a closer economic and monetary union. The political and the binding aspects of EEC were becoming clearer, and the opposition in Sweden stronger.

Prime Minister Palme was increasingly dependent on the left-wing elements in his own party and on the communists. To appease them, or to hold them in the fold, he announced on March 18, 1971 that there was no longer a question of Swedish membership in EEC. At an earlier stage Sweden had sought "association" with right of withdrawal. But from 1971 on the only real possibility was a special trade agreement to be negotiated on an individual basis, gaining what privileges the Community was willing to grant. The great disadvantage was that it left Sweden with vital economic interests on the continent but with no voice in the councils of the European body. The agreement reached in the fall of 1972 was more favorable in its purely economic terms than observers had expected. And "nothing is forever." Also, dismembered EFTA would remain for an indefinite period. With these arrangements and with the move of certain of her factories into EEC countries, such as Denmark and Belgium, Sweden would carry on.

The Swedish attitude is well epitomized in two quotations, first that of Kjell-Olof Feldt, budget chief in the government (1969):

It is of course true that we are influenced by that which happens around us, that we must always adapt our policies to changes in the international milieu. However, there is an essential difference between the type of influence that we encounter when we have the freedom to decide ourselves how we will respond to it, and that influence that occurs when we have bound our freedom of action through a surrender of decision-making power to supra-national organizations. [10]

The other is a statement made by then Prime Minister Tage Erlander in 1959:

We wish to play our part in promoting more extensive relations between nations, increasing the exchange of ideas in the cultural sphere, and in furthering personal contacts. But if we are to be able to do all this we must not commit ourselves deeply to either side in the political struggle between East and West or to any other groups.[11]

This is the prescription of friendly isolationism. Each of the northern countries builds its policy on somewhat different foundations, and the end result is that Denmark is the only one of them that has become a member of the European Economic Community; each of the others operates with a separate trade agreement. How much of internal Nordic economic cooperation can survive is a question for which no one has an answer.

Is There a Nordic Common Front?

Yes, there is. But it is based not on formal documents but on common interests and patterns of doing things. Binding agreements are shunned; ad hoc cooperation is welcomed. Relationships within this family of nations frequently puzzle outside

---

10. Address of November 23, 1969, in *Utrikesfrågor* [Foreign policy questions] (Stockholm: Utrikesdepartementet, 1970), p. 156.

11. Quoted in Nils B. E. Andrén, *Power Balance and Non-alignment: A Perspective on Swedish Foreign Policy* (Stockholm: Almquist and Wiksell, 1967), pp. 198–200.

observers. One recent visitor who could not understand the attitudes he felt about him asked a native, "Do you Danes and Swedes
really dislike each other?" The immediate answer was "No, we
hate each other. It's an important part of our family relationship."
And it has been cynically remarked that these five countries cooperate beautifully in the things that don't matter much. The record
shows both failures and successes, definitely more successes than
among other neighbor-nations groups such as in the Balkans, the
Middle East, or Africa.

Through past centuries there was more bloody slaughter than
loving collaboration. While the Swedes and the Danes were bitter
rivals for hegemony in the Baltic, the Norwegians repeatedly
struck from the rear. Again and again attempts failed to build
partial or complete union in the North. Longest lived was the uni-
tary kingdom which for seven centuries governed Swedes and
Finns. The fourteenth-century union of Sweden and Norway did
not last through the lifetime of King Magnus Eriksson. The 400-
year union of Denmark and Norway was smashed by Sweden, and
the Norwegian-Swedish union lasted less than 100 years. Iceland,
associated first with Norway and then with Denmark, took the
earliest opportunity to detach herself. Only for one brief period
was the entire North held together by Margareta in the fragile
structure of the Union of Kalmar (ca. 1389–1520). At the time of
Denmark's anguish in the mid-nineteenth century, and despite a
wave of romantic "talk-brotherhood," pan-Scandinavianism did
not function. The forces of separatism proved always stronger
than either conquest or the will to unite. Yet the urge for community was persistent.

After the disastrous experiences of World War II there arose a
felt need for mutual support. The American proposal for a large
North Atlantic alliance would happily have embraced all of Scandinavia. But not all of these states welcomed an organization
wherein they would be only minor partners. Sweden felt strong
enough and was independent-minded enough to propose an alliance with Denmark and Norway based on neutrality. The idea
was appealing and yet, although Sweden had a good airplane and
munitions industry, it was not good enough to give her neighbors
a sufficient sense of security. Sweden felt she was offering a great
sacrifice in spreading her neutrality umbrella over the North as a

whole, but she would not yield the principle of neutrality. She could not, for instance, sanction acceptance of arms from the United States except on a strictly commercial basis, and the Norwegians feared this might be both too costly and too limited. Hence the three western states associated themselves with NATO, Finland was left with her nonaggression treaty (of 1948) with the Soviet Union, and Sweden became more solidly confirmed in her "alliance-free" policy.

Out of the failure of these defense negotiations grew the determination to create another organ of cooperation, outside the military realm, and in 1952 all five countries got together in the Nordic Council. Here each preserves independence but finds an institution through which common problems can be discussed and common legislation can be developed. Every year selected representatives from the parliaments and the administrations meet in one of the capital cities for a week. Investigating commissions of experts probe throughout the year into problems such as a bridge over Öresund, pollution of air and water, the Lapps, divorce law, Nordic labor market, and a great variety of matters of mutual interest. By the 1970s the independent countries of Scandinavia had more legislation in common than did the states of the United States.

On a very practical basis the cooperative societies of the separate countries have proved that they can cooperate. The Scandinavian Airlines System (SAS) is a highly successful business arrangement in which Sweden has three parts of the investment and three of the directors, Norway and Denmark two each. In the 1970s further cooperation is developing in which the transportation-communication network may be vastly improved: the plan is that Denmark will build a bridge across the Great Belt and, in combination with SAS, a huge airfield on Saltholm, an island in the Sound between Denmark and Sweden, while Sweden builds a bridge and tunnel connecting mainland Sweden with the airport and with the Danish mainland. One of the results will be a still greater conurbation in the Copenhagen-Malmö area. But political and financial difficulties may prove insurmountable.

Most dramatic example of successful cooperation came with the "Kennedy-Round" negotiations of 1966–67 (so called because instigated by President Kennedy, with the purpose of reducing in-

ternational tariff barriers and stimulating trade). Without the
guarantees and sanctions of a permanent treaty relationship,
without integration of political authority, Denmark, Finland, Norway, and Sweden came together on an ad hoc basis and agreed to
pool their interests and act through one negotiator. The weak-
nesses of four small countries vis-à-vis the great conglomerations
of political and economic strength—the United States, the United
Kingdom, Japan, and the European Community—were overcome. Four small countries that had to beg for privileges became
one economic power that could command concessions. The Great
Powers, astonished, had to face the fact that when acting together
the Scandinavian states became an equal, for the North *as a whole*
was more important in the trade of EEC than was the United
States. Nils Montan, representative of this group-become-one,
was taken into the council of major states, and out of the negotiations came an international agreement with benefits for the Nordic countries that they could not have dreamed of achieving while
acting separately.

The next step was to try to consolidate this cooperation in a permanent five-state economic union—Nordek. Negotiations led to
an agreement that was initialed in Reykjavik in February 1970.
But it appeared that this agreement might lead to the entry of
Nordek as a whole into EEC; the Finns realized that such a development would be highly displeasing to the USSR, and their second thoughts led to their reneging on the agreement, and thus to
the collapse of the whole project.

This sad dénouement surprised many and disappointed all the
advocates of cooperation. Finland had participated as an associate
member of EFTA and her big eastern neighbor did not seem to
object. And EFTA had been an enormous success. As indicated
above, in the treatment of trade the Scandinavian countries had
all profited greatly from the relaxation of trade barriers. It was a
bit ironic that Scandinavian cooperation had succeeded only when
these states combined with outside states like Britain, Portugal,
Switzerland, and Austria. Then, worse than the stillborn death of
Nordek, came the crippling of EFTA by Great Britain's shift to
the Common Market. In the 1970s the dark cloud on the horizon
was the division within Scandinavia regarding relations with the
European Community. The portents indicated that Danish inter-

ests and loyalties would draw this southern flank away from her northern colleagues and more and more into the embrace of the Continent.

Nevertheless, despite the disappointments of the past or difficulties of the present there is a functioning Nordic common front. Its ingredients may be classified in five broad categories: geography, language, cultural heritage, philosophical outlook, and flow of social communication.

Physical and political geography are factors of obvious significance. But propinquity guarantees neither conflict nor collaboration. The most that can be said is that geographical proximity facilitates cooperation when other factors are present to promote it. Certain characteristics of the political geography of Scandinavia may, however, positively encourage cooperation.

Smallness induces a similar small-state psychology in all of them. The tacit acceptance by each people of the necessity for a policy of adjustment vis-à-vis the Great Powers creates a bond of sympathy. Erik Scavenius, foreign minister and prime minister of Denmark in the early years of World War II, adjusted too much to be popularly acceptable, yet the statesmen of the North have had to live by the philosophy he expounded in his apologia, *Forhandlingspolitiken under Besaettelsen.*[12] True, each state has different powerful neighbors to whom it must adjust, but this divergence may itself facilitate sympathy and understanding. For instance, Sweden, which must adjust to several powers, takes a tolerant attitude toward Finland's attempts to maintain peaceful coexistence with Russia, as well as toward Denmark's position with respect to Germany and Norway's with respect to Russia and Great Britain. Every citizen of the North is aware that his government cannot dominate world events but at most can influence in a minor way and attempt to remain independent. The fact that no single common enemy forces the Scandinavian states to unite is of small significance, for the shotgun marriages commanded by such external threats do not in any case survive beyond the lifespan of the threat.

Size is of significance in the relations among these states them-

---

12. *Forhandlingspolitiken under besaettelsen* [The politics of adjustment during the Occupation] (Copenhagen: Steen Hasselbachs Forlag, 1948).

selves. Not only have Denmark and Sweden renounced their ancient imperial ambitions, but now no one of these states is strong enough to coerce another. Hence, though there may be jealousy and even resentment against the most prosperous one, there is no fear among them.

In brief, geography demands nothing, and it makes neighborhood possible.

Language, often considered a unifying force, is almost as neutral as geography. The major Anglo-Saxon powers get along with each other fairly well despite "the common language through which Englishmen and Americans misunderstand one another," while the Swiss, using four distinct languages, have managed through centuries to maintain effective national unity. But the Arabs, who have both language and religion in common, can unite only in their hatred of the Jews. As for Scandinavia, neither Icelandic nor Finnish is useful in their international conferences. But with Danish for the Icelanders as well as the Danes, Swedish for the Finns as well as the Swedes, and Norwegian for the Norwegians—three basic languages make it possible for everyone to speak his first or second tongue and to understand his neighbors in their languages. It may not always be easy, but translation is unnecessary. It is established practice within the Nordic Council that committee reports are left in the language of the chairman. (At Nordic professional conferences sometimes English becomes the common denominator, and there is fear that this may become the "wave of the future" and that it may portend the end of real Scandinavianism.) Literary works are often translated from one Nordic speech to another, but that is because of the laziness of the average reader, not because he *could* not understand if he would.

The significant and positive thing is that, although words may have developed different spellings and differing connotations, concepts and ideals have retained a common meaning. One Northerner does not have to explain to another what he means when he says "democracy" or "justice." Linguistic similarities mean also, from a very practical standpoint, that small businesses which cannot afford interpreters can easily trade with their neighbors. In essence, the languages of the North pose no real barriers for men who wish to act together. The languages provide effective vehicles of communication, and they encourage the feeling among Northerners that the peoples are related to each other more closely than to "outsiders."

Thus the first two of our categories are at least a little more than neutral in effect; the next three are strongly positive.

The cultural heritage is that factor which, above all, produces a distinctive Northern way of life and that "mutual compatibility of main values" which Karl Deutsch calls the first essential for a viable security community. The basic cultural heritage is the same from Kuopio to Reykjavik, from Varangerfjord to Slesvig.

The preponderance of Lutheranism might be considered a basis for peaceful relations—but it is only partly so. Through many past centuries, when religion was a more vital force than it seems to be in the twentieth century, these peoples eagerly cut each others' throats. Christianity as a whole does not appear to have checked or ameliorated bloody strife, any more than has Islam or Hinduism. Perhaps nothing in which man believes passionately can be expected to reduce passion, even within the body of believers. However that may be, the faith men profess does carry with it side effects: in the case of Lutheran Christianity, for example, similar customs in the celebration of Easter and Christmas, the same code of honor, the same set of values. The traditions of religious custom have so fixed themselves upon the society that "atheist" socialist leaders have their children baptized and confirmed in the state church, and almost to a man they are "buried in white clothes." The teaching of a common faith results in common practices, makes possible mutual and instant understanding, and thus lays the basis for mutual trust.

Even in the more distant heritage of Thor and Odin there is common ground, and in the ancient literature of the sagas, and in the old folk beliefs in nature. So also in the concepts that individual powers count as heavily as birth and that each person is responsible for his actions and his fate—or at least for the manner in which he faces his fate. Such ideas serve as foundation for the dignity and the self-assertion of the common man.

The heritage of conflict has itself produced some notable cooperation. Because of the very multiplicity of their devastating feuds and the varying points of view taught in the schools, the Scandinavians were among the first, if they were not *the* first, to set up commissions to examine each others' textbooks in history and to try to eliminate the nationalist distortions that aggravate pride in one's own accomplishments and institutions and contempt for one's neighbors'. Through these procedures the folk memories of war and pillage have become at least somewhat muted.

Most relevant of all the facets of the common cultural heritage are the concepts and institutions of democracy, from the aristocratic democracy of the Vikings to the welfare democracy of today. Democracy in the sense of individualism is an ancient inheritance. Democracy in the sense of majority rule, one man one vote, toleration of the opinions of others, is recent. This modern practical democracy has been attained throughout the North by similar processes that are roughly parallel in time in the various countries. Written constitutions were adopted in Sweden in 1809, in Norway in 1814, in Denmark in 1849. Extension of the suffrage proceeded independently but in roughly simultaneous fashion. Social democratic parties and principles made headway at about the same rate, and at one time (in the early 1950s) all five governments were under social democratic leadership. This parallelism in politics was due to a combination of factors, fundamentally to that common heritage which bred a common response and which produced a similar pattern for democracy throughout the North.

Other parallelisms have existed at other points in time. The codes of laws passed on through oral tradition from a dim Germanic past were alike in spirit even if different in detail. When the Jutes and the Skåningar wrote their laws in the thirteenth century, Goths and the Upplanders and the men of Gulathing and Frostathing wrote theirs too. An illuminating sidelight on Scandinavian solidarity is provided in Västgötalag (the law of medieval Västergötland), which required rather mild fines for the murder of a German or an Englishman but stiffer penalties for the killing of a Dane or a Norwegian—though it must be added that the price for a fellow-Swede was still higher. The ancient law remains the foundation for modern law. And law, along with the concept of justice and social order, is so central in Nordic thought that it may be labeled the cultural focus of the society.

Through these and other forces, including nature and climate, there has developed through the centuries a uniting Northern view of life, with stress on the worth of the individual, freedom of conscience, and devotion to justice and law-bound order. Out of such things grows the "mutual compatibility of main values" essential for integration and for a distinctive way of life. But even these things are not enough by themselves.

Fourth of the major factors making possible an effective common front is the philosophical outlook. In the North a pervasive pragmatism is a distinguishing characteristic. It is exemplified even in art which insists on beauty in the things of everyday utility. What counts is what will work, and abstruse theory plays a small role indeed. As far back as we know the Scandinavians, and whether the highest acknowledged leadership was Thor or Jesus, the attitude was like that of Benjamin Franklin: "Trust God but keep your powder dry." These peoples never yielded even theoretically to the Islamic idea of complete surrender to God's will. God would help only him who helped himself.

On the other hand, neither did the Northerners accept the absolutes of Cartesian logic which result in an all-or-nothing position. In their arguments between laborers and employers, in their repeated political adjustments (often involving coalition governments), they take the view that the important thing is to get something done. They can proceed gradually and informally; they can, as illustrated in the Kennedy-Round negotiations, work as partners without alliance. Yet more importantly, they can accept partial achievement if the complete program is unattainable. When the Nordic Union failed in 1949 the peoples concerned set up the Nordic Council (1952) which at least provides a forum and a means of cooperation in a multitude of common interests. Meantime, agitation and discussion continues concerning closer economic cooperation.

This kind of approach recognizes both the *I* and the *We* and works for that which is advantageous if not ideal. It prevents the utter stalemate of negotiations, such as is all too common in recent international relations.

Another facet of the political pragmatism of the Scandinavians has been mentioned before: their attitude toward the state as an agent to be used for the general good, not as an enemy to be thwarted.

To the cultural mutuality and the all-Nordic pragmatic attitude toward getting things done one must add the fifth category: free-flowing social communication. The Deutsch group of integration analysts speaks of the need for mobility and multiplicity of ranges of contact and for compensation of flows and interchange of group roles. The North enjoys all these attributes, as Ray Lindgren, in lending his Scandinavian expertise to the theoretical analysts, well illustrates.[13] Communication by telephone and mail, travel by rail and plane, all are provided by technically excellent service. Danes go skiing in Norway, Swedes go to Denmark to buy butter and cheese, Norwegian graduates go to Copenhagen to celebrate, some 200,000 Finns go to Sweden to work. Throughout the North workers and others now move back and forth without passports and can collect social security from the country in which they last work. Mobility is as unrestricted as between the states of the United States. The ranges of contact are not only multiple but well-nigh infinite: The political parties of the North are sufficiently similar in ideology and problems that their representatives find it valuable to compare notes with one another; associations of scientists and lawyers and historians, of young people and especially students, of labor leaders and ordinary workers in exchange jobs, ministers of the cloth and ministers of state, sports competitors—the list of those who move across national lines to hold meetings large and small is all but endless. People come to know one another and to recognize that frequently their problems can be met on a Scandinavian level better than on the national or local level.

Much of this intercommunication has been fostered by the various Norden Societies which in 1969 began the celebrations of their fiftieth anniversaries. These wholly private societies have worked ever since World War I for the improvement of relations among the Northern peoples. Through publications, lectures, and conferences they have inspired young people who have

13. *Norway-Sweden: Union, Disunion, and Scandinavian Integration* (Princeton: Princeton University Press, 1959).

grown up to be legislators, business men, officials, and who have maintained their interest and helped to implement their youthful ideals. For example, Nils Herlitz, professor of law in Stockholm, was as a young man active in the founding of Swedish "Norden" in 1919; a few decades later he pushed for the establishment of the Nordic Council and served as chairman of the Swedish delegation to the Council through its early years; at age eighty he was still writing about it. Frantz Wendt is a long-lived and effective agent of Nordic cooperation who has moved from Norden to the secretaryship of the Nordic Council in Denmark. The Nordic Cultural Commission, established in 1947, and the institutions established under its auspices are important in their own right, and as stimulators of additional interchange and activity. The Nordic Council (1952–) is the political keystone of the arch of Nordic cooperation, the institutionalization of the common front.

In brief, the Scandinavian common front is a cultural phenomenon growing out of common tradition, idealistic promotion, a pervasive pragmatic philosophy, and active interpersonal relations. It has been propagated by devoted and intelligent leadership, inspired by idealism and seeking practical goals. Governments give it enthusiastic support. Its success rests on voluntarism, the willingness of all to let each nation follow its own inclinations in foreign policy and in any other sphere where independence is felt to be more important than group action.

6 *Scandinavian-American Crosscurrents*

The American way of life and the Scandinavian way of life differ in various ways, but the values and the purposes of the two societies are basically similar. The bonds between us stretch back to Leif Ericson and now embrace several million Americans of Scandinavian origin. They include a continual interchange of people and goods and ideas. We read each other's literature and ride in each other's automobiles, we cooperate in the functioning of the United Nations, and when we have differences we talk to each other frankly—even sometimes heatedly. The vital thing is that we understand each other. These countries of the North are the most "Americanized" in Europe, as has been often remarked. We too have received much from them, much besides the smorgasbord and the ombudsman. Interrelations are multifold and deep.

First Explorers and Settlers

Leif Ericson's discovery of Vinland was premature. After the settlements in Russia and Normandy and Sicily and the British

Isles and the land-taking in Iceland, too few Vikings remained to people the great New World in the West. Greenland was far from the home base, and its settlements degenerated after a few centuries; Vinland was both too vast and too far, although it was but one step more.

Vinland colonization, however, was not impossible, it was only impractical. There stood no important barrier of either cold or distance to repel sailors who for 400 years crossed the North Atlantic from Norway to Greenland and who never ceased trading between Iceland and Europe. Several colonies were established in North America, but they were short-lived, wrecked by personal dissensions, trouble with Indians and weather, and most of all by lack of motivation. We have brief saga-accounts of some of the seaboard establishments, especially Leif's own wintering about the year 1000, and the horror of the Amazon Freydis' murder spree some fourteen years after. Evidences of later (fourteenth century?) Scandinavian enterprises in America are sparse and tantalizing, only enough to prove that the Northerners did reach North America.

Not until the seventeenth century did the Northerners put down permanent roots in America. The farseeing imperial eye of Gustav II Adolf visioned a Swedish colony across the Atlantic, and in 1638, six years after his death, groups of Swedes and Finns were sent to the Delaware. They brought the log cabin to America, building their cottages and their barns in the style of the homeland 4000 miles away. This was the log cabin which became both the home-building pattern and the social symbol of the American frontier. The colony was soon overwhelmed by the Dutch and then by the English, but the people remained. They gradually blended into the larger community, and left upon it a moral as well as an architectural influence. They were a sober and industrious group, whose pastors came direct from Sweden until the end of the eighteenth century.

The Old World Awakens to the New

Europe itself was reinvigorated by the discovery and development of America—wasn't it Europe's find and creation? In far-off Finland men breathed deeper because of the widening of their horizons. Peter Kalm, student of the famed Karl von Linné (Linnaeus), visited and studied in North America in the mid-eighteenth century and reported back to Europe on the wonders of the flora and fauna and the society where "each man is a king in his own house." Axel von Fersen was one of the adventurous and liberty-loving Swedish noblemen who played his dashing role in the American Revolution before he became involved with Marie Antoinette. The Crown Prince of Sweden (later Gustav III) became so enamored of Benjamin Franklin, the scientist and "worthy bourgeois," that he advocated (1768) reconstruction of the Swedish school system in accord with the principles laid down by Franklin for Pennsylvania.

The Norwegian constitution-makers of 1914 studied carefully the constitution of the United States and the separate state constitutions. Their constitution of Eidsvold carried out the Montesquieu theory and American practice of the separation of powers. One draft incorporated a direct translation of Article XXX of the constitution of Massachusetts, stating the principle of separation of powers and ending with the same dictum that government "should be a government of laws and not of men." Here was a principle inherent in the ancient Norwegian tradition as well as in the state and federal constitutions of the United States. One of the Norwegian constitution-makers christened a son George Benjamin after the two great Americans.

America was in those days for Europe both reality and dream—and probably most important as dream. With the opening of the New World began the "boom period" in European history.

The Migration That Helped Build America

Those small Finnish-Swedish settlements on the Delaware left some interesting marks on American history. John Hanson, descendant of the early Swedish settlers, was first president of the Congress. Nils Collin, last of the pastors sent out from Sweden in the eighteenth century to the colony on the Delaware, founded the historical society of Pennsylvania; he was one of those lively and intelligent persons who recognized the crudities and difficulties of early America and still appreciated it. Norwegians and Danes were fewer in the early United States than the Swedes and Finns, but gradually they too began to move and soon the stream was a torrent.

The first group migration from Norway sailed in the 54-foot, 39-ton sloop *Restauration* in 1825. In the families which crowded onto the little ship were fifty-two people, fifty-three by the time they landed in New York. Except for the birth of the baby the monotony of the long trip was relieved only by the capture of a floating wine keg near the Madeira Islands. This find caused the thirsty emigrants to rock into port at Madeira without their flag hoisted and nearly brought about their arrest and detention. But they were allowed to sail on, and after a voyage of forty-six days they landed in New York. Here more troubles awaited them, for the number of passengers exceeded the limits of the immigration regulations. But again there was leniency. They sold their ship (at a loss) and most of them moved to Orleans County, New York, where they bought small farms along the Erie Canal and tried to settle down. Then the beckoning prairies of Illinois led them on westward in the mid-1830s, to the Fox River Valley.

From here their glowing letters home lured more families and young men and young women. The America fever was beginning to burn, and the Middle West became the promised land. For four generations it beckoned, and called with a voice heard throughout Scandinavia.

The "America letters" sent home by ardent pioneers bragged and romanticized; they also contained much sound sense and occasionally money or steamship tickets. Some of the letters made a direct materialistic appeal, like one of 1856: "and I can tell you that here we do not live frugally, but one has eggs and egg pancakes and canned fish and fresh fish, and fruit of all kinds, so it is different from you who have to sit and suck herring bones." [1] Gustaf Unonius, who founded the Swedish settlement at Pine Lake, Wisconsin, wrote many a persuasive letter home. A passage in his diary gives some clues to his own thinking and that of many another. He wrote of America:

Work, and honest occupation, is no disgrace. Conventional prejudices, class interest, meanness of public opinion, tyranny of fashion are not present to hamper every step. Why should I not go to America, to that country which looms like a shining Eldorado before the eyes of every adventurous youth, to that country whose fabulous history compelled our

1. Quoted in Florence E. Janson, *The Background of Swedish Immigration, 1840–1930* (Chicago: University of Chicago Press, 1931), p. 23.

attention from our earliest years at school. That country which has become the grave of old prejudices, a cradle for true civic liberty and equality and principles of social beneficence for new generations.[2]

After years of hardship and disappointment in Wisconsin and Illinois, Unonius returned to Sweden, and argued against emigration. Later he said ruefully in his memoirs that he had made two great mistakes in life: first in going to America, second in leaving it. Many warnings were sounded that life in America was not all ease, that the changeable rigors of the climate took terrible toll in illness and death. Ole Rynning, a noble-spirited and educated young Norwegian, a leader of the ill-fated Beaver Creek colony in Illinois, wrote (in 1838) a judicious *True Account of America,* which became a popular book in Norway and one of the best guides for emigrants. But Rynning died the next September. Those of his colleagues who survived the fever soon fled from their little cabins in the malarial swamplands. Many must have yearned for Norway, but they could not return; they had spent everything they had on the journey and the land. They died silently, or they lived to rebuild their fortunes from nothing, some at last to own good farms. It was the living and the successful who wrote home, or who went back to visit with high beaver hat and gold watch chain. The dead and the broken were voiceless; the saga of America was a saga of success. To warnings only those listened who wanted to listen.

So new and greater waves of migrants broke from the past and sought the better life in the land across the sea.

Ole Rölvaag in his *Giants in the Earth* has told in universal terms the tense drama of those who struggled with nature on the stormswept prairies of the Dakotas. The Danes who settled in Iowa or eastern Nebraska faced conditions somewhat less rugged, as did the later Icelanders and the Finns in Massachusetts and northern Wisconsin. But, as with immigrants in general, the first generation had to endure the uncertainties and risks of change and carry the burden of back-breaking work. They turned the virgin sod of the western prairies, they felled the timber in the northern forests,

---

2. Condensed from Unonius's *A Pioneer in Northwest America, 1841–1858,* I, ed. Nils William Olsson (Minneapolis: University of Minnesota Press for the Swedish Pioneer Historical Society, 1950), p. 6.

they did housework for those who had migrated a generation or two earlier, they built railroads and carried bricks and stoked furnaces in the steel mills, they laid foundations for a new civilization.

Occasionally some Scandinavian writer or scientist came to view this brave new world and to report to his own people and to Europe. As Peter Kalm had come in the mid-eighteenth century, so came Fredrika Bremer in the mid-nineteenth. The opportunity and the "restless on-ward striving" made a deep impression on this sensitive Swedish writer. She felt the sharp difference between earnest New England and the West, where freedom was "still sowing its wild oats." She reflected the European wonder at the eager search for speed and the mobility of people, "the incessant change from place to place." She analyzed the ideal of the American man as "purity of intention, decision in will, energy in action, simplicity in manner, and demeanor." The woman's ideal she found to be "independence of character, gentleness." She discovered in the New England spirit the "two mainsprings . . . the one is a tendency toward the ideal of moral life, the other impels it to conquer the earth." She recognized America to be the "land of experiment." In her book she frankly said that in America "children have a better prospect . . . for their future than at home. They are admitted into schools for nothing; receive good education, and easily have an opportunity for maintaining themselves." Though slavery and politics worried her, her report in *America of the Fifties* [3] was favorable indeed, and gave another impetus to the growing migratory movement.

One of the most dramatic and full-bodied accounts of migration is Vilhelm Moberg's trilogy: *The Emigrants, Unto a Good Land,* and *The Last Letter Home.* It is fiction based on much research and a deep sympathy for the subject, for Moberg's thirteen aunts and uncles were all emigrants; to Moberg as a boy the words "cousin" and "American" were synonymous. He tells the story of a group of Swedes moving from the poverty and the stifling rigidity of life in rural Småland to the upper Mississippi Valley, a wilderness that offered hope of a new life. Jan Troell has created from this saga a memorable movie of the struggles of this determined band, with Liv Ullman representing Kristina, the reluctant pioneer woman,

3. *America of the Fifties,* ed. A. B. Benson (New York: American Scandinavian Foundation, 1924), passim.

and Max von Sydow as Karl Oskar the indomitable pioneer with a vision ahead into the distance of time.

The upsurging migration of the 1850s was halted by the War between the States, gained new momentum in the later sixties stimulated by a classic push and pull: crop failures and distress in the north of Europe, the Homestead Act of 1862 and the prospects of cheap land in America. After a pause brought by the economic crisis of the early 1870s a new wave reached peak proportions in the 1880s when more than 650,000 Scandinavians came to the United States. In the twentieth century the Viking inundation began to recede, and by the 1930s the movement was not into but out from the United States. But already some 2,500,000 Scandinavians had migrated to the New World; hardly a family was left in the Northland without a brother or a cousin in America—in Minneapolis or Rockford, Fitchburg or Worcester, Decorah, Dana, Chicago, Seattle. . . .

A few adventurous spirits went to South America or Africa, and many to Canada, but 98 percent of Swedish emigrants found their new homes in the United States, 96 percent of Norwegians and 88 percent of Danes. Most of these settled in the upper Mississippi Valley.

They were attracted by the cheap good land and by jobs. They were drawn by the demands of a new society for brain and sinew, by a higher reward for their abilities than they could ever expect to gain at home. And they were drawn too by the principles of social equality in democratic America; many an "America letter" rejoiced that the settler no longer had to tip his hat to the clergyman and that he had a voice in the affairs of the community. Such letters circulated in Scandinavia from household to household, sometimes were copied dozens of times and passed on, or were published in the local papers. The vision of America was painted in rosy hues; imagination and hope only deepened the colors.

Steamship agents fanned the ardor and the returned "local boy made good" enhanced the legend—the legend which was more than half truth. Migration fed on itself and grew.

On they came, thousands and hundreds of thousands, rogues and saints and in-betweens, from the neat thatched cottages of Denmark, from the overpopulated woodlands of Småland, from far north in the land of the midnight sun. They came to the land where life was young. In the first generation they drew together in their own national groups, held by their common background, and by their distance from it. They brought with them many of their old-world prejudices. For example, many retained a strong anticlericalism, and it took them a few years to realize that in a society with no state church the issues of clericalism were simply not relevant. Many bore through life a sense of loss and rootlessness, a feeling poetically expressed by Arthur Landfors, a twentieth-century emigrant from northernmost Sweden, in "The Tree that barely leafs":

> I took a birch that grew in the woods
> and planted it beside my house.
> It got good nourishment and it got good light
> and all the care it could want,
> And every spring it came out in leaf.
> But never did it grow vigorous
> like other trees in forest and field.
> Half green it stood there, half withered,
> with a trunk scraggy and distressed.

> We came here from the Old World,
> when we were pulled up and torn loose
> from the earth that fostered us,
> from the milieu, from the culture
> that once had given us birth.
> Here we found a place in the sun,
> but seldom did our roots go
> deep enough down in the soil
> to take from it the strength it can give.
> However fertile the place may be
> we remain but stunted plants.[4]

Gradually these transplants out of the North adjusted to the new environment. They Americanized no more rapidly but at least as thoroughly as other immigrants. They became aware of issues such as slavery and public education and temperance, and they began to speak their minds. They joined hands with the

---

4. Translated from the title poem in *Träd som bara grönska* [Tree that barely leafs] (Stockholm: FIBs Lyrikklub, 1962); original and my translation printed also in my article "Literature in Periodicals of Protest of Swedish-America," *Swedish Pioneer Historical Quarterly,* 16 (October 1965), 193–215.

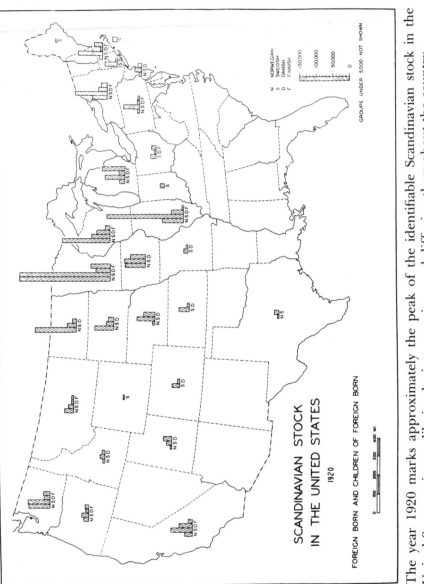

The year 1920 marks approximately the peak of the identifiable Scandinavian stock in the United States, prior to dilution by intermarriage and diffusion throughout the country.

Greeks and the English, the Germans and the Irish and the Poles, and built a new and great society. They furnished thousands of the "common man," sturdy backbone of America.

They came from a background of discontent in the old country, sometimes from a background of protest. This was why they had left. And they didn't always find that America lived up to expectations. Emigrants from the integral society of rural Scandinavia, the community-conscious villages and mountain settlements, were often appalled at the ruthless competitiveness, the "rugged individualism," of capitalistic America. They found the old ideal better than the new reality. Hundreds of Swedish immigrants in the period around World War I entered radical socialist activities and the still more radical IWW (Industrial Workers of the World), and some were deported back home. Legendary Joe Hill, the IWW song writer, was executed. Radical also were those earlier Norwegian immigrants who became the rigid backbone of the populist movement and who provided votes and leadership for the Non-Partisan League and the Farmer-Labor Party—men like Andrew Volstead, Halvor Steenorson, and Asle Grønna. Among the great labor leaders were Andrew Furuseth and Marcus Thrane. They were attuned to ideas of economic self-sufficiency and the cooperative spirit. Horatio Alger and the success myth were not their heroes. Where, as in Minnesota and North Dakota, they concentrated in adequate numbers they made their "voice of protest" heard. Out of this Norwegian background came Thorstein Veblen, maverick and one of the keenest critics of all.

More commonly the Scandinavians were scattered thinly among the population of natives and other immigrants and could not effectively express themselves. Most of them also, though reformist in spirit, adapted not to the left side but to the moderate mainstream or to the right. From their ranks came Senators Henrik Shipstead, Irvine Lenroot, Knute Nelson, Governor and Chief Justice Earl Warren. In fields other than politics the annals of America are studded with Scandinavian names of the first and second and third generations: Lauritz Melchior, Greta Garbo, and Ingrid Bergman; Charles Lindbergh and the astronaut Ed Aldrin; Victor F. Lawson of the *Chicago Daily News;* Vilhjalmur Stefansson the explorer and writer; Eliel Saarinen the architect and Carl Milles the sculptor; Anton J. Carlsson the Chicago scientist; Carl Sandburg, poet and biographer of Lincoln; John Ericsson, builder of the *Monitor,* and hundreds of engineers after him.

Craftsmen and engineers from the North have brought overseas their training and techniques in carpentry, glassmaking, interior decorating, metallurgy, and the building of bridges. In the seventeenth century they cut down trees and built log cabins; in the twentieth century they measured stresses and strains and built skyscrapers. They were a part of the "migration of skills."

In all walks of life, in positions of leadership and management, in individual roles as artists and writers, in essential but less publicized supporting parts, one found these dependable and intelligent offspring of the North. By the late twentieth century most of them were so wholly a part of America that their origin was forgotten—by others if not by themselves. Their inherited ideals and patterns of life were basically the same as the ideals and patterns earlier established in American life and appropriate to the American environment.

Their churches gradually changed from the use of the mother tongue to the English of the new society and of the second generation. Their schools and colleges retained something of the stamp of church and nationality but more and more began to serve a larger community. The day may come when Rock Island's Augustana College is no more Swedish than Notre Dame is Irish. The same will be true of the colleges of St. Olaf, Luther, Dana, Upsala, and Lindsborg. The consciousness and the characteristics of national background are gradually lost in the process of living and working together. But the process is slow. The sense of owning a dual heritage survives in many a Nordic descendant as he strives to retain the memories and something of the values of his ancestors while at the same time he is wholly an American.

The American Impact on Scandinavia

The mass movement of peoples created the new America; it also helped to transform the old Europe.

Even before 1900 authorities in Scandinavia became concerned over the flow of young blood to the West. The predominance of young men in migration upset the ratio of the sexes (leaving only some 100 men for every 105 women), and became a factor in a declining birth rate. Ministers preached that the Lord intended people to live where they were born, and societies against emigration appealed to the young to help build their own countries. Governments asked what was wrong, and the social legislation of the late nineteenth and early twentieth century was partly "appeasement," to try to hold at home the youth who were tempted to emigrate. The legal status of the lower classes was improved, women's rights were extended, and labor gained greatly in power. Or, as with the cotters in Norway,[5] the class itself was eliminated by emigration; it declined from one-quarter of the total population in 1845 to 3 percent in 1920.

Sometimes the appeal for social reform came directly from across the Atlantic. P. A. Berg and his wife left Norway for economic reasons, and also, as was often the case, because their dissenting religious opinions made them social outcasts. From Wisconsin Mr. Berg wrote back to the liberal Norwegian Prime Minister Johan Sverdrup that they enjoyed their Methodist fellowship, but he added: "You, Mr. Sverdrup, are fighting the good fight for democracy and freedom in Norway; keep it up, we are for you, for we have three sons and two daughters still in Norway, and we want them to enjoy at home the freedom which we could get only by leaving." [6]

Another Norwegian, who had never been to America, held up the United States as the model of all things wise and good. Sören Jaabaek was a radical politician, a Stortingsman (congressman), close to Sverdrup and other political leaders who were friendly to the United States. From 1865 to 1879 Jaabaek published a small paper with a big rural circulation (for then) of 17,000. He compared the "unjust inequality" of Norway with the assumed new equality of Negroes and whites in the United States; he condemned the suffrage restrictions in Norway and called attention to the coming universal suffrage in America. He praised the early income tax law of the United States, the lack of pensions, the fruitfulness of the land, and the stimulus given to work. He serialized a history of the United States and gave information about migration.

5. The cotters, or *husmaend*, farmed small plots of land, but earned most of their meager living by working for the owners of large farms; they were sharecroppers.
6. Original, dated from New Centerville, Wisconsin, January 17, 1874, is in Sverdrup Papir, Riksarkiv, Oslo.

Migration was escape for the downtrodden and the embittered; the threat of it was a bludgeon with which to force reform from the vested powers. As Brynjolf Hovde points out with regard to the adoption of religious freedom in Scandinavia: it "was due in no small part to the knowledge that people were emigrating for the lack of it." [7] Jaabaek and others deliberately used the fear of emigration to pry reform from reluctant government and to speed the process of social and economic change.

Migration itself was a potent force in Sweden as well as in Norway. In the early years of the twentieth century employers in industry and agriculture worried about the depletion of the labor supply, and officials were concerned about the "bloodletting of the Swedish nation," especially the loss of military manpower. Others did their best to capitalize on this concern in order to bring about change in Swedish society. The sociologist E. H. Thörnberg, who assisted in the great Emigration Inquiry of 1907–1913, stated openly that "we reformers used [emigration] as a vehicle for social legislation." [8] The right-wing maverick Adrian Molin worked strenuously to promote individual homeowning and settlement in northern Sweden in order to hold potential emigrants in their mother country. The Swedish minister to Washington, Herman Lagercrantz, developed a plan for bringing back to Sweden men and women who had worked in America long enough to learn industrial skills and to become imbued with the American initiative and lust to work; such people would challenge Sweden to new achievement. This scheme was quickly scuttled by the disapproval of Theodore Roosevelt!

Nevertheless, in the course of the years large numbers of emigrants did remigrate homeward—about a fifth of those who left Sweden in the years between 1881 and 1930. No man can assess with accuracy what effect such remigrants had on Swedish indus-

7. B. J. Hovde, *The Scandinavian Countries, 1720–1865,* 2 vols. (Boston: Chapman and Grimes, 1943), II, 660.

8. Quoted in B. J. Hovde, "Notes on the Effects of Emigration upon Scandinavia," *Journal of Modern History,* 6 (1934), 268n51. Thörnberg was a collaborator in the great Emigration Inquiry and author of *Sverige i Amerika, Amerika i Sverige* (Stockholm: Bonniers, 1938). Similar purposes manifested themselves in Norway, as attested by Hovde. See also my articles "Sören Jaabaek, Americanizer in Norway," *Norwegian-American Studies and Records,* 17 (1952), 84–107; and "The Study of the Effects of Emigration," *The Scandinavian Economic History Review,* 8 (1961), 170 and passim.

trial growth, though it is known that they brought several useful techniques, if not too much "lust for work." Furthermore, those who returned took American earnings home with them, and those who stayed abroad sent back remittances that helped many a family to buy food or clothing or new equipment for the farm, and sometimes tickets for the steamship across the ocean. For Sweden the amount of such remittances was estimated at eight to ten million dollars per year for the period 1906–1930, which represented 25 percent of the balance of payments with foreign countries in the 1920s, or 0.4 percent of gross national income. In the late 1930s O. B. Grimley estimated that for Norway contributions from America during a hundred years had amounted to $600,000,000.

By the end, in 1930, of the long epoch of active migration hardly a family in the North was without a brother or a cousin in the "land of opportunity." Letters and visits and travel reports spread such a feeling of acquaintance with America that the editor of the Emigration Inquiry had to comment that for some Swedes the United States did not seem to be a foreign country, but "the rightful homeland."

Diplomatic Relations

The United States' first treaty with a nonbelligerent was that with Sweden in 1783. Thus early began the cooperation of the new state overseas with one of the small but commerce-minded monarchies of Europe. Both countries were interested in maintaining freedom of the seas. This first step led on to others and, during the 1820s, to separate treaties between the United States and Denmark, Norway, and Sweden which abolished many of the old mercantilistic restraints on trade. Thereafter the ships of the Scandinavian countries could trade freely with the United States, and vice versa, carrying either their own goods or the goods of other countries. The Scandinavian governments were pleased too with the Monroe Doctrine and with the way in which Great Britain and the United States together blocked the reconquest of the Spanish American republics.

The countries were still both small and far apart, however, in the late eighteenth century and the early nineteenth, and connections were not always close. In 1780 John Quincy Adams was of the opinion that the North of Europe thought very seldom about America, and that this was a very healthy state of affairs that he did not wish to disturb. The United States often had very meager consular and diplomatic representation in Scandinavia. As late as 1810 the government used a British citizen as consul at the important port of Gothenburg.

This underestimation of real interests, the failure to appreciate the worldwide ramifications of commerce and of war, almost led to complications in the Napoleonic period. Then a vigorous young Philadelphian had himself appointed as vice-consul in Gothenburg. He, Richard Smith, was in Gothenburg from 1810 to 1812 because he had shipped as supercargo on one of his uncle's vessels bound to Russia. War conditions made the trip on to Russia seem too risky and he and the consignments for which he was responsible were stranded in Sweden. By 1812 Gothenburg played host to some 1200 foreign merchant vessels, anchored far up and down the river, all afraid of capture by the French or the English. The Americans had been protected often in British convoy, but times were changing. Smith expected a United States declaration of war on Britain. When word arrived in Gothenburg, five weeks after the outbreak of the War of 1812, the vice-consul's alertness saved 40 ships from capture.

The major depredations on American commerce were, however, due in this period to France and to her ally Denmark-Norway, and the claims arising out of these seizures cluttered the diplomatic docket for many years to come. Part of the claims dated back to John Paul Jones, some of whose prizes the Danes had given back to the British. In 1898 twenty-three American prizes were held in Norwegian ports at one time. After long negotiation Denmark in 1830 agreed to pay $650,000 and there was a mutual renunciation of claims. It is only such claims against Denmark and Sweden and disputes over the interpretation of clauses in the commercial treaties that comprised the early diplomatic controversies between the United States and the Scandinavian countries.

Another aspect of diplomatic relations had to do with colonial possessions. As early as 1783, and again in 1845, the Swedish government wanted to sell the island of St. Bartholomew in the West Indies to the United States. In the latter instance it was James

Buchanan who rejected the offer on the ground that the United States had never considered it desirable to acquire distant islands as colonies.

But conditions changed. By 1917, after fifty years of intermittent negotiations, the United States was glad indeed to get new footholds in the West Indies and bought the Danish possessions in the Virgin Islands. Despite the high price of $25,000,000, the Danish conservatives and some of the Left strongly opposed the sale, but the people as a whole were not so proud in their nationalism, and a plebiscite approved the agreement. The Danes also obtained from the United States a recognition of Denmark's sovereignty over all Greenland.

More significant and more fruitful than these bilateral agreements and disagreements has been the cooperation of the United States and the Scandinavian states in international affairs. Norway especially and the United States have been concerned with the codification of maritime law. Citizens of the small Northern states have often been able to accomplish the kind of things which the United States wanted done, but which it was difficult for Americans to do because of the suspicions aroused by great power activity. Fridtjof Nansen and Count Folke Bernadotte are two outstanding examples. The story of Scandinavian contributions to international enterprise is a long and glorious one, studded with the names of able statesmen: Stauning, Undén, Hambro, Trygve Lie, Dag Hammarskiöld. In the League of Nations and in the early years of the United Nations the Scandinavian states and the United States often saw eye to eye and acted arm in arm. The Northerners were called on time and again to provide peacekeeping forces, for example, in Cyprus and the Arab lands (especially after the Israeli-Arab war of 1967), and Ambassador Gunnar Jarring attempted for years to negotiate peace in the Near East.

Tensions and fundamental divergences developed especially between the United States and Sweden. The United States was disappointed when Sweden in 1949 attempted to form a Nordic union separate from NATO. The proposal fell through because the other small countries of the North could not bring themselves to depend on each other for defense. Hence Denmark, Iceland, and Norway joined NATO while Sweden and Finland stayed out.

Sweden's hospitality to American draft evaders and deserters from the forces in Germany and Vietnam annoyed Washington, but her right to such a policy was recognized. Real antagonism began to develop when Olof Palme, then a cabinet minister, marched in a May Day parade in Stockholm with the North Vietnam ambassador (1968). When Jerome Holland went to Sweden as ambassador in the spring of 1970 he was repeatedly insulted by roughneck elements. By courageous and effective visits throughout the country he won respect but at length had to travel with a bodyguard. There were demonstrations against the American Embassy in Stockholm and frequent damage. The problem was the intensity of public reaction against American policy in Vietnam, a reaction which the government in Washington felt was encouraged by the Swedish administration. Certainly Olof Palme, now prime minister, minced no words in condemnation of the war. When Ambassador Holland returned to the United States in the fall of 1972 no successor was appointed. When the Swedish ambassador in Washington, Hubert deBesche, was transferred to Copenhagen the State Department requested that his replacement should be delayed. Not until the spring of 1974 were formal diplomatic relations resumed.

In a speech to the Riksdag on January 31, 1973, after the peace agreement had been signed, Palme again damned the war as cruel, destructive, and meaningless. "The guilt of western civilization is great." He praised the young people of Sweden and the labor movement and the churches for their show of opposition to the war and pointed to 2,000,000 signatures on a petition for peace. He reminded his people of the "risk in our time of a hegemony of the super-powers in the world," and asserted the right of all small nations (and he referred to Czechoslovakia, and Vietnam and Sweden) to exist and to express themselves. Specifically with regard to the United States he spoke of the grave differences of opinion and added only: "The American government has chilled down our diplomatic relations. This was not our wish. Our wish is that normal diplomatic relations shall exist between us." The whole imbroglio was caused in the first place by a disastrous error in American foreign policy that was then made an issue in Sweden's new policy of "active neutrality." It was exacerbated by a personality conflict between Olof Palme and Richard Nixon.

Cultural Crosscurrents

"Government of the people, by the people, for the people." Abraham Lincoln thus epitomized American democracy; quite independently and twenty years earlier Johan Sverdrup of Norway used exactly the same terms—only in Norwegian. It was natural for each, because each was giving expression to the political philosophy of his own society. Henrik Wergeland and Walt Whitman, though they did not know each other, gave voice to common ideals and aspirations; and Wergeland, Norway's romantic nationalist poet of the nineteenth century, proposed a triune federation of Scandinavian states patterned after the federal union of the United States.

The traditions of Scandinavia are the traditions too of America and center about the struggle for personal freedom and democratic equality. The men of the Icelandic sagas sound much like American frontiersmen, though placed in different surroundings. Hard work and the incessant struggle with nature have characterized both Scandinavian and American. The resultant likeness in thought has made easier all phases of cultural exchange, from religion to industry.

For religion was a field of active interchange. In America the Scandinavian immigrants established their own religious organizations, and they were deeply affected by the evangelistic movements of the midwest in the nineteenth century. The Methodists, the Baptists, the Mormons, and other sects also reached across the ocean to preach and convert in Scandinavia. To this day the peoples of the North are amazed at the religious diversity and fervor in America—"The land of revivals, churches, chapels, congregations."

A Presbyterian Sunday School worker from New Jersey, Robert Baird, was one of the most effective apostles to Scandinavia. Mr. Baird went to Europe in the 1830s to preach religious toleration and temperance. He won the highest sponsorships for his temperance program in Scandinavia as well as in Germany. King Carl Johan was deeply impressed by Baird's book (in French) on the American temperance movement, and had it translated and published in Sweden and distributed to every pastor in the kingdom. It was spread in Finland as well.

It was the psychological moment, for the Swedes had begun to worry about themselves. The English pastor, George Scott, helped to promote the movement, as did Swedish leaders like Per Wieselgren. In 1826 the Swedes had shown interest in the work of the American Temperance Society. In the 1830s temperance societies grew up rapidly, Baird traveled about like a conquering hero, and in less than a decade the consumption of *brännvin* and other strong liquors declined from forty-eight quarts per capita to less than six. In Norway legislation aided the cause; many little distilleries went out of business; and coffee replaced *brännvin* as the national drink.

When in the 1890s this wave had exhausted itself, a new working-class movement sprang up to fight demon rum, and this too had strong American support. Yet temperance was but one of the many social reform movements stimulated by American experience and precept.

Religious intolerance was not usually brutal in Scandinavia, but social and political ostracism often plagued dissenters. The Erik Janssonists were something of an exception, yet they as a group of dissenters were thrust out of Sweden in the mid-nineteenth century, and migrated to set up the Bishop Hill colony in Illinois. Law and practice grew more liberal, but men and women opposed to the state church made up an unusual proportion of emigrants. Visiting preachers from America left their imprint in Scandinavia, as did the "America letters" and the stories told by returned emigrants. The Nordic countries remained Lutheran but became tolerant. By the twentieth century considerable congregations of Methodists, Baptists, Mission Friends, and Mormons flourished. They and their Sunday Schools, which reached with moving religious force the worker elements of the population, played a significant part in the education and inspiration of the labor and government leadership of the Northern lands.

Prison reform in the United States concerned Fredrika Bremer, as it had even earlier interested Crown Prince Oscar. The Prince studied the Philadelphia system of single cells and the Auburn system of common work. In 1840 he published a book dealing with the American experiments that was influential in the creation of new prisons and new penal methods, more humane and more effective in crime prevention. In the early twentieth century the Scandinavians looked carefully at American theory and experience with the indeterminate sentence, honor system, and parole, and legal authorities like Harald Salomon and Arne Omsted made extensive study tours in the United States and published their views at home. Norwegian authorities used American experience in railroad law, and they quoted John Marshall on the power of the courts. In the 1970s the tables are turned and it is the Americans who are studying the innovative prison systems of the North, especially Sweden.

The cooperative movement is the most noted example of recent Scandinavian influence on the United States. Marquis Childs' *Sweden, The Middle Way* won an amazing vogue in the United States and worried sober Swedes, who knew that their angels' wings had been pictured as too lily-white. Through the Hoover Commission and its report and the visits of cooperative-minded Americans the Scandinavian countries became an ideological and practical pattern for that movement in the United States. In 1949 the Danes themselves were amazed at the popularity of the course on cooperatives which they offered to American graduate students in Copenhagen.

In 1911 Niels Poulsen, a wealthy Danish-American businessman, established the American-Scandinavian Foundation which has been continuously active in promoting understanding of Scandinavian culture in the United States and in sending American students to study in the North. The Foundation has also published *The American Scandinavian Review,* one of the most distinguished journals of any ethnic group in the United States. It has served as an interpreter of Scandinavia to all Americans and as a bond with the ancestral lands for Americans of Northern descent. The Foundation has also published, and continues to publish, classics from the wealth of Scandinavian literature and modern books of interpretation. Complementing the work of the American-Scandinavian Foundation have been the independent but cooperating societies established in the northern countries: Sverige-Amerika Stiftelsen (Sweden America Foundation), Danmark-Amerika Fondet (The Denmark America Fund), Norge-Amerika Foreningen (The Norway America Society), and Islenzk-Ameriska Félagid (Icelandic American Society). During World War II a Finnish-America Society was organized and it has become active in the postwar period.

Partly through these sister societies of the American Scan-

dinavian Foundation and also through a variety of other sponsorships, immediately after 1945 scores and hundreds of Scandinavians flocked to the United States to study dentistry, banking,
education, journalism, science—though few in the social sciences
and humanities. Their own universities had been seriously hurt
by war. Germany was closed and England could not be as hospita-
ble as of old. The center for foreign study, for Scandinavians as
for other people, had shifted across the Atlantic. In 1949
Congress passed an act authorizing the use of the remainder of
the Finnish debt payments to the United States for scholarships to
Finnish students to come to America to study (an $8,000,000 ges-
ture).

Even prior to this postwar surge the cultural ties between Scandinavia and the United States had been peculiarly strong in certain fields. To American library schools, for instance, had come
more student-librarians from Norway than from any other country. The organizer of the city library in Oslo had spent seven years
at the Newberry Library in Chicago, and the director (Arne Kildal) of the widespread library extension service of Norway got
his own training and inspiration in the United States. The
builders of the city library in Stockholm made a tour of United
States libraries and many ideas thus gained were incorporated in
the new structure as the Swedes adapted and remolded them to fit
their needs. Scandinavian pedagogues had come to the United
States as early as the 1840s, and they kept on coming to learn of
classroom architecture, teaching devices, and "progressive education." In recent years have come also hundreds of young Scandinavian bank clerks, skilled workers, business managers, to learn
the practical aspects of their work by experience.

Among the notable former fellows in this two-way educatonal
exchange are: Henrik Dam (who won the Nobel Prize for his discovery of the vitamin K); Harold C. Urey, atomic physicist, another Nobel winner; Robert Hillyer, Pulitzer prize poet; Bryn
Hovde, former president of the New School for Social Research, a
Guggenheim fellow; the Swedish brain surgeon Herbert Olive-
crona. Some Scandinavian scholars have succeeded better than
Americans in explaining Americans to themselves—notably Gunnar Myrdal, author of *An American Dilemma*. Others have become
in actuality binational as well as bilingual.

In America rather few Scandinavian authors and books are known. Ibsen and Strindberg and Hans Christian Andersen and Sigrid Undset of the older writers; Vilhelm Moberg and a handful of others for the current generation. But there is a rich literature to be tapped, and an increasing number of items get translated. The bibliography at the end of this volume lists some of the most significant writings. American books are read avidly in Scandinavia, many in translation. But these are often read in the original, for Scandinavians know English well. Even before World War II the public libraries of both Oslo and Stockholm loaned more American than English fiction and far more than German or any other: Jack London, Upton Sinclair, Dos Passos, Hemingway, Sinclair Lewis, as well as the old standbys like James Fenimore Cooper and Mark Twain. More recently it is Eugene O'Neill, between whom and the Swedes a real love affair developed.

Music, often an easy international language, has been interchanged freely. Americans have loved the grave and powerful symphonies of the Finnish Sibelius and the mysterious blend of the gay and the somber that is found in Norwegian Edvard Grieg. From America the Scandinavians have taken the Sankey-Moody hymns, translated them over and over, and sung them into their own souls. America has modified and popularized the music of Africa and sent it on to the North. There it contrasts oddly with the old folk music but it dominates the dance. In 1948 the master of jazz, Dizzy Gillespie, began his triumphal European tour in Gothenburg—an extraordinary exchange for Jenny Lind, the Swedish nightingale, and for Ole Bull, the Norwegian violinist, both of whom won vast popularity in American tours a century earlier.

One's thoughts race on through the innumerable avenues and bypaths of Scandinavian-American cultural interchange. The first private banks of the North in the 1850s were patterned on American models. Many American buildings, some of the most notable skyscrapers, have been built by architects and engineers from Scandinavia. When after World War II a medical mission from the United States went to assess the needs for aid in Poland and northeast Europe, it arrived at last in Helsinki. There the members were so impressed with the practical architectural improvement they saw that they warned their colleagues in New

York to postpone further hospital construction until the travelers could give them information on the new devices built into Finnish hospitals. In the other direction a Swedish committee planning a children's hospital to be given to Norway made a flying tour to inspect the most recent developments in the United States. Hundreds of engineers from the Scandinavian countries have toured the United States and gained new insights into factory management, technical appliances, new products.

Groups of industrial laborers have been brought across the Atlantic to observe and work in American factories for brief periods. Perhaps American labor and management can learn from them some of the reasons why industrial labor relations operate more smoothly in the Scandinavian environment than in the American. These visitors are impressed by the mass productiom of the great factories, by the mechanical aids that lessen the human burden, and by the fine cars driven to work by the American workers. They consider their housing superior to that of the American workers.

However, such phenomena as these are superficial in comparison with the deep whirlpools in the cultural crosscurrents of the immigrants. They adapted well to America, yes, but their roots had been cut; their associations, their memories, were of people and institutions far away. To be complete they had to retain what they could of their past, they must realize the fullness of their dual heritage. As Dr. Lars W. Boe has epitomized it:

To us has been given the task of mediating a culture, of preserving and transferring to our children in a new land the cultural and spiritual values bound up in the character, act, music, literature, and Christian faith of a generation no longer found even in the land from which the fathers came.[9]

Hence they founded newspapers and churches and clubs. Interestingly, the few attempts to make such institutions "Scandinavian" soon foundered. Each had to be Danish or Finnish or Icelandic or Norwegian or Swedish, or even provincial. The felt need was for something as familiar as the old language (even dialect). Their churches, whether Lutheran or of the dissenting

9. Quoted in the *Norwegian-American Historical Association Newsletter*, no. 31 (August 1954), p. 2.

denominations, changed slowly from mother tongue to English to accommodate the younger generation (and to meet the opposition to their foreignness that arose during World War I); later still most of them merged with the larger associations of like faith that were originally American. Their newspapers lost their raison d'être as their special language clientele gradually disappeared, and so the dailies became weeklies and then slowly vanished from the scene. But both churches and newspapers had done their work of bridging the chasm of cultural transition.

Colleges founded to educate in the old language and culture were built from the first on the American pattern and were never wholly exclusive. They served an expanding community with success. The lodges and singing clubs and other societies could rather easily adapt both to a mixing of the generations and to the interethnic scene, for they were not dependent on language affiliation. They, along with the other organizations, have helped to transfer to a wider American society institutions such as the smörgåsbord and St. Lucia's Day, and they have preserved for themselves festivals and holidays such as the Norwegians' seventeenth of May.

Most persistent may be the cultural societies that demand less total allegiance but that deliberately appeal to the lasting elements in the heritage. These organizations do not depend on nostalgia or on the search for identity of rootless immigrants, although such impulses do appear in their activities and publications. Their purposes are less emotional and more akin to the scholarly search for understanding of cultures outside America. This kind of academic interest has been growing rapidly in the universities.

Some significant trends are brought into the light by an extensive survey conducted in 1970–1972 by Gene Gage and published in successive issues of *Scandinavian Studies:* Danish language courses were taught in 1970 in fourteen universities and two colleges, Norwegian in fifteen universities and five colleges, Swedish in twenty-two universities and five colleges; adding the advanced courses in literature the total number of institutions giving such courses was fifty-five and the number of students 4072. This latter figure was almost double the numbers of 1939. Social science courses devoted to Scandinavia enrolled 720 students. Most revealing of all was that of twenty-nine candidates for the Ph.D. in

Scandinavian subjects only six had any Nordic blood in their veins. Only a few of them had come out of the Scandinavian colleges. The meaning of this is, of course, that the immigrant factor has ceased to be of importance. American students are seeking to know the Scandinavian languages and literature solely because of the value of that literature, they are studying the history and sociology and economics and other aspects of Nordic culture because these countries are laboratories of social significance.

Programs of college study abroad have stimulated some of the preliminary study in American universities. The big boost came in the years immediately after World War II with the GI grants and the Fulbright scholarships. One hundred GIs went to Stockholm in 1946 and a group to Copenhagen in 1948. Since then several colleges have established "junior year abroad" courses in Denmark, two of the California university systems have year-long programs based in Uppsala and Lund, and for a quarter of a century the University of Oslo has conducted a summer school attracting hundreds of Americans of college age and above. Scores more, often on the advanced doctoral level, have gone on their own or through grants from various foundations, to study chemistry, history, forestry, religion, government . . . in these same institutions or in Finland or Iceland. The movement of students in both directions is remarkably active and rewarding alike to the individuals and the countries concerned.

Within Scandinavia and for their own students teaching about America was meager until very recently. English language teaching was universal, but it had to be "Oxford English" and the literature taught was primarily English. It was evidently felt that "American" was a cross between a Swedish-American brogue and gangster slang. Since World War II perceptible change has brought the establishment of American institutes in Uppsala and Oslo and a generally increased schedule of studies in American literature and American history and institutions. One of the special branches in which Scandinavian professors and students have become involved is the study of emigration, and a rich harvest of dissertations has begun to appear. Archives and museums of emigration have been established in Växjö and Karlstad.

Denmark has a unique American institution in the form of a park at Rebild in Jutland. Here a gift from a Danish-born Chicagoan has preserved a large section of natural Danish heath and has established a museum complete with covered wagon, Indian headdresses, and American flags. Nearby in Ålborg a Danish-American archive was created, with valuable material on migration (in 1949 moved to Copenhagen). At Rebild on each Fourth of July American tourists and native Danes in numbers up to 40 — and 50,000 assemble for a huge picnic and lengthy oratory. It is a Denmark-America love feast, and lacks only a baseball game to make an American feel fully at home.

The tourists to Rebild and the thousands of others who have sailed to the North Cape or traveled by air and land in the picturesque North have left in their wake American dollars, millions of them. Immigrant sons and daughters of these lands have sent home parts of their earnings. Long before the epoch of the Marshall Plan some of the "surplus profits" of a rich America were going back to make life easier in lands which had for centuries "lived on the margin of the possible," lands which are now themselves well-to-do.

An interesting recent example, given much publicity in the Swedish press, was of a Swedish emigrant boy who became a successful doctor in Oregon. He bethought himself of his little village in southern Sweden and of his own difficulties in getting an education. He gave $3000, as a beginning, for the use of deserving boys of that village who wanted further education. "It happens every day"—almost.

The manifold influences and ideas from America continue to be significant. The ideas were felt at first largely through missionaries and returned emigrants and therefore affected the lower classes more powerfully than the intelligentsia. Among the working groups the influence was so direct that, for example, when a controversy within the Independent Order of Good Templars split the organization in the United States the division was mirrored within every Good Templar lodge in Sweden.

The men and women of the North have been deeply moved by American-expressed ideals like the Gettysburg Address and the Four Freedoms, but often they see that American realities do not match the high ideals. They become confused and even embittered at reports of racial intolerance in the United States, of bigotry and materialism and waste and the ruthlessness of man to man. This is partly because they have been taught to think of the United States as a kind of Utopia and they hate to be disillusioned; it is partly that in the homogeneity of their own society it is difficult to appreciate the complex problems of the heterogeneous community across the Atlantic, a community great with potentialities but still lacking the unity and stability of the ancient nations of northern Europe.

Yet these two societies, the small and the large, the old and the new, have reacted powerfully on one another. By direct imitation of techniques and by subtle pervasive ideals the United States has helped to make the modern Scandinavia and Scandinavia has helped to make the United States. The New World has been a testing ground for theories born in the Old World; it has helped prove possible "things before held impossible." Now American society has aged and the Scandinavian societies lead, for better or for worse, in innovativeness. Interaction can still be productive.

Appendices
Suggested Reading
Index

Appendix 1. Norden population statistics.

POPULATION TRENDS

Country	1800	1900	1950	1973 (Jan. 1)
Denmark	929,000	2,450,000	4,281,000	5,008,000
Faroe Islands	5,000	15,000	32,000	39,000
Greenland	—	12,000	24,000	48,000
Finland	833,000	2,656,000	4,030,000	4,708,500 (1974)
Iceland	47,000	78,000	144,000	213,000
Norway	883,000	2,240,000	3,279,000	3,997,000 (1975)
Sweden	2,347,000	5,136,000	7,042,000	8,175,000 (1975)

URBAN POPULATIONS

Country	City	Including suburbs	City proper
Denmark	Copenhagen	1,353,777 [a]	—
	Århus	244,840 [a]	—
	Odense	167,772 [a]	—
	Ålborg	155,264 [a]	—
	Esbjerg	77,780 [a]	—
Faroe Islands	Torshavn	10,810 [b]	—
Greenland	Godthåb	7,974 [b]	—
Finland	Helsinki	829,473 [a]	514,166 [c]
	Tampere	228,266 [a]	170,000 [c]
	Turku (Åbo)	225,619 [a]	165,000 [c]
	Lahti	117,307 [a]	95,000 [c]
	Oulu	107,939 [a]	97,000 [c]
	Vantaa	—	108,000 [c]

Country	City	Including suburbs	City proper
Iceland	Reykjavik	97,848 [a]	—
Norway	Oslo	—	468,514 [d]
	Bergen	—	214,580 [d]
	Trondheim	—	133,213 [d]
	Stavanger	—	84,359 [d]
	Kristiansand	—	58,975 [d]
	Drammen	—	50,513 [d]
Sweden	Stockholm	1,350,929 [a]	671,453 [d]
	Gothenburg	688,069 [a]	445,482 [d]
	Malmö	451,845 [a]	246,622 [d]
	Uppsala	—	137,447 [d]
	Norrköping	—	119,488 [d]
	Västerås	—	117,985 [d]
	Örebro	—	117,527 [d]
	Jönköping	—	108,152 [d]
	Linköping	—	108,028 [d]
	Borås	—	105,544 [d]
	Helsingborg	—	102,116 [d]

Source. Nordisk statistisk årsbok, 1973, pp. 28, 30. Figures for 1975 are from the national information services reports.

[a] Jan. 1, 1973.
[b] Jan. 1, 1972.
[c] 1974.
[d] Jan. 1, 1975.

Appendix 2. Norden area statistics.

	Square kilometers	Square miles
Denmark		
Metropolitan total	43,000	17,000
Jutland	29,000	11,400
483 islands	13,400	5,600
Faroe Islands	1,400	540
Greenland	—	840,000
		(about 16% ice-free)
Finland	337,000	130,000
Iceland	103,000	40,000
Norway	324,000	125,000
Sweden	450,000	174,000

Sources: Nordisk statistisk årsbok, 1973; Denmark: An Official Handbook (Copenhagen: Ministry of Foreign Affairs, 1970); Frederick G. Vosburgh, ed., *National Geographic Atlas of the World,* 3d ed., rev. (Washington: National Geographic Society, 1970).

Suggested Reading

From a profusion of riches ample reading matter can be selected to broaden and deepen knowledge of Norden. In their own languages the Scandinavians produce the world's highest percentages of books per capita, and English-language books and articles are flowing increasingly from the presses. Many of the scholarly publications in Nordic tongues carry English summaries, and the statistical yearbooks always run titles in English as well as in the native language. Informational pamphlets on varied subjects, including constitutional documents, are often published in English and are available from the embassies in Washington, the information services in New York and other cities, or establishments in the home countries such as the Swedish Institute in Stockholm. Since the early 1950s the Nordic Council has published a *Yearbook of Nordic Statistics* which is especially good for summary and comparative purposes. The following list emphasizes recent titles and English-language materials.

GENERAL

Among recent books on Scandinavia as a whole the following can be particularly recommended:

William R. Mead and Wendy Hall. *Scandinavia.* New York: Walker, 1972. A broad-based treatment by two English geographers.
Brian Fullerton and Alan F. Williams. *Scandinavia: An Introductory Geography.* New York: Praeger, 1972. Geographic and economic description.
Donald S. Connery. *The Scandinavians.* New York: Simon and Schuster, 1966. People and society.

John H. Wuorinen. *Scandinavia*. Englewood Cliffs, N.J.: Prentice-Hall, 1965. A brief paperback history stressing the twentieth century.

Jørgen Bukdahl et al. *Scandinavia, Past and Present*. 3 vols. Copenhagen: Edvard Henriksen [ca. 1959]. An extensive cooperative history, a mine of information.

Axel Sømme, ed. *A Geography of Norden*. Oslo: Cappelen, 1960.

Among the most useful periodicals are:

The American Scandinavian Review.   New York.
The Scandinavian Economic History Review.   Copenhagen.
Economy and History.   Lund.
The Norseman.   Oslo.
The Scandinavian Times.   Copenhagen.

General treatments of individual countries include:

Denmark: An Official Handbook. Copenhagen, 1974. An excellent 900-page illustrated book of information, published by the Danish Foreign Office.

Stewart Oakley. *A Short History of Denmark*. New York: Praeger, 1972. Contains a good bibliography.

Palle Lauring. *History of Denmark*. Copenhagen, 1961. Brief.

P. M. Mitchell. *A History of Danish Literature*. New York: American Scandinavian Foundation, 1958. A valuable survey.

John Danstrup and Hal Koch, eds. *Danmarks Historie*. 14 vols. Copenhagen: Politiken, 1969–.

The Danish Journal (formerly the *Danish Foreign Office Journal*). General articles, illustrated.

W. Glyn Jones. *Denmark*. London and New York: Praeger, 1970. A history with emphasis on the nineteenth and twentieth centuries.

Eino Jutikkala. *History of Finland*. New York: Praeger, 1962. Strong on pre-twentieth century political history.

John H. Wuorinen. *A History of Finland*. New York: Columbia University Press, 1965. Emphasizes twentieth-century development.

W. R. Mead. *Finland*. New York: Praeger, 1968. Broadly interpreted geography.

Hillar Kallas and Sylvia Nickels, eds. *Finland, Creation and Construction*. Helsinki, London, and New York: Praeger, 1968. Selected topics by various authors.

Jaakko Ahokas. *A History of Finnish Literature*. New York: American Scandinavian Foundation, 1973.

Elias Lönnrot. *The Kalevala, or Poems of the Kaleva District*. Cambridge: Harvard University Press, 1963. Trans. and ed. Francis P. Magoun, Jr., and *The Old Kalevala and Certain Antecedents*, ibid., 1969.

Knut Gjerset. *History of Iceland*. New York: Macmillan, 1924. Although long out of date, this is the most extensive treatment of Icelandic history in English.

Stefan Einarsson. *A History of Icelandic Literature.* New York: The Johns Hopkins Press for American Scandinavian Foundation, 1957.

Iceland, 1966. Reykjavik: Central Bank of Iceland, 1967. A thorough, recent compendium of information.

Atlantica and Iceland Review. Reykjavik. A beautiful and enlightening monthly, containing a small bulletin insert of statistical data.

Barthi Guthmundsson. *The Origin of the Icelanders.* Lincoln: University of Nebraska Press, 1967.

Karen Larsen. *History of Norway.* Princeton: Princeton University Press, for the American Scandinavian Foundation, 1948. Good one-volume account in English.

T. K. Derry. *A Short History of Norway.* London: Allen and Unwin, 1957.

John Midgaard. *A Brief History of Norway.* Oslo: Tanum, 1963, 1964. Paperback.

Magne Helvig and Viggo Johannessen. *Norway: Land—People—Industries.* Oslo: Tanum, 1966.

Egil Tveterås. *The Norway Yearbook, 1967.* Oslo: Tanum, 1966.

Edvard Bull, Wilhelm Keilhau, et al. *Det norske folks liv og historie.* 11 vols. Oslo: Aschehoug, 1929–1938.

Ingvar Andersson. *A History of Sweden.* New York: Praeger, 1956. The best history for pre-twentieth century. OP.

Stewart Oakley. *A Short History of Sweden.* New York: Praeger, 1966. Similar to his *Short History of Denmark.*

Irene Scobbie. *Sweden.* New York: Praeger, 1972. Recent, accurate, and readable.

Kurt Samuelsson, *From Great Power to Welfare State.* London: Allen and Unwin, 1968. Good.

Steven Koblik, ed. *From Poverty to Affluence.* Minneapolis: University of Minnesota Press, 1975. Swedish history from the eighteenth to the twentieth century; topical essays by outstanding Swedish authorities.

Sten Carlsson and Jerker Rosén. *Svensk historia.* 2 vols. Stockholm: Bonniers, 1960, 1962. Standard Swedish textbook.

Den svenska historien. 10 vols. Stockholm: Bonniers, 1966–1968. An expanded, illustrated, and popularized version of the text listed immediately above.

Hans W. Ahlmann et al. *Sverige: Land och folk.* 3 vols. Stockholm: Natur och Kultur, 1966. Superb illustrated geography.

Alrik Gustafson. *A History of Swedish Literature.* Minneapolis: University of Minnesota Press for the American Scandinavian Foundation, 1961. Encyclopedic in coverage, readable in style.

Sweden Now. Stockholm. Monthly news and feature magazine.

THE HERITAGE

The native-language works on the heritage are so voluminous that we will restrict ourselves here to translations and works written in English, French, or German.

Geoffrey Bibby. *The Testimony of the Spade.* New York: Knopf, 1956. Popular-scientific archaeology, entire North.

Viggo Starcke. *Denmark in World History.* Philadelphia: University of Pennsylvania Press, 1968. Stone Age to Middle Ages.

Sven B. F. Jansson. *The Runes of Sweden.* Stockholm: Norstedt, 1962. Small but good introduction.

Eric Linklater. *The Ultimate Viking.* New York: Harcourt Brace, 1955. Fictional but essentially "right."

Ole Klindt-Jensen. *Viking Art.* Ithaca: Cornell University Press, 1966. A magnificent book.

Charles H. Haskins. *The Normans in European History.* Boston: Houghton Mifflin, 1915. A classic.

Peter G. Foote and David M. Wilson. *The Viking Achievement.* London and New York: Praeger, 1970. Emphasis on home and social background.

Gwyn Jones. *A History of the Vikings.* New York: Oxford University Press, 1968. Emphasis on the outward thrusts.

Henry Goddard Leach. *Pageant of Old Scandinavia.* Princeton: Princeton University Press, for the American Scandinavian Foundation, 1946. A fascinating anthology.

Halvdan Koht. *The Old Norse Sagas.* New York: Norton, 1931. Interpretive.

Heimskringla: History of the Kings of Norway, by Snorri Sturluson. Trans. Lee M. Hollander. Austin and New York: American Scandinavian Foundation, 1964. The best translation of a fundamental classic.

Theodore M. Andersson. *The Icelandic Family Saga.* Cambridge: Harvard University Press, 1967. Synopses and analyses of several sagas. Many editions are available of the various sagas; read especially *The Saga of Burnt Njal, The Saga of Egil Skallagrimsson.*

Gwyn Jones. *The Norse Atlantic Saga.* New York: Oxford University Press, 1964.

R. A. Skelton et al. *The Vinland Map and the Tartar Relation.* New Haven: Yale University Press, 1965. Despite the challenge to the authenticity of the Vinland Map, this remains a valuable book.

For the Middle Ages a reader almost has to go to works in the Scandinavian languages, though the best single-volume survey is in French.

Lucien Musset. *Les peuples scandinaves au moyen age.* Paris: Presses Universitaires, 1951.

L. M. Larson. *The Earliest Norwegian Laws.* New York: Columbia University Press, 1935.

Wilhelm Holmquist. *Sveriges forntid och medeltid.* Malmö: Malmö Ljustrycksanstalt, 1949. Abundantly illustrated by a leading Swedish authority.

Halvdan Koht. *Drottning Margareta och kalmarunionen.* Stockholm: Natur och Kultur, 1956. A great Norwegian scholar's treatment of an extraordinary woman and the brief period of Nordic union.

Vilhelm Moberg. *A History of the Swedish People: From Pre-History to the Renaissance.* New York: Pantheon, 1972. A "popular history of the Swedish common man."

Sigrid Undset. *Kristin Lavransdatter.* New York: Knopf, 1929. Historical fiction at its best.

Beginning with the early modern times the good works in English multiply:

Michael Roberts. *The Early Vasas: A History of Sweden, 1523–1611.* Cambridge: Cambridge University Press, 1968.

——— *Gustavus Adolphus: A History of Sweden, 1611–1632.* 2 vols. London: Longmans, 1953, 1958.

——— *Essays in Swedish History.* London: Weidenfeld and Nicolson, 1967. On Charles XI, Christina, and special subjects.

——— ed. *Sweden as a Great Power, 1611–1697: Government: Society: Foreign Policy.* London and New York: St. Martin's, 1968. Collection of documents.

——— ed. *Sweden's Age of Greatness, 1632–1718.* London and New York: St. Martin's, 1973. Essays by Swedish specialists.

(For most of this dramatic middle period of Swedish history Professor Roberts has written and compiled works that not even the Swedes can match).

Curt Weibull. *Christina of Sweden.* Stockholm: Bonniers, 1966. Translated from the Swedish.

Jill Lisk. *The Struggle for Supremacy in the Baltic, 1600–1725.* New York: Funk and Wagnalls, 1968.

Ragnhild Hatton. *Charles XII of Sweden.* London: Weidenfeld and Nicolson, 1968. Most modern treatment.

Oscar Haintz. *König Karl XII von Schweden.* 3 vols. Berlin: W. de Gruyter, 1958. Germanic in scholarship and interpretation as well as in language.

Claude Nordmann. *Grandeur et liberté de la Suède (1660–1792).* Paris: Béatrice-Nauwelaerts, 1971. An interpretive narrative, well written.

H. S. K. Kent. *War and Trade in Northern Seas: Anglo-Scandinavian Economic Relations in the Mid-18th Century.* Cambridge: Cambridge University Press, 1973. Some new facets.

Beth Hennings. *Gustav III: En biografi.* Stockholm: Norstedt, 1957. A general biography by the leading Swedish authority on the enigmatic monarch.

Knut Hagberg. *Carl Linnaeus.* London: Jonathan Cape, 1952.

Vilhelm Moberg. *A History of the Swedish People: From Renaissance to Revolution.* New York: Pantheon, 1973. Continuation of his work mentioned above, and all that Moberg completed before his death in 1973.

A drastically curtailed list of books on the nineteenth and early twentieth centuries:

Brynjolf J. Hovde. *The Scandinavian Countries, 1720–1865.* 2 vols. Boston: Chapman and Grimes, 1943. Reissued by Cornell University Press, 1948. Firstrate social history.

Erica Simon. *Réveil national et culture populaire en scandinavie: La genèse de la højskole nordique, 1848–1878.* Copenhagen: Gyldendal, 1960. An excellent study of Nordic educational developments, broader than title indicates.

Franklin D. Scott, *Bernadotte and the Fall of Napoleon.* Cambridge: Harvard University Press, 1935.

T. K. Derry. *A History of Modern Norway, 1814–1972.* London: Oxford University Press, 1973.

Oscar Falnes. *National Romanticism in Norway.* New York: Columbia University Press, 1933.

Theodore Jorgenson. *Norway's Relation to Scandinavian Unionism, 1815–1871.* Northfield, Minn.: St. Olaf College Press, 1935.

L. D. Steefel. *The Schleswig-Holstein Question.* Cambridge: Harvard University Press, 1932.

W. Carr. *Schleswig-Holstein, 1815–1848: A Study in National Conflict.* Manchester: University Press, 1963.

Eli F. Heckscher. *An Economic History of Sweden.* Cambridge: Harvard University Press, 1954. This pioneering work in economic history is somewhat outdated but still valuable.

Arthur Montgomery. *The Rise of Modern Industry in Sweden.* London: P. S. King & Son, 1939.

Sten Carlsson. *Ståndssamhälle och ståndspersoner, 1700–1865.* Lund: Gleerup, 1973. On the replacement of the old estate society in Sweden by a class society. With good summary in English.

Douglas Verney. *Parliamentary Reform in Sweden, 1866–1921.* Oxford: Clarendon Press, 1957.

O. Fritiof Ander. *The Building of Modern Sweden: The Reign of Gustav V, 1907–1950.* Rock Island: Augustana Book Concern, 1958.

FUNCTIONING SOCIAL DEMOCRACY

Government

Nils Andrén. *Government and Politics in the Northern Countries.* Stockholm: Almquist-Wiksell, 1964.

J. A. Lawerys, ed. *Scandinavian Democracy: Development of Democratic Thought and Institutions in Denmark, Norway, and Sweden.* Copenhagen: Danish Institute and others, 1958.

Scandinavian Political Studies. Helsinki, 1966–. (Distributed by Columbia University Press, New York.) A yearbook of scholarly articles published by the Political Science Associations of Denmark, Finland, Norway, and Sweden.

Åke Sparring. *Kommunismen i Norden och den Världskommunistiska Rörelsens Kris.* Stockholm: Aldus/Bonniers, 1965.

A. F. Upton. *Communism in Scandinavia and Finland.* Garden City: Doubleday, 1973.

Nils Herlitz. *Elements of Nordic Public Law.* Stockholm: Norstedt, 1969.

Danish and Norwegian Law. Ed. The Danish Committee on Comparative Law. Copenhagen: Gad, 1963.

Kenneth E. Miller. *Government and Politics in Denmark.* Boston: Houghton Mifflin, 1968.

John Logue. "Parties and Politics in Denmark." *American Scandinavian Review* 62 (June 1974), 140–150.

Jaakko Uotila, ed. *The Finnish Legal System.* Helsinki: The Finnish Lawyers Publishing Co., 1966.

Jaakko Nousiainen. *The Finnish Political System.* Cambridge: Harvard University Press, 1971.

Harry Eckstein. *Division and Cohesion in a Democracy: A Study of Norway.* Princeton: Princeton University Press, 1966.

James Storing. *Norwegian Democracy.* Oslo: Universitetsforlag, 1963.

Herbert Tingsten. *The Swedish Social Democrats: Their Ideological Development.* Totowa, N.J.: Bedminster, 1973. Translation of Tingsten's classic *Den svenska socialdemocratins idéutveckling* (1941).

Raymond Fusilier. *Le parti socialiste suèdois: Son organisation.* Paris: Les Editions Ouvrières, 1954.

Dankwart Rustow. *The Politics of Compromise: A Study of Parties and Cabinet Government in Sweden.* Princeton: Princeton University Press, 1955.

Olof Ruin. *Mellan Samlingsregering och Tvåpartisystem, 1945–1960.* Stockholm: Bonniers, 1968. A detailed study.

Gunnar Adler-Karlsson. *Functional Socialism: A Swedish Theory for Democratic Socialization.* Stockholm: Prisma, 1969.

Nils Elvander. *Intresseorganisationerna i dagens Sverige.* Lund: Gleerup, 1966. On the strong role played in government by extragovernmental special interest organizations.

Social Welfare

George R. Nelson, ed. *Freedom and Welfare: Social Patterns in the Northern Countries of Europe.* The ministries of Social Affairs of Denmark, Finland, Iceland, Norway, and Sweden, 1953.

Herbert Hendin. *Suicide and Scandinavia: A Psycho-analytic Study of Culture and Character.* New York: Grune & Stratton, 1964.

Orla Jensen. *Social Welfare in Denmark.* 2d ed. Copenhagen: Danske Selskab, 1961.

Peter Manniche. *Denmark, a Social Laboratory.* Copenhagen: Gad, 1939.

Pekka Kuusi. *Social Policy for the 60s: A Plan for Finland.* Helsinki: Finnish Social Policy Association, 1964.

Kaare Salvesen. *Social Legislation in Norway.* Oslo: Norwegian Joint Committee on International Social Policy [and Tanum], 1967.

Karl Evang. *Health Services in Norway.* 3d ed. Oslo: Tanum, 1969.

Jämlikhet (Equality). Första rapport från SAP-LOs arbetsgrupp för jämlikhets frågor [First report from the Socialist Workers Party and Labor Organization Working Group for Equality-questions]. Stockholm: SAP-LO, 1969.

The National Insurance in Norway. Oslo: Ministry of Social Affairs, 1966.

Richard F. Tomasson. *Sweden, Prototype of Modern Society.* New York: Random House, 1970.

Albert H. Rosenthal. *The Social Programs of Sweden.* Minneapolis: University of Minnesota Press, 1967.

Murray Gendell. *Swedish Working Wives: A Study of Determinants and Consequences.* Totowa: Bedminster, 1963.

Frederic Fleisher. *The New Sweden: The Challenge of a Disciplined Democracy.* New York: McKay, 1967.

Birgitta Linnér. *Sex and Society in Sweden.* New York: Random House, 1967.

Housing

Housing in the Nordic Countries. By the housing authorities of the five northern countries. Copenhagen, 1968.

Anna Louise Strong. *Planned Urban Environments: Sweden, Finland, Israel, The Netherlands, France.* Baltimore: Johns Hopkins University Press, 1971.

Labor Relations

Walter Galenson. *The Danish System of Labor Relations.* Cambridge: Harvard University Press, 1952.

——— *Labor in Norway.* Cambridge: Harvard University Press, 1949.

Herbert Dorfman. *Labor Relations in Norway.* Rev. ed. Oslo: Tanum, 1966.

Folke Schmidt. *The Law of Labour Relations in Sweden.* Uppsala: Almquist-Wiksell, 1962. Laws on labor courts, collective bargaining, etc., translated into English, comprise 100 pages of the book.

Democratization of Education

Cyril W. Dixon. *Society, Schools, and Progress in Scandinavia.* New York: Oxford University Press, 1965.

Thomas Rørdam. *The Danish Folk High Schools.* Copenhagen: Danske Selskab, 1965.

Aksell Nellemann. *Schools and Education in Denmark.* Copenhagen: Danske Selskab, 1964.

Fridlev Skrubbeltrang. *The Danish Folk High Schools.* Copenhagen: Danske selskab, 1964.

Ingeborg Lyche. *Adult Education in Norway.* Oslo: Universitetsforlag, 1964. (Pamphlet.)

Gunnar Mortensen and Sven Persson. *Vocational Training in Norway.* Oslo: Norwegian Joint Committee on International Social Policy, 1964.

Torsten Husén et al. *Differentiation and Guidance in the Comprehensive School.* Stockholm: Almquist-Wiksell, 1959.

——— *Educational Research and Educational Change: The Case of Sweden.* New York: Wiley, 1967.

Adèle Heilborn. *Travel, Study and Research in Sweden*. Stockholm: Sweden-America Foundation, 1975. A guide to programs, institutions, and how to do things; kept up to date by successive revisions.

Franklin D. Scott. *The American Experience of Swedish Students*. Minneapolis: University of Minnesota Press, 1956.

Gunnar Mortensen and Sven Persson. *Vocational Training in Norway*. Oslo: Tanum, 1964.

Olav Hove. *The System of Education in Norway*. Oslo: Tanum, 1968.

Arne Evensen. *Social Defence in Norway*. Oslo: Ministry of Social Affairs, 1965.

Jonas Orring. *Comprehensive Schools and Continuation Schools in Sweden*. Stockholm: K. Eckliastikdepartment, 1962.

The Ombudsman and Citizen Protection

Alfred Bexelius. *The Swedish Institution of the Justitieombudsman*. Stockholm: Swedish Institute, 1966. Brief account in English by the ombudsman himself.

Stephan Hurwitz. *The Ombudsman*. Copenhagen: Danske Selskab, 1962. By the Danish ombudsman and major propagandizer.

Walter Gellhorn. *Ombudsmen and Others*. Cambridge: Harvard University Press, 1967.

The Cooperative Society Movement

Marquis W. Childs. *Sweden: The Middle Way*. Rev. ed. New Haven: Yale University Press, 1951. The book that popularized the idea of the "middle way."

Axel Gjöres. *Cooperation in Sweden*. Manchester: The Co-operative Union, 1937. Old now, but by one of the prime movers.

Report of the Inquiry on Cooperative Enterprise in Europe. Washington: G.P.O., 1937.

Clemens Pedersen, *The Danish Cooperative Movement*. Copenhagen, 1966.

THE ECONOMIES OF THE NORTHERN COUNTRIES

Sima Lieberman, *The Industrialization of Norway, 1800–1920*. Oslo: Universitetsforlag, 1970.

Seymour E. Harris. *Economic Planning*. New York: Knopf, 1949. Among the Northern countries Harris deals only with Norway.

L. R. Klein. "Planned Economy in Norway." *American Economic Review*, 38 (December 1948), 795–814.

OECD Economic Surveys, *Norway*. Paris: Organization for Economic Co-operation and Development, June 1967.

Arthur Stonehill. *Foreign Ownership in Norwegian Enterprises*. Oslo: Aschehoug, 1965.

Norwegian Long Term Programme, 1970–1973. Parliamentary Report, no. 55, 1968–1969.

Leif Johansen and Harald Hallaråker. *Economic Planning in Norway*. Oslo: Universitetsforlag, 1970.

Ahti Karjalainen. *A National Economy Based on Wood: What Finland Lives on and How.* Helsinki: Tammi, 1957.

Ilmari Hustich. *Finland Förvandlas.* Helsinki: Holger Schildt, 1967. Stresses industrial development.

Very helpful for following developments are the monthly or quarterly bank bulletins, such as: *The Bank of Finland Monthly Bulletin,* the Kansallis-Osake-Pankki *Economic Review,* and Nordiska Föreningsbankens *Unitas.*

William C. Chamberlin. *The Economic Development of Iceland through World War II.* New York: Columbia University Press, 1947. Studies in History, Economics, and Public Law, no. 531.

Erik Dahmén. *Entrepreneurial Activity and the Development of Swedish Industry, 1919–1939.* Homewood, Ill.: Richard D. Irwin, 1970.

Olle Gasslander. *History of Stockholms Enskilda Bank.* Stockholm: By the bank, 1966. Industrial development as well as banking history.

Douglas Verney. *Public Enterprise in Sweden.* Liverpool: Liverpool University Press, 1959.

Lennart Jörberg. *Growth and Fluctuations of Swedish Industry, 1869–1912.* Stockholm: Almquist-Wiksell, 1961.

Ernst Söderlund et al. *Sveriges industri.* Stockholm: Industriförbundet, 1967.

Svensk ekonomi 1971–1975 med utblick mot 1990: 1970 års långtidsutredning huvudrapport. Stockholm: Statens Offentliga Utredningar, 1970: 71.

Åke Burstedt et al. *Social Goals in National Planning: A Critique of Sweden's Long-Term Economic Survey.* Stockholm: Prisma, 1972.

Lars Nabseth et al. *Svensk industri under 70-talet med utblick mot 80-talet.* Stockholm: Industriensutredningsinstitut, 1971. This is the same as SOU (Statens Offentliga Utredningar), 1971, no. 5.

The Swedish Budget, 1974–75. Stockholm: Ministry of Finance, 1974.

Economic Survey of Denmark. Copenhagen: Ministry of Foreign Affairs, annual.

THE SEARCH FOR SECURITY

Folke Lindberg. *Scandinavia in Great Power Politics, 1905–1908.* Stockholm: Almquist-Wiksell, 1958.

Paul Vigness, *The Neutrality of Norway in the World War.* Stanford: Stanford University Press, 1932.

W. M. Carlgren, *Neutralität oder allianz.* Stockholm: Almquist-Wiksell, 1962. In German, on World War I.

Lucien Maury. *Les problèmes scandinaves: Le nationalisme suèdois et la guerre 1914–1918.* Paris: Perrin et Cie., 1918.

Olav Riste. *The Neutral Ally: Norway's Relations with Belligerent Powers in the First World War.* Oslo and London: Universitetsforlag, 1965.

Troels Fink. *Ustabil Balans . . . 1894–1905.* Aarhus: Universitetsforlag, 1961. Denmark's foreign and defense policy.

Raymond E. Lindgren. *Norway-Sweden: Union, Disunion, and Scandinavian Integration.* Princeton: Princeton University Press, 1959.

Steven Koblik. *The Neutral Victor.* Lund: Läromedelsförlag, 1972. Sweden's relations with Great Britain and the United States during World War I.

Juhani Paasivirta. *The Victors in World War I and Finland.* Helsinki: Finnish Historical Society, 1965.

Nils Örvik. *The Decline of Neutrality, 1914–1941.* New York: Humanities Press, 1971. A popular and updated version of the author's *The Changing Concept of Neutrality,* with a supplementary chapter on "since 1952."

Herbert Tingsten. *The Debate on the Foreign Policy of Sweden, 1918–1939.* New York: Oxford University Press, 1949.

Viggo Sjöquist. *Danmarks udenrigspolitik, 1933–1940.* Copenhagen: Gyldendal, 1966.

Arnold J. Toynbee, ed. *The War and the Neutrals.* London: Oxford University Press, 1956.

Nils Morten Udgaard. *Great Power Politics and Norwegian Foreign Policy: A Study of Norway's Foreign Relations November 1940–February 1948.* Oslo: Universitetsforlag, 1973.

Carl J. Hambro. *I Saw It Happen in Norway.* New York: Appleton Century, 1940.

Johs. Andenaes et al. *Norway and the Second World War.* Oslo: Tanum, 1966.

Richard Petrow. *The Bitter Years: The Invasion and Occupation of Denmark and Norway, April 1940–May 1945.* New York: William Morrow, 1974. A debunking book.

Ralph Hewins. *Quisling: Prophet without Honour.* New York: John Day, 1966. A not very successful attempt to rehabilitate Quisling's reputation.

Odd Nansen. From Day to Day. New York: G. P. Putnam's, 1949. Memoirs of the concentration camp.

Tuomo Polvinen. *Finland i stormaktspolitiken, 1941–1944.* Helsingfors: Schildt, 1969.

Stig Jägerskiöld, *Gustaf Mannerheim, 1918.* Stockholm: Bonniers, 1967–.

The Memoirs of Marshal Mannerheim. New York: Dutton, 1954.

A. F. Upton, *Finland in Crisis, 1940–1941.* Ithaca: Cornell University Press, 1964.

John H. Wuorinen, ed. *Finland and World War II, 1939–1944.* New York: Ronald, 1948.

Max Jakobson. *The Diplomacy of the Winter War.* Cambridge: Harvard University Press, 1961.

Leonard Lundin. *Finland in the Second World War.* Bloomington: Indiana University Press, 1957. Critical.

Jeremy Bennett. *British Broadcasting and the Danish Resistance Movement, 1940–1945.* Cambridge: Harvard University Press, 1966.

Erik Scavenius. *Forhandlingspolitiken under Besaettelsen.* Copenhagen: Steen Hasselbach Forlag 1948. A significant apologia and analysis of a small state's dilemma.

Sveriges förhållande till Danmark och Norge under Krigsåren. Stockholm: Norstedt, 1945. Sweden's official whitebook.

Nils Örvik. *Trends in Norwegian Foreign Policy.* Oslo: Norwegian Institute of International Affairs, 1962.

Max Sörensen and Niels J. Haagerup. *Denmark and the United Nations.* New York: Manhatten, 1956.

Swedish Institute of International Affairs. *Sweden and the United Nations.* New York: Manhattan for Carnegie Endowment, 1956.

Nils Andrén and Åke Landquist. *Svensk utrikespolitik efter 1945.* Stockholm: Almquist-Wiksell, 1965. Valuable document collection.

Nils Andrén. *Power Balance and Non-alignment.* Stockholm: Almquist-Wiksell, 1967.

Wilhelm M. Carlgren. *Svensk utrikespolitik, 1939–1945: Aktstykken utgivna av utrikesdepartementet.* n.s. 2, no. 26 Stockholm: Allmänna Förlaget, 1973. Important wartime documents issued by the Foreign Office.

Finnish Foreign Policy. Helsinki: Finnish Political Science Association, 1963. Fourteen essays on varied aspects of history and policy, sponsored by the Finnish Political Science Association.

Urho Kekkonen. *Neutrality: The Finnish Position.* Enlarged ed. London: Heinemann, 1973.

Per Frydenberg, ed. *Peace-Keeping, Experience and Evaluation—The Oslo Papers.* Oslo: Norwegian Institute of International Affairs, 1964. Problems concerning international peace-keeping forces in crisis spots.

Ingemar Dörfer. *System 37 Viggen: Arms, Technology, and the Domestication of Glory.* Oslo: Universitets Forlag, 1973. A significant study of the relations between government and technology in Sweden in connection, especially, with the Viggen military airplane.

Frantz Wendt. *The Nordic Council and Cooperation in Scandinavia.* Copenhagen: Munksgaard, 1959.

Vegard Sletten. *Five Northern Countries Pull Together.* Oslo: Nordic Council, [1967].

Stanley V. Anderson. *The Nordic Council.* Seattle: University of Washington Press, and New York: American Scandinavian Foundation, 1967.

Einar Löchen. *Norway in European and Atlantic Cooperation.* Oslo: Universitetsforlaget, 1964.

Göran von Bonsdorff. *Regionalismen i den internationella politiken.* Helsingfors: Natur och Kultur, 1967.

———— "Regional Cooperation in the Northern Countries." *Cooperation and Conflict,* I (1965).

Hans Karl Gunther, *German-Swedish Relations, 1933–1939.* Ann Arbor: University Microfilms, 1954. Much on German concept of Nordicism.

IMMIGRATION AND CROSS-CURRENTS

Amandus Johnson. *The Swedish Settlements on the Delaware.* 2 vols. Philadelphia: University of Pennsylvania Press, 1911. The classic account.

John H. Wuorinen. *The Finns on the Delaware, 1638–1655.* New York: Columbia University Press, 1938.

Theodore C. Blegen. *Norwegian Migration to America.* 2 vols. Northfield, Minn.: Norwegian-American Historical Association, 1931, 1940. Thorough and readable.

Einar Haugen. *The Norwegians in America.* New York: Teachers College Press, 1967. Pamphlet emphasizing places to visit, etc.

Kenneth Bjork. *Saga in Steel and Concrete.* Northfield, Minn.: Norwegian-American Historical Association, 1947.

Ole Rynning's "True Account of America." Ed. by T. C. Blegen. Minneapolis: Norwegian-American Historical Association, 1926. Original issued in Norway in 1838.

Arlow W. Andersen. *The Immigrant Takes His Stand.* Northfield, Minn.: Norwegian-American Historical Association, 1953. The nineteenth-century Norwegian-American press. The N.A.H.A. has published a long shelf of books and "Studies," the most thorough and most scholarly treatment accorded any immigrant group.

Ole Rølvaag. *Giants in the Earth.* New York: Harper, 1927. The best novel of immigration to America.

William A. Hoglund. *Finnish Immigrants in America, 1880–1920.* Madison: University of Wisconsin Press, 1960.

John I. Kolehmainen and George W. Hill. *Haven in the Woods: The Story of the Finns in Wisconsin.* Madison: State Historical Society of Wisconsin, 1965.

Jacob A. Riis. *The Making of an American.* New York: Macmillan, 1901.

Kristian Hvidt. *Flight to America: The Social Background of 300,000 Danish Emigrants.* New York: Academic Press, 1975. Translation of a large part of his extensive *Flugten til Amerika* (Århus: Universitetsforlaget, 1971).

Jon Wefald. *A Voice of Protest: Norwegians in American Politics.* Topical Studies no. 1. Northfield, Minn.: Norwegian-American Historical Association, 1971.

George M. Stephenson. *The Religious Aspects of Swedish Immigration.* Minneapolis: University of Minnesota Press, 1935.

Gustaf Unonius. *A Pioneer in Northwest America, 1841–1858.* 2 vols. Chicago: Swedish Pioneer Historical Society, 1950, 1960.

Nils William Olsson. *Swedish Passenger Arrivals in New York, 1820–1850.* Chicago: Swedish Pioneer Historical Society, 1967. Personal details of origin and destination.

Franklin D. Scott. *Wertmüller: Artist and Immigrant Farmer.* Chicago: Swedish Pioneer Historical Society, 1963.

———— "Sweden's Constructive Opposition to Emigration." *Journal of Modern History,* 37 (September 1965), 307–335.

———— *The American Experience of Swedish Students.* Minneapolis: University of Minnesota Press, 1956.

Franklin D. Scott, ed. *Baron Klinkowström's America, 1818–1820.* Evanston: Northwestern University Press, 1952.

Vilhelm Moberg, *The Emigrants: Unto a Good Land;* and *The Last Letter Home.* Stockholm: Bonniers, 1949–1959. Later English editions, New York: Simon and Schuster. This is the epic three-part novel that was made into a two-part movie on Swedish emigration.

Harald S. Naess and Sigmund Skard, eds. *Americana Norvegica,* vol. III: *Studies in Scandinavian-American Interrelations Dedicated to Einar Haugen.* Oslo: Universitetsforlag, 1971. See also vols. I (1966) and II (1968).

H. Arnold Barton, ed. *Scandinavians and America: Essays Presented to Franklin D. Scott.* Chicago: Swedish Pioneer Historical Society, 1974. Identical to *Swedish Pioneer Historical Quarterly,* 25, nos. 3 and 4.

————— ed. *Letters from the Promised Land.* Minneapolis and Chicago: The Swedish Pioneer Historical Society, 1975.

Allan Kastrup. *The Swedish Heritage in America.* Minneapolis: The Swedish Council of America, 1975.

The Swedish Pioneer Historical Quarterly. Chicago: Swedish Pioneer Historical Society, 1950–.

BIBLIOGRAPHIES AND OTHER GUIDES

Excerpta Historica Nordica. Copenhagen: Gyldendal, 1955–. Summaries, usually in English, of recent historical publications in northern Europe. Biennial or triennial.

Sven Groennings. *Scandinavia in Social Science Literature.* Bloomington: Indiana University Press, 1970. English language literature; quite thorough, up-to-date publication. Index of authors.

Erling Grönland. *Norway in English.* Oslo: Norwegian Universities Press, 1961.

Nils Örvik. *Norwegian Foreign Policy.* Oslo: Universitetsforlaget, 1968.

Bure Holmbäck. "About Sweden 1900–1963: A Bibliographical Outline." *Sweden Illustrated.* Stockholm: Sweden Illustrated, 1968. 5000 books in English under about 180 subject titles. Sponsored by the Swedish Institute.

Suecana Extranea. A bulletin of the Royal Library, Stockholm, listing new books on Sweden in various non-Swedish languages. Since 1967, twice yearly.

P. M. Mitchell. *A Bibliography of English Imprints of Denmark.* Lawrence, Kansas: University of Kansas Libraries, 1960.

Erland Munch-Petersen. *A Guide to Danish Bibliography.* 1965. Copenhagen: Royal School of Librarianship, 1965.

Index

(The Scandinavian letters å, ä and ö, ø are here alphabetized as if they were simple a or o.)

The American Foreign Policy Library

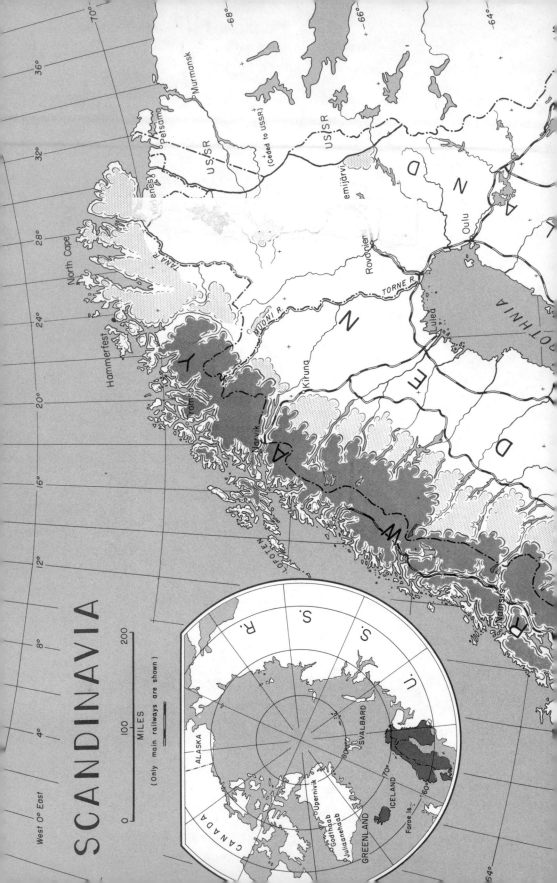